# ▄▄ MOSAIC II

## A READING SKILLS BOOK

# MOSAIC II

## A READING SKILLS BOOK

**Second Edition**

**Brenda Wegmann**

**Miki Prijic Knezevic**

**Marilyn Bernstein**

McGRAW-HILL PUBLISHING COMPANY

New York   St. Louis   San Francisco   Auckland   Bogotá   Caracas
Hamburg   Lisbon   London   Madrid   Mexico   Milan   Montreal   New Delhi
Oklahoma City   Paris   San Juan   São Paulo   Singapore   Sydney   Tokyo   Toronto

This is an EBI book.

Mosaic II
A Reading Skills Book

2  3  4  5  6  7  8  9  DOH  DOH    9  4  3  2  1  0

ISBN 0-07-557566-3

This book was set in 10/12 Aster by Jonathan Peck Typographers.
The editor was Mary Gill;
the designer was Naomi Schiff;
the cover designer was Cheryl Carrington;
the photo researcher was Judy Mason;
the project editor was Stacey C. Sawyer;
R. R. Donnelley & Sons Company was printer and binder.

**ACKNOWLEDGMENTS**
**Pp. 4–6**  Jamake Highwater, "Native Americans" in *TV and Teens*, 1982. Published by Addison-Wesley, Reading, MA. Reprinted with permission of Action for Children's TV; **pp. 10–12** from *Becoming a Master Student* by David B. Ellis, copyright 1984; **pp. 16–18**  from *The Story of English* by Robert McCrum, William Cran, and Robert MacNeil. Copyright © 1986 by Robert McCrum, William Cran, and Robert MacNeil. All rights reserved. Reprinted by permission of Viking Penguin Inc., and Faber & Faber Ltd., **pp. 31–35**  L. P. Hartley, "A High Dive" in *The Complete Short Stories of L. P. Hartley*, Hamish Hamilton Ltd. Copyright © 1973 The Executors of the Estate of L. P. Hartley. "A High Dive" originally appeared in *Two for the River*; **pp. 39–41**  from *Never Cry Wolf* by Farley Mowat. Copyright © Farley Mowat. By permission of Little, Brown and Company in association with the Atlantic Monthly Press, and the Canadian publisher, McClelland and Stewart Limited, Toronto; **pp. 47–51**  Urban Lehner, "For Better or for Worse, Arranged Marriages Still Thrive in Japan," *The Wall Street Journal*, July 29, 1983. Reprinted by permission of *The Wall Street Journal*. © Dow Jones & Company, Inc. 1983. All rights reserved; **pp. 55–59**  Signe Hammer, "Anatomy of a Difference" reprinted by permission of the author. (This article first appeared in *Health*, July, 1983); **pp. 63–65**  "I Want a Wife" by Judy Syfers, 1971. Reprinted with permission of the author; **p. 67**  "Oh, When I Was in Love with You," by A. E. Housman. Copyright 1939, 1940, © 1965 by Holt, Rinehart and Winston. Copyright © 1967, 1968 by Robert E. Symons. Reprinted from *The Collected Poems of A. E. Housman*, by permission of Henry Holt and Company, Inc.; **p. 71**  from *Money Should Be Fun* by William Hamilton. Copyright © 1980 by William Hamilton; **pp. 71–73**  Richard Blodgett, "Against All Odds." Reprinted from GAMES Magazine (810 Seventh Avenue, New York, NY 10019). Copyright © 1983 PSC Games Limited Partnership; **pp. 79–84**  Frank Stockton, "The Lady or the Tiger?" in *The Best Short Stories of Frank R. Stockton*, Charles Scribner's Sons, 1957; **pp. 86–89**  from *Speaking of Chinese* by Raymond Chang and Margaret Scrogin Chang, by permission of W. W. Norton & Company, Inc., and Andre Deutsch Ltd. Copyright © 1978 by W. W. Norton & Company, Inc.; **pp. 97–99**  from *The Lifetime Book of Money Management*. Copyright © by Grace W. Weinstein, reprinted by permission of New American Library, a Division of Penguin Books USA Inc.; **pp. 102–104**  from *Among the Believers*, by V. S. Naipaul. Copyright © 1981 V. S. Naipaul. Reprinted by permission of Alfred A. Knopf, Inc., and Aitken & Stone Ltd.; **pp. 108–110**  excerpt from "Human Waves" by Leon Bouvier. With permission from *Natural History*, Vol. 92, No. 8; Copyright the American Museum of Natural History, 1983; **pp. 117–121**  Stephen Singular, "A Memory for All Seasonings." Reprinted with permission from *Psychology Today Magazine*. Copyright © 1982 (PT Partners); **p. 118** photo by Brian Payne/Black Star; **pp. 127–130**  from *The Mind of Man* by Nigel Calder.

# ▦ Contents

# CHAPTER 4

# Mysteries Past and Present    69

# CHAPTER 5

# Transitions    95

# CHAPTER 6

# The Mind    115

# CHAPTER 7

# Working    145

# CHAPTER 8

# Energy and Matter    171

# CHAPTER 9

# The Arts    197

# CHAPTER 10

# Ethical Questions    219

# CHAPTER 11

# Medicine    247

# CHAPTER 12

# The Future     273

# ▄▄ Preface to the Second Edition

---

## MOSAIC: THE PROGRAM

*Mosaic* consists of eight texts plus two instructor's manuals for in-college or college-bound nonnative English students. *Mosaic I* is for intermediate to high-intermediate students, while *Mosaic II* is for high-intermediate to low-advanced students. Within each level, I and II, the books are carefully coordinated by theme, vocabulary, grammar structure, and, where possible, language functions. A chapter in one book corresponds to and reinforces material taught in the same chapter of the other three books at that level for a truly integrated, four-skills approach.

Each level, I and II, consists of four books plus an instructor's manual. In addition to *A Reading Skills Book*, they include:

- *A Content-Based Grammar I, II:* Each grammar chapter relates to a specific theme, so the exercises focus on contexts and ideas. There is a wide variety of communicative, functional activities.

- *A Content-Based Writing Book I, II:* These books provide students with short readings on the chapter themes and include many pre-writing, revision, and vocabulary-building exercises. The books focus on the writing process, particularly on techniques for gathering ideas, such as "brainstorming" and "freewriting," and on using feedback to rewrite.

- *A Listening-Speaking Skills Book I, II:* These books teach study skills and language functions through active listening activities based on lectures on chapter themes and sample conversations. A variety of speaking activities to reinforce language functions is also included. A cassette program with instructor's key accompanies each text.

- *Instructor's Manual I, II:* These manuals provide instructions and guidelines for use of the books separately or in any combination to form a program. For each of the core books, there is a separate section with teaching tips and other suggestions. The instructor's manuals also include sample tests.

# MOSAIC II: A READING SKILLS BOOK

## Rationale

The main purpose of the *Mosaic II* reader is to polish and perfect the English skills of the intermediate student that will enable him or her to deal effectively with sophisticated reading materials of both a scientific and humanistic nature. In other words, it aims to bring the student from a basic level of comprehension of the English language to the higher competence necessary for tackling more difficult work, such as that of the college classroom. While the orientation is primarily academic, the book is also helpful for students who simply wish to read English with a deeper understanding. When used in conjunction with the other *Mosaic* components (grammar, writing book, and listening/speaking book), it provides continuous reinforcement of vocabulary, grammar structures, and thematic ideas through reading.

The *Mosaic II* reader differs from the *Mosaic I* reader in several ways. *Mosaic II* emphasizes the advanced skills of interpretation, inference, critical analysis, evaluation, and application; it presents but gives less weight to more basic comprehension skills like skimming, scanning, and guessing meaning from context. It includes more work with charts, tables, and graphs; more discussion of style and tone; more technical and literary terminology, and longer, more varied, and more difficult selections. In general, *Mosaic II* covers the reading skills for the high-intermediate/advanced level as recommended by the guidelines of numerous universities throughout the country. The second half of *Mosaic II* contains a number of special exercises that focus on the acquisition and practice of study skills, such as underlining, glossing, outlining, and study mapping.

Like *Mosaic I*, the *Mosaic II* reader is designed to guide the student in the development of a conscious, reflective attitude toward reading, to teach him or her to anticipate the context, to evaluate the difficulty and decide on the level of understanding desired, to distinguish between different types of selections and different purposes for reading and avoid wasting time in a useless mechanical thoroughness. For this reason, particular types of timed readings are included in the second half of the book, even though speed reading for its own sake is not generally encouraged at this level.

The reading selections were drawn from a variety of sources: scientific, literary, textbook, trade book, periodical. They were chosen to be relevant and interesting to a multicultural readership and to present in a challenging way representative customs, personalities, values, and ways of thinking of Americans and Canadians.

# Chapter Organization

Every chapter begins with a brief introduction to the chapter theme. This can be used as a starting point to set the stage for later discussion and to give both teacher and students an idea of the class' knowledge and prejudices on the subject. The introduction is followed by two or more reading selections, each one preceded by one or two prereading exercises and followed by comprehension and skill-building exercises. These are usually accompanied by a "Talking It Over" section and occasionally by activities, such as group problem solving, discussions that require expressing reactions or applying what has been read to new situations, composition or library research assignments. These latter features are optional and are included primarily to give the book greater flexibility for those programs that do not include the other *Mosaic II* components. Also included are sections called "Stories Behind Words," which focus on particular aspects of vocabulary: word origins, nuances, the relationship between word choice and cultural attitudes, and the current sensitivity to what is perceived as sexist language. There are also exercises that deal with ways of coping with technical terms, slang, idioms, and some differences between American, British, and Canadian English. Chapters 6 to 12 include a graduated series of exercises aimed at developing study skills.

A quick glance through the book will show you that there is no set sequence of exercises repeated chapter after chapter. The types of exercises vary according to the difficulties particular to each selection and to the skills being emphasized. This variety lessens the chance that the student will relapse into a mechanical approach of nonreflective reading. Previously presented skills are reinforced throughout, however, often by using different styles of exercises to review the same skill.

The principal aim of the prereading exercises is to condition students to stop and think before plunging into a reading. Some of them concentrate on finding clues that can help a reader to anticipate the style, contents, or organization; others work at helping students to determine the level of understanding needed for more difficult, abstract material; others reinforce the important skills of guessing the meaning of words from context and coping with technical terms, idioms, slang, abbreviations, and archaic words.

In the first chapters, the skill-building exercises that follow each selection focus on reviewing basic skills such as skimming, scanning, and vocabulary analysis. Later chapters emphasize more advanced skills while reviewing basic ones. Among the advanced skills presented are the following: making and supporting inferences, separating fact from opinion, identifying and evaluating points of view, applying what has been read, summarizing and paraphrasing, reading critically, finding support for or against ideas and opinions, comparing interpretations, and reading charts, tables and graphs. These exercises at times practice and reinforce a skill that has been introduced in a prereading exercise. Optional timed readings also appear in the second half of the book along with comprehension quizzes that offer practice in reading for a set purpose and under a time constraint.

## Teaching Suggestions

The prereading exercises may be used in different ways depending on the level of the students. At first a teacher will probably do them orally with the class as a means of introducing each selection and ascertaining class level. These exercises, especially the ones using direct quotations from the selection, can act as a bridge helping students over some of the difficult sections of the article. If, after a few weeks, the class seems to have little problem with the readings, however, these exercises can be assigned for homework and corrected quickly at the beginning of the class.

A good way of adding spontaneity to the completion of the exercises following the selections is to occasionally reserve some challenging ones for group work, especially if there are no group activities included in the lesson. The class may be divided into small groups and given ten or fifteen minutes to do the exercise, with one of the group members reporting results to the class afterwards. In any event it is a good idea at times to assign only some of the exercises to be done with the reading as homework. Then, if time permits, the others can be worked out in class, adding an element of the unexpected. When an exercise aimed at reviewing a skill is used in this way, one of the more extroverted students might be asked to play the role of teacher (perhaps after having been warned in advance). This is a sure way of gaining class attention, since everyone wants to see if the new "teacher" will make a mistake, and it also serves to challenge a confident, highly motivated student who might otherwise begin to lose interest.

Answers to certain puzzles and problem-solving exercises as well as to the "You Be the Judge" article will be found in the back of this book.

## Changes to the Second Edition

1. A number of selections were dropped based on reactions from teachers, and other selections were added to replace them.
2. All material was updated.
3. More emphasis was given to vocabulary acquisition in exercise work.
4. New types of prereading exercises were added.
5. There is a new design and layout, and new photos and artwork were added as necessary.

# ACKNOWLEDGMENTS

Our heartfelt thanks go to several teachers who aided us with their suggestions and constructive criticism: Patricia K. Werner, of the University of Wisconsin at Madison; Seaneen Fulton, of the Yellowhead Tribal Council ; Brenda Walls of Victoria Composite High School, and Mary Mitchell Church. Special appreciation is due to Marian Kowler of Grant MacEwan Community College for her helpful evaluation of certain reading materials and exercises. Our thanks also to the following reviewers, whose comments, both favorable and critical, were of great value in the development of the first edition: Laurie Blass; Sheila Brutton, Southern Illinois University; Suzanne Flynn, Massachusetts Institute of Technology; Nancy Herzfeld-Pipkin, San Diego State University; Cynthia Holliday, State University of New York, New Paltz; Patricia Johnson, University of Wisconsin, Green Bay; Gail Kellersberger, University of Houston; Susan Martel, University of Southern Illinois; Betsy Soden, University of Michigan; Elizabeth Templin, University of Arizona; and thanks to the following reviewers of the first edition for their help in shaping the second edition: Miriam Barton, Orange Coast College; James Burke, El Paso Community College; Annette Fruehans, Orange Coast College; Nicki S. Giroux de Navarro, University of Arizona; Brandy Harrell, Tacoma Community College; Grace Hauser, El Paso Community College; Vivian P. Hefley, Iowa State University; Ellen J. Kisslinger, Boston University; Linda Levine, Orange Coast College; Catherine Mason, University of Minnesota; Blanca Moss, El Paso Community College; Joseph Pettigrew, Boston University; Fran Schmittdiel, California State University, Northridge.

We also wish to thank Mary McVey Gill for her excellent help, tolerance, and cooperation. Finally, a very special thank you to Yen Tang, Anné Knezevic, and our husbands Tom and Ivan for their valuable comments, and to our children, parents, and friends for their patience and encouragement.

*B. W.*
*M. P. K.*
*M. B.*

# ◨ MOSAIC II

## A READING SKILLS BOOK

# Language and Learning

Not all American and Canadian citizens grow up speaking English. Some, like the author of the first selection in this chapter, must learn it when they arrive at school. He describes his first encounters with English, the language that finally helped him to overcome his feelings of being an outsider to the dominant culture. The second selection discusses how to use the library, a valuable resource center that offers books and much more. The third selection traces the rise of today's most popular international language, English.

## SELECTION ONE

# Native Americans

English is the official language of the United States and one of the two official languages of Canada (French is the other), but many people born in these countries do not grow up speaking it. For them, English is a second language that they learn at a later time. In some cases this is because their parents are immigrants or because they grow up in an ethnic neighborhood where Spanish, Chinese, or another language is spoken by almost everyone. For a small percentage it is because their ancestors were the original natives of this continent, the Indians who were here before the arrival of the European settlers in the sixteenth century. Is this situation unique to North America? Or can you think of other parts of the world in which many people learn the official language of their country as a second language? Do people like this have a harder time succeeding in society? Does this situation make a society weaker or stronger?

The author of the following selection, Jamake Highwater, is a Native American Indian and a well-known author who writes in English. He speaks of the terrible shock that certain English words caused him when he first learned them at school. As you read, try to understand Highwater's attitudes toward the two languages and the two cultures that have formed him.

## Prereading Exercise: Guessing the Meaning of New Words from Context

### PART A

Try to guess the meanings of unfamiliar words as you read. Skimming a selection first (reading very quickly for main ideas) helps a great deal. Other ways of understanding a new word include breaking it apart into

smaller words, prefixes, and suffixes, and finding a synonym or explanation near the word. Practice these skills by writing your own definitions for the italicized words in the following sentences taken from
the selection. Use the hints to help you.

1. "We are born into a cultural *preconception* that we call reality and
   that we never question." (*Hint:* Do you know the meaning of the
   prefix *pre-* and the word *concept*?)

   *preconception:* _____

2. "We essentially know the world in terms of that cultural package
   or preconception, and we are so unaware of it that the most liberal of us go through life with a kind of *ethnocentricity*." (*Hint:* The
   word *ethnic* means "belonging to a particular culture or group."
   What do you think *centr-* means?)

   *ethnocentricity:* _____

3. "I grew up in a place that was called a *wilderness*, but I could
   never understand how that amazing ecological park could be
   called '*wilderness*,' something wild that needs to be harnessed."
   (*Hint:* What part of the sentence explains the meaning of
   *wilderness*?)

   *wilderness:* _____

4. "Nature is some sort of foe, some sort of *adversary*, in the dominant culture's mentality." (*Hint:* Because of the repetition of the
   words *some sort of*, you can see that there is another word that is
   very close in meaning to *adversary*. What word is this?)

   *adversary:* _____

**PART B**

If you cannot break a word apart or find a nearby synonym or explanation, you simply have to guess a likely meaning to fit the context.
Choose what you think is the best word to substitute for each italicized
word in the following sentences from the selection.

1. "The bird had a very particular *significance* to me because I desperately wanted to be able to fly too."

   a. beauty  b. meaning  c. appearance  d. name

2. "When I was ten years old, my life changed *drastically*. I found
   myself adopted forcefully and against my parents' will."

   a. slowly  b. happily  c. easily  d. violently

3. ". . . They were considered *inadequate* parents because they could
   not make enough money to support me."

   a. unintelligent                b. wealthy
   c. not suitable                 d. not interesting

4. "...I was even more confused when I found out that the meaning of the verb 'to duck' came from the bird and not *vice versa*."
   a. the other way around
   b. from something else
   c. with many meanings
   d. written in a different way

5. "...We are so unaware of it that the most liberal of us go through life with a kind of ethnocentricity that automatically *rules out* all other ways of seeing the world."
   a. eliminates   b. emphasizes   c. includes   d. improves

6. "...I could never understand how that amazing ecological park could be called 'wilderness,' something wild that needs to be *harnessed*."
   a. changed   b. set free   c. controlled   d. appreciated

7. "I grew up in a culture that considers us *literally* a part of the entire process that is called nature, to such an extent that when Black Elk called himself the brother of the bear, he was quite serious."
   a. in an imaginative way
   b. in reality
   c. intellectually
   d. poetically

8. "The earth is such an important symbol to most primal people that when we use European languages we tend to capitalize the *E* in much the same way that the word *God* is capitalized by people of the dominant culture. You can imagine my *distress* when I was ten years old to find out that synonyms for the word *earth—dirt* and *soil*—were used to describe uncleanliness on the one hand and *obscenity* on the other."
   *distress:*   a. fear   b. joy   c. suffering   d. laughter

   *obscenity:*   a. correct speech and manners
                  b. offensive language and actions
                  c. religious customs
                  d. objects considered beautiful

9. "I could not possibly understand how something that could be dirty could have any kind of negative *connotations*."
   a. sounds connected to a word
   b. ideas associated with a word
   c. ways of spelling
   d. ways of writing

## Native Americans

When I was about five years old, I used to watch a bird in the skies of southern Alberta from the Blackfeet Blood Reserve in northern Montana where I was born. I loved this bird; I would watch him for hours. He would glide effortlessly in that gigantic sky, or he would come down and light on

5  the water and float there very majestically. Sometimes when I watched him
he would creep into the grasses and waddle around not very gracefully. We
called him *meksikatsi*, which in the Blackfeet language means "pink-colored
feet"; *meksikatsi* and I became very good friends.

   The bird had a very particular significance to me because I desperately
10  wanted to be able to fly too. I felt very much as if I was the kind of person
who had been born into a world where flight was impossible, and most of
the things that I dreamed about or read about would not be possible for me
but would be possible only for other people.

Blackfoot Indians

DEPARTMENT LIBRARY SERVICES/AMERICAN MUSEUM OF NATURAL HISTORY

   When I was ten years old, my life changed drastically. I found myself
15  adopted forcefully and against my parents' will; they were considered inadequate parents because they could not make enough money to support me,
so I found myself in that terrible position that 60 percent of Native Americans
find themselves in: living in a city that they do not understand at all, not in
another culture but between two cultures.

20  A teacher of the English language told me that *meksikatsi* was not called
*meksikatsi*, even though that is what my people had called that bird for
thousands of years. *Meksikatsi*, he said, was really "duck." I was very disappointed with English. I could not understand it. First of all, the bird didn't
look like "duck," and when it made a noise it didn't sound like "duck," and I
25  was even more confused when I found out that the meaning of the verb "to
duck" came from the bird and not vice versa.

This was the beginning of a very complex lesson for me that doesn't just happen to black, Chicano, Jewish, and Indian children but to all children. We are born into a cultural preconception that we call reality and that we never question. We essentially know the world in terms of that cultural package or preconception, and we are so unaware of it that the most liberal of us go through life with a kind of ethnocentricity that automatically rules out all other ways of seeing the world.

As I came to understand English better, I understood that it made a great deal of sense, but I never forgot that *meksikatsi* made a different kind of sense. I realized that languages are not just different words for the same things but totally different concepts, totally different ways of experiencing and looking at the world.

As artists have always known, reality depends entirely on how you see things. I grew up in a place that was called a wilderness, but I could never understand how that amazing ecological park could be called "wilderness," something wild that needs to be harnessed. Nature is some sort of foe, some sort of adversary, in the dominant culture's mentality. We are not part of nature in this society; we are created above it, outside of it, and feel that we must dominate and change it before we can be comfortable and safe within it. I grew up in a culture that considers us literally a part of the entire process that is called nature, to such an extent that when Black Elk called himself the brother of the bear, he was quite serious. In other words, Indians did not need Darwin to find out that they were part of nature.

I saw my first wilderness, as I recall, one August day when I got off a Greyhound bus in a city called New York. Now that struck me as being fairly wild and pretty much out of hand. But I did not understand how the term could be applied to the place where I was from.

Gradually, through the help of some very unusual teachers, I was able to find my way into two cultures rather than remain helplessly between two cultures. The earth is such an important symbol to most primal people that when we use European languages we tend to capitalize the *E* in much the same way that the word *God* is capitalized by people in the dominant culture. You can imagine my distress when I was ten years old to find out that synonyms for the word *earth—dirt* and *soil—*were used to describe uncleanliness on the one hand and obscenity on the other. I could not possibly understand how something that could be dirty could have any kind of negative connotations. It would be like saying the person is godly, so don't go near him, and I could not grasp how these ideas made their way into the English language.

**Jamake Highwater**

## Recalling Information

Fill in the blanks of this summary with key words from the selection.

**AN INDIAN BOY MEETS THE ENGLISH LANGUAGE**

When Jamake Highwater was ten years old, he had to move

from the _____₁ to a _____₂. At school a
teacher told him that the *meksikatsi* he loved was really called

a _____₃. He had grown up in a culture that

considered people as part of _____₄. He thought that

he saw his first "wilderness" when he went to _____₅.
At first he felt he was between two cultures, but he became
part of both of them with the help of some unusual

_____₆. He finally got over his shock at finding out

that in English synonyms for the word _____₇ had

negative _____₈: they were used to describe

_____₉ on the one hand and _____₁₀ on the
other.

# Talking It Over

1. Why did the duck have a special significance for Jamake Highwater when he was very young?

2. What drastic change occurred when he was ten years old? Why
   did he describe himself then as "not in another culture but
   between two cultures"?

3. Can you give an example of ethnocentricity that you have seen?
   Do you think that some people are more ethnocentric than others?
   Why?

4. Why didn't the author like the word *duck*? What are some English
   words that have surprised or displeased you? Explain.

5. According to Highwater, what difference is there between Native
   American Indians and the dominant American culture with regard
   to nature?

6. Do you know who Charles Darwin is? (If not, how can you find
   out?) Why does the author say that the Indians did not need him?

7. Why did it bother the author that in English obscene words and
   jokes are often referred to as "dirty" words and jokes? They are
   also sometimes called "off-color." In some cultures, obscene jokes
   are referred to as "green stories." Is there any color associated
   with them in your culture? How are they referred to?

8. Was the author's attitude toward English negative or positive
   when he first started to learn it? Why? What part of the selection
   tells us that his attitude changed later? Why do you think that it
   changed?

## Finding Verbs with Precise Meanings

It is obvious that Jamake Highwater has mastered his second language well. Reread his description of the *meksikatsi* bird in the first paragraph and find the verbs that he used instead of the more ordinary ones given in the sentences that follow. Note how the ideas listed in parentheses are included in the meaning of these verbs and do not need to be expressed.

1. The bird would *fly* in the sky (without moving his wings):

   _____

2. Then he would come down and *land* on the water (gently and without making a splash): _____

3. Afterward the bird would *come* (slowly and carefully) into the grasses: _____

4. There he would *walk around* (swaying from side to side) not very gracefully: _____

## Stories Behind Words: Expressions Associated with Animals

Highwater speaks of his disappointment when he learned that the verb "to duck" came from the animal and not vice versa. Actually, many English verbs and adjectives (and even some nouns used with special meanings) do come from the names of animals. Usually some well-known characteristic of the animal provides the basis for the association. For example, people sometimes say they had "a *whale* of a good time." Since a whale is very big, the word *whale* intensifies the idea and means a *very* good time. Animals are also used in expressions such as "slow as a turtle" and "hungry as a bear." However, animals are often perceived differently by different cultures, so the English expression "clumsy as an elephant" surprises people from India. They know elephants quite well and claim that they are among the most graceful of all animals. This caused some embarrassment for the Indian gentleman who once told an American lady that she "walked like an elephant." He couldn't understand why she got angry! Read the following sentences and guess the meanings of the italicized words. Try to explain what quality and animal are associated with each one.

1. He *wolfed* down his dinner with his eye on the clock.

   _____

   _____

2.  The people *craned* their necks to see the famous actor.

    _____

    _____

3.  She worked at the task with *dogged* determination.

    _____

    _____

4.  A sparkling river *snaked* through the lush green valley below.

    _____

    _____

5.  The teacher got angry because the students were *horsing* around.

    _____

    _____

6.  That professor has an *elephantine* memory.

    _____

    _____

7.  The new boy was a *bully* who liked to scare the other children.

    _____

    _____

8.  She *fished* around in her purse until she found her glasses.

    _____

    _____

9.  The general *cowed* the rebel soldiers with his fiery speech.

    _____

    _____

10. After winning the Nobel Prize, the scientist was *lionized* by the crowd of reporters.

    _____

    _____

Can you think of any other such phrases? Can you give examples of words from the language of your culture that are associated with animals?

# ▓ Library: The Buried Treasure

Libraries are one of the marks of civilization. They provide the depository for the accumulated wisdom of previous generations. Recent advances in technology are changing the modern library in remarkable ways. In the following article you will read about some of them.

## Prereading Exercise: Reading for Information

The following selection is taken from the book *Becoming a Master Student*. Judging from its title, why do you think people read this book? Looking at the title of the selection, what do you think the author means when he refers to "buried treasure"?

_____

_____

Look at the photo and headings in the selection. Then make a list of three specific pieces of information that you think you might learn from the article.

1. _____

2. _____

3. _____

Compare these items with those of your classmates. Add to your list and correct the list as you read. This is a good technique to use when reading for specific information.

## Library: *The Buried Treasure*

Books. That's what most people imagine when a library is mentioned. Books occupy a lot of space in a library, but they are only a small part of what is really there.

Most libraries have books. They also have, for your use, records, artwork,
5  maps, telephone directories for major cities, audiovisual equipment, microfiche, slide programs, film strips, magazines, dictionaries and encyclopedias of all varieties, research aids, computer searches, and people.

### The Best Resource Is Not Made of Paper

People who work in libraries are trained explorers. They know how to search out information that might be located in several different places. They can
10  also act as guides for your own expedition into the data jungle. Their purpose is to serve you. Ask for help.

RAFAEL MACIA/PHOTO RESEARCHERS, INC.

Recent advances in technology are changing the modern library
in remarkable ways.

Most libraries have a special reference librarian who can usually let you
know right away if the library has what you need. He may suggest a different
library or direct you to another source, such as a business, community agency,
15 or government office.

You can save hours by asking.

### Any Book You Want

Most libraries now have nearly every book you could ever want through a
service known as interlibrary loan. This sharing of materials gives even the
smallest library access to millions of books on any subject you could imagine.
20 Just ask that the book be ordered from another library. It often takes only a
few days.

### Periodicals

The magazines and newspapers a library carries depend mostly on the
location and purpose of the library. A neighborhood branch of a public library
may have copies of the local paper and magazines right from the grocery
25 store aisle. A library in a business school is more likely to have the *Wall
Street Journal* and trade journals for accountants and business managers.
Law libraries subscribe to magazines that would probably bore the socks off
a veterinarian.

### Reference Material

The card catalog lists books available in that library and their location. It is
30 an alphabetical listing that is cross-referenced by subject, author, and title.

Each card carries the author's name, the title, the publisher, the date of publication, the number of pages and illustrations, the Library of Congress or Dewey decimal system number (for locating the book), and sometimes a brief description of the book. *Books in Print* is a list of most books currently
35  in publication in the United States. Like the card catalog, it is organized by subject, author, and title.

*The Reader's Guide to Periodical Literature* catalogs articles found in most magazines. By subject, you can find titles of articles from a wide variety of magazines. The magazine name, date, and page numbers will be listed.
40  If you want an older magazine, many libraries require that you fill out a form requesting the magazine so it can be retrieved from storage in closed stacks.

Other guides to what has been recently published include: *New York Times Index, Business Index, Applied Science and Technology Index, Accountants' Index, General Science Index, Education Index, Humanities Index,*
45  *Art Index*, and many others. These indexes help you find what you want in a hurry.

Abstracts are publications that summarize current findings in specific fields. You can review condensed versions of specialized articles by reading *Chemical Abstracts, Psychological Abstracts,* or *Education Abstracts.* . . .
50  Resources listed in indexes or *Reader's Guide* but not available at a particular library are usually available through interlibrary loan.

General and specialized encyclopedias are found in the reference section. Find what you want to know about individuals, groups, places, products, words, or other books. Specialized examples include: *Encyclopedia of World*
55  *Authors, Encyclopedia of Music and Musicians, Encyclopedia of Religion and Ethics, Encyclopedia of Associations, Thomas Register of American Manufacturers,* and *Encyclopedia of the Arts.*

Dictionaries of all sizes and specialties are also available in the library. Technical disciplines (medicine, computer science, engineering) often have
60  their own dictionaries. Of special value to your writing projects is the thesaurus, a type of dictionary. You will find single words that have a very similar meaning to the word you look up (synonyms). Instead of standard definitions, a thesaurus provides fast relief when you just can't think of the word you want.
65  Computer networks now provide information and resource materials to most libraries. DIALOG, ORBIT, and BSR are the three major electronic information vendors, and each contains several dozen data bases. Up-to-the-minute reports (stock prices set in the past fifteen minutes, yesterday's *New York Times* stories) can be retrieved almost instantly on a video terminal.
70  Gaining familiarity with all these resources and services is crucial to the success of most students. And to some, even more valuable than access to information is the convenient, comfortable, quiet, and dependable atmosphere for study to be found in a library.

**David B. Ellis**
*Becoming a Master Student*

HUGH ROGERS/MONKMEYER PRESS PHOTO SERVICE

Library at the National Autonomous
University of Mexico in Mexico City. The
mosaic tells the story of the history of
Mexico.

## Scanning for Specific Information

Can you tell in what library source you could find each of the pieces of
information given below? If you took notes or have a very good memory,
perhaps you can simply write all of the correct information down. If
not, use the *scanning* technique.

   To scan, move your eyes quickly over the article until you come to
the specific piece of information that you want. If you remember that
it is given in the middle or toward the end of the article, start your
search there. Do not be distracted by other items. (Remember that you
are not trying to get a general idea of what the article is about; that is
a different technique called *skimming*.) Concentrate. When you find what
you are looking for, stop and immediately write it down. Then go on to
the next point.

   In the blanks provided, write a correct source for each of the following pieces of information.

**EXAMPLE**   You are writing a report on acid rain for your political
science class and need recent information on the subject:

*The Reader's Guide to*
*Periodical Literature*

1. You are preparing an exam in your music course and need to
   know the year in which the composer Beethoven wrote his famous

   ninth symphony: _____

2. You have bought some stock and someone told you that just a few hours ago it jumped way up in price. You want to find out how

   much you have earned: _____

3. You once met a man from Vancouver on an airplane trip and now are planning to visit there. You remember his full name and that he lives near the university but would like to find out his phone

   number: _____

4. You will be having dinner with an engineer who works with super-conductors and you want to read some recent information on this

   field: _____

5. You are writing an essay for your English course and have used the word *increase* four times and want to replace two of these with

   a synonym: _____

6. You have been assigned the topic of "Television and Its Influence on Children" for your speech class and need to find some current

   magazine articles for background: _____

7. You have heard of a recent book on management techniques written by an author named Le Boeuf and would like to know the

   title: _____

## Talking It Over

1. What does the author mean when he says "the best resource is not made of paper"? When should you use this "resource"? How would you ask for help?

2. What is interlibrary loan? When would you use this service?

3. What services or sources have you used in the library? Have you had any trouble using them?

4. Why do you think that many people find the atmosphere of the library conducive to study? Which part of the library do you think is the best place to study in?

## Word Detective

Using the following clues and your *scanning* technique, find the words from the article that correspond to the descriptions. The words are given in the order of their occurrence.

1. A word of French origin that starts with an *m* and means "small sheets of film containing information that can be viewed under a

   special apparatus": _____

2.  A slang expression consisting of a four-word phrase that means "be very uninteresting to": _____

3.  A phrase of two words, each beginning with a *c*, that refers to the alphabetical listing of all the books in a library, by subject, author, and title: _____

4.  A word beginning with the letter *p* and used as one of the headings; it means "magazines and newspapers": _____

5.  A noun rhyming with the word *packs* that means the shelves used for the storage of books and other materials: _____

6.  A word beginning with an *a* that refers to a brief summary of a scientific or technical article or of the current findings in a particular field: _____

7.  An adjective beginning with a *c* and meaning "very important, decisive": _____

SELECTION THREE

# ▦ An English-Speaking World

Just how important is English in the world today? Why has it risen to such prominence over other languages? The following selection gives answers to these and other questions about the English language.

# Prereading Exercise: Skimming for the Main Idea

*Skimming* is a useful technique to develop. Sometimes all you want to know is the main idea of a short reading. But even if you intend to do a careful reading of a selection, it is a good idea to skim it first. Research shows that knowing the main idea in advance makes reading faster and more efficient.

Take two minutes only to skim the selection, which is taken from the book *The Story of English*. Move your eyes quickly through the reading, without stopping for details or worrying about words or phrases you don't understand. Try to grasp the main idea of the whole piece. Write down here what you think is the main idea:

_____

_____

Now read the selection and do the exercises that follow.

## *An English-Speaking World*

In September of 1977, the American spacecraft *Voyager One* blasted off on its historic mission to Jupiter and beyond. On board, the scientists, who knew that *Voyager* would one day spin through distant star systems, had installed a recorded greeting from the people of the planet earth. Preceding a brief
5  message in fifty-five different languages for the people of outer space, the gold-plated disc plays a statement from the Secretary General of the United Nations, an Austrian named Kurt Waldheim, speaking on behalf of 147 member states—in English.

The rise of English is a remarkable success story. When Julius Caesar
10  landed in Britain nearly two thousand years ago, English did not exist. Five hundred years later, *Englise*, incomprehensible to modern ears, was probably spoken by about as few people as currently speak Cherokee*—and with about as little influence. Nearly a thousand years later, at the end of the sixteenth century, when William Shakespeare was in his prime, English was
15  the native speech of between five and seven million English people and it was, in the words of a contemporary, "of small reatch, it stretcheth no further than this iland of ours, naie not there over all."

Four hundred years later, the contrast is extraordinary. Between 1600 and the present, in armies, navies, companies, and expeditions, the speakers
20  of English—including Scots, Irish, Welsh, American, and many more—traveled into every corner of the globe, carrying their language and culture with

---

*Cherokee*  an American Indian language

them. Today English is used by at least 750 million people, and barely half of those speak it as a mother tongue. Some estimates have put that figure closer to one billion. Whatever the total, English at the end of the twentieth
25  century is more widely scattered, more widely spoken and written, than any other language has ever been. It has become *the* language of the planet, the first truly global language.

The statistics of English are astonishing. Of all the world's languages (which now number some 2,700) it is arguably the richest in vocabulary. The
30  compendious *Oxford English Dictionary* lists about 500,000 words; and a further half million technical and scientific terms remain uncatalogued. According to traditional estimates, neighboring German has a vocabulary of about 185,000 words and French fewer than 100,000, including such Franglais as *le snaque-barre* and *le hit-parade*. About 350 million people use the
35  English vocabulary as a mother tongue: about one-tenth of the world's population, scattered across every continent and surpassed, in numbers, though not in distribution, only by the speakers of the many varieties of Chinese. Three-quarters of world's mail, and its telexes and cables, are in English. So are more than half the world's technical and scientific periodicals: it is the
40  language of technology from Silicon Valley to Shanghai. English is the medium for 80 percent of the information stored in the world's computers. Nearly half of all business deals in Europe are conducted in English. It is the language of sports and glamour: the official language of the Olympics and the Miss Universe competition. English is the official voice of the air, of the
45  sea, and of Christianity: it is the ecumenical language of the World Council of Churches. Five of the largest broadcasting companies in the world (CBS, NBC, ABC, BBC, CBC) transmit in English to audiences that regularly exceed one hundred million.

English has a few rivals, but no equals. Neither Spanish nor Arabic, both
50  international languages, have this global sway. Another rival, Russian, has the political and economic underpinning of a world language, but far from spreading its influence outside the Soviet empire, it, too, is becoming mildly colonized by new words known as *Russlish*, for example *seksapil* (sex appeal) and *noh-khau* (know-how). Germany and Japan have, in matching
55  the commercial and industrial vigor of the United States, achieved the commercial precondition of language power, but their languages have also been invaded by English, in the shape of *Deutschlish* and *Japlish*.

The remarkable story of how English spread within predominantly English-speaking societies like the United States, Canada, Australia, and
60  New Zealand is not, with the benefit of hindsight, unique. It is a process in language that is as old as Greek, or Chinese. The truly significant development, which has occurred only in the last one hundred years or so, is the use of English, taking the most conservative estimates, by three or four hundred million people for whom it is not a native language. English has
65  become a *second* language in countries like India, Nigeria, or Singapore,

where it is used for administration, broadcasting, and education. In these
countries, English is a vital alternative language, often unifying huge territories
and diverse populations. When Rajiv Gandhi appealed for an end to the
violence that broke out after the assassination of his mother, Mrs. Indira
70   Gandhi, he went on television and spoke to his people in English. In anglo-
phone Africa, seizures of power are announced in English. Then there is
English as a *foreign* language, used in countries (like Holland or Yugoslavia)
where it is backed up by a tradition of English teaching or where it has been
more recently adopted—Senegal, for instance. As a foreign language, it is
75   used to have contact with people in other countries, usually to promote trade
and scientific progress, but to the benefit of international communication
generally. A Dutch poet is read by a few thousands. Translated into English,
he or she can be read by hundreds of thousands.

**Robert McCrum, William Cran, and Robert MacNeil**
*The Story of English*

## Identifying the Order of Secondary Ideas

Besides the main idea, every reading also presents a number of ideas
of lesser importance that relate to the main idea. Tell which of the six
paragraphs of the selection presents each of the following secondary
ideas, placing the numbers 1 to 6 in the appropriate blanks.

_____ English is widely used as a *second* language in many
countries where it is not the mother tongue.

_____ The early history of English is not very impressive.

_____ In general, English has a larger vocabulary and is more
widely used than other languages.

_____ English was chosen by the United Nations for a message
sent out to other beings in the universe.

_____ The other international or important languages are not as
universal as English.

_____ Between 1600 and the present, English has grown in
importance to be the first truly global language.

## Refining a Statement of the Main Idea

Now that you have reviewed the secondary ideas presented in the selection, look back at the statement of the main idea that you wrote in the
prereading exercise. Can you expand upon it and correct it so that it
includes some of the secondary ideas without making it too long? Work-

ing by yourself or with a partner, write a two- or three-sentence summary of the main idea of the selection. Try to write it so that someone
who had not read the selection would learn something and become
convinced of the main idea.

_____

_____

_____

_____

_____

## Talking It Over

1. What examples are given in the article to show that English
   is now the language of business and science and global
   communication?
2. Do you think another language will replace English in these roles
   sometime in the future? If so, which one?
3. What is meant by *Franglais, Russlish, Deutschlish,* and *Japlish*?
   Why have these new words appeared?
4. Do you know any words from other languages that are widely
   used and understood in English?
5. In which countries of the world is English used as an important
   *second* language? Why is it used there?

## Using Punctuation to Unravel Meaning

The use and placement of punctuation often helps us to understand the
ideas being expressed. Read the comments on punctuation, then answer
the questions about the excerpts from the reading.

1. "Between 1600 and the present, in armies, navies, companies,
   and expeditions, the speakers of English—including Scots, Irish,
   Welsh, American, and many more—traveled into every corner
   of the globe, carrying their language and culture with them."
   *Comment:* Writers of English often interrupt the main idea of a
   sentence to insert a secondary idea, separating it off with dashes
   before and after. They insert it right after the word or phrase it
   is related to. What is the main idea of this sentence? What is the
   secondary idea? How are they related?

   _____

   _____

2. "It has become *the* language of the planet, the first truly global language."
   *Comment:* One of the uses of italics is emphasis. How does its use in this sentence modify the meaning?

   _____

   _____

   It can also alter the pronunciation. How would you say the sentence aloud?

3. "About 350 million people use the English vocabulary as a mother tongue: about one-tenth of the world's population, scattered across every continent and surpassed, in numbers, though not in distribution, only by the speakers of the many varieties of Chinese."
   *Comment:* Usually the use of the colon signifies that what is before it and what is after it are equal or identical. In this sentence, what equals what?

   _____

   _____

   Commas are used to separate different parts of a complex idea. Look at the end of the sentence. Does English or Chinese have a larger number of users? Does English or Chinese have a larger distribution? How can you tell?

   _____

   _____

## Understanding a Shaded Map

Look at the map of the world, read its legend, and answer the questions that follow it.

1. What do the shaded parts of the map indicate?

   _____

2. What is the difference between the two types of shading?

   _____

3. Looking at the map, tell on what continents English is spoken (in some countries) as the mother tongue.

   _____

   _____

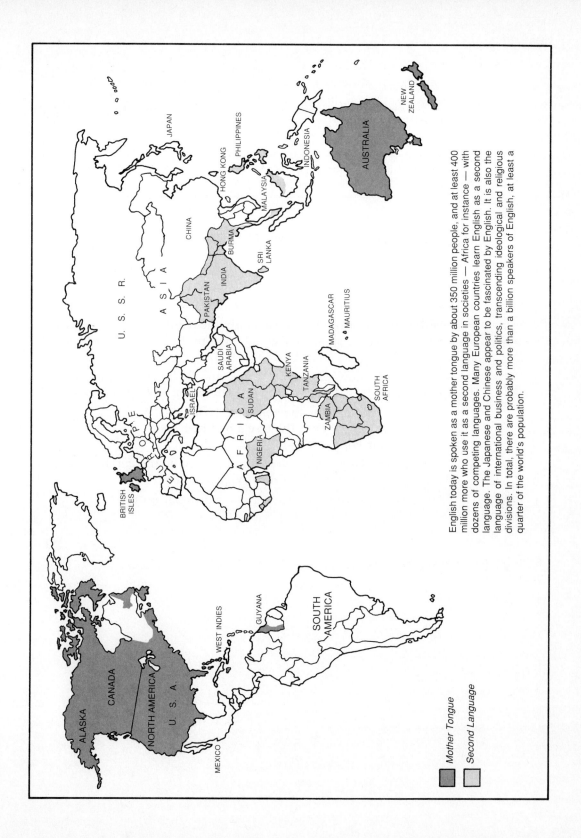

English today is spoken as a mother tongue by about 350 million people, and at least 400 million more who use it as a second language in societies — Africa for instance — with dozens of competing languages. Many European countries learn English as a second language. The Japanese and Chinese appear to be fascinated by English. It is also the language of international business and politics, transcending ideological and religious divisions. In total, there are probably more than a billion speakers of English, at least a quarter of the world's population.

*Mother Tongue*

*Second Language*

4. On what continents is English spoken as a second language?

_____

_____

5. Which of these two groups is larger? Which is more important for the status of English as a *global* language?

_____

## Famous Quotations on Education

Which of the following quotations relates most directly to your own personal ideas about education? Why?

"Knowledge is power."—Francis Bacon, 1561–1626

"Education is a thing of which only the few are capable. Teach as you will, only a small percentage will profit by your most zealous energy."—George Gissing, 1857–1903

"We do not know what education could do for us, because we have never tried it."—Robert Maynard Hutchins, 1899–1977

"'Tis Education forms the common mind:
Just as the twig is bent the tree's inclined."
—Alexander Pope, 1688–1744

"There are two ways of spreading light: to be the candle or the mirror that reflects it."—Edith Wharton, 1862–1937

"Experience is the best teacher."—traditional proverb

CHAPTER 2

# Danger and Daring

Why take risks? Why face danger and even death when it is possible simply to stay at home in safety and comfort? Throughout history there have been many who dared: explorers, mountain climbers, travelers, soldiers, religious leaders. Some have done it for fame or fortune; some for sport or curiosity. The first selection focuses on some present-day adventurers who have become famous for their daring. The second is a short story that examines some different attitudes toward risk taking. The third selection is a true account of a Canadian naturalist and writer who went to live among wild animals and found that the experience led to an important discovery—about himself.

## SELECTION ONE

# Adventurers of Today

Helen Keller once wrote that a life without risk is not worth living. She had good reason to know. Blind and deaf from an early age, she became a renowned writer who later traveled and gave speeches in various parts of the world. Many people share her sentiments. In fact, today, more than ever, people attempt feats that are difficult to achieve. Consider marathon races, weight lifting, and hang gliding. Additionally, many people pursue professional goals that ensure competition and with it the possibility of failure. Why do you think so many of us are willing to attempt these feats? What character traits are necessary for people to take these risks?

In the space below, write one of the major risks you have taken in recent years. What happened?

_____

_____

_____

What did you learn from this experience?

_____

_____

_____

## Prereading Exercise: Formulating Questions About a Reading in Advance

The following selection is an informative essay based on recent items in the news. Before beginning to read, you should try to get a general idea of what the selection is about and imagine key questions about the topic. Then you will be able to read more efficiently, skipping over difficult sections unless they relate directly to the central topic or the key questions.

Look at the title and illustrations. What is the article about?

_____

Take three minutes to skim the entire selection. Then write three important questions about the topic that you think will be answered in the reading.

1. _____

2. _____

3. _____

Now compare your questions as a class. Which ones were asked by the most students? Which ones relate to several parts of the article or to the article as a whole instead of to just one part? Decide on the questions you think are the most important and focus on these as you read.

## Adventurers of Today

"The future doesn't belong to the fainthearted, it belongs to the brave."
Former President of the United States Ronald W. Reagan

**March 20, 1985**
Libby Riddles, a 28-year-old Canadian residing in Teller, Alaska, a village on the Seward Peninsula, became the first woman to win the 1,135-mile (1,827-kilometer) Anchorage-to-Nome Iditarod Trail International Race, the world's longest and most difficult dog-sled race. This was the thirteenth year the race
5   had been run and the third year in which Riddles had competed. After nearly eighteen days, her thirteen huskies beat sixty teams for the $50,000 top prize. Riddles had taken the lead during the final days of the race by pushing into a snowstorm that other contestants decided to sit out. She crossed the finish line some three hours ahead of the second-place finisher.

**March 13, 1986**
10   Susan Butcher became the second woman to win the race in a record time of eleven days, fifteen hours, and six minutes. Butcher repeated her victory in 1987 and 1988, and so became the only participant in history to win three consecutive Iditarods.

**December 23, 1986**
Dick Rutan, 48, and Jeanna Yeager, 34, became the first pilots to circle the
15   world without making a stop or refueling. Their plane, the *Voyager*, designed by Dick's brother, Burt Rutan, made the 25,012-mile (40,254-kilometer) flight

in nine days. Five times during their flight, typhoons and other storms had forced them to change course or climb to a higher altitude. Occasionally, the lightweight craft had been tossed about as if it were a toy.

20      The most frightening five minutes of the journey came seven and a half hours away from landing, when the plane plummeted some 3,500 feet (1,000 meters) from its altitude of 8,500 feet (2,600 meters) over the coast of California. The rear engine had stalled upon drawing in air from a near-empty fuel tank, and the pilots had had to switch to the front engine to save the 25    plane.

The journey was the longest flight made without a stop, and the continuous nine days, three minutes, and forty-four seconds the two pilots spent in the air set an aviation endurance record.

The crew of the space shuttle Challenger, who died in the explosion of the shuttle upon takeoff in 1986

### January 28, 1986

The space shuttle *Challenger* exploded shortly after takeoff. All seven mem-
30    bers of the crew died in the explosion. The disaster, the worst in the American space program, occurred only seventy-four seconds after launching at 11:38 A.M. from Cape Canaveral, Florida.

The seven *Challenger* crew members had a variety of proficiencies and specialties. Three of them were trained pilots.

35      Francis R. (Dick) Scobee, 46, flight commander, had logged more than 6,500 hours of flight in forty-five types of aircraft. He was making his second space shuttle mission, having piloted the *Challenger* mission in 1984. He was a former combat pilot, married and the father of two grown children.

U.S. Navy Commander Michael J. Smith, 40, pilot of the *Challenger*, was
40    a former jet training teacher and instructor of Navy test pilots. The flight was his first space mission. Smith was married and the father of three children.

Ronald E. McNair, 36, was a physicist and an expert in lasers. He flew on the tenth space shuttle mission in 1984. On this one, he was to have
45 launched a small science platform to study Halley's Comet. McNair was the second black American astronaut in space. He was also a karate expert and saxophonist. He was married and the father of two children.

U.S. Air Force Lieutenant Colonel Allison S. Onizuka, 39, born in Hawaii, flew on a secret space shuttle flight in 1985. He was an aerospace engineer.
50 He was married and the father of two children.

Judith A. Resnik, 36, a research scientist before becoming an astronaut, had logged 144 hours and 57 minutes in space and was the second American woman astronaut to travel in space. She held an electrical engineering degree and was a classical pianist. She was single.

55 Gregory B. Jarvis, 41, an engineer with Hughes Aircraft Co., was making his first space flight. He was to have conducted experiments in fluid dynamics. He was married.

Sharon Christa McAuliffe, 37, was a high school social studies teacher from Concord, New Hampshire. She was to have taught science lessons on
60 television over the Public Broadcasting Service to schoolchildren throughout the country. McAuliffe was selected from more than eleven thousand applicants as NASA's first "citizen in space." She was a native of Boston, married, and the mother of two children.

The tragedy of the *Challenger*, viewed on television by millions of people,
65 sent a shock wave through the world and ignited an ongoing controversy on all aspects of America's space program.

**July 20, 1986**
Teiichi Igarashi, born September 21, 1886, climbed snowcapped Mt. Fuji at age 99 years, 302 days.

Igarashi topped the 12,388-foot mountain to become the oldest climber
70 on record to achieve such a remarkable feat.

**April 1987**
Skydiver Gregory Robertson, 35, made one of the most daring rescues in skydiving history. Fellow skydiver Debbie Williams, 31, while attempting to join three other divers in a hand-holding ring formation, slammed into the backpack of another chutist and was knocked unconscious. She was floating
75 through the air like a limp rag doll.

Within seconds, Robertson, a veteran instructor with 1,700 jumps to his credit, assessed the situation and decided to attempt rescue. Assuming a rocket-like vertical position, Robertson pinned his arms to his body, crossed his ankles and plummeted in a "no-lift" dive at a speed of around 200 miles
80 per hour toward Williams. At 3,500 feet, about ten seconds before impact, Robertson caught up with Williams and angled her in the right position so that her chute could open. With six seconds left, at 2,000 feet, Robertson

85 yanked the ripcord on William's emergency chute, then pulled his own. The two sky divers floated to the ground. Williams landed on her back and suffered injuries, but thanks to Robertson's daring rescue, she is alive and has recovered.

AP WIREPHOTO

Skydivers in ring formation

### November 11, 1987

90 Erik Fiederer, 10, set a record for cross-country speed and distance transcontinental flight for persons in his age group. Accompanied by his mother, U.S. Air Force Col. Nancy Fiederer, Erik piloted his Cessna Centurion P-210 from Fort Lewis, Washington, to Miami in a total flying and ground time of thirty-one and a half hours including fifteen hours in the air. The sixth-grader from Santa Maria, California, with only three months of flying experience, said he was happy knowing he had done it. "I wanted to fly ever since I was four," he added.

## Using Facts to Explode Myths

People often have opinions on subjects that they don't know many facts about. Tell what facts from the article support the following opinions and what facts contradict them.

1. Only the young participate in dangerous activities; older people are too concerned with safety and security.

2. Nowadays people are too selfish to risk their lives for the benefit of others.

3. Children who make important achievements are usually helped along by their parents.

4. Men are stronger and braver than women, so most acts of danger and daring are performed by them.

5. No airplane will ever circle the globe without refueling, because if it is light enough to attain the required speed it will not be able to withstand the winds and storms.

6. The honor of being an astronaut in the American space program is reserved for male WASPs (White Anglo-Saxon Protestants).

7. Marriage and children do not necessarily mean the end to adventure.

## Comparing and Evaluating Answers

Write answers to the questions you wrote for the prereading exercise. Then, as a class or in small groups, compare your answers. Do they use specific information from the reading? Are they clear and concise? Are they too concise? Choose one or two good answers to each question and read them aloud or write them on the board.

## Making Inferences About Character Traits

Inferences are conclusions we draw from facts. For example, if someone is frowning, we infer that he or she is sad or angry. The article discusses several modern-day adventurers. It does not say what traits (qualities) of character they have, but it does give you information about what they have done. Look at the following list of traits. Do you know what all of the words mean? Tell which traits you think the adventurers have and from what information you have inferred this.

| | | |
|---|---|---|
| persistence | ambition | timidity |
| self-confidence | courage | intelligence |
| laziness | decisiveness | |

## Talking It Over

1. Which of the adventures mentioned in the article do you think is the most interesting? Which of the people described is the most worthy of admiration? Why?

2. Have you ever done something dangerous or daring? If so, what was it and why did you do it? Give an example of something adventurous you might like to do some day.

3. What do you think of the American space program? Should it be discontinued and the money used for something else? Should the focus be changed to unmanned missions? Explain your opinion.

4. The most famous quotation about the dangerous sport of mountaineering is from adventurer George Leigh Mallory. On a lecture tour in 1923, he was asked, "Why do you want to climb Mt. Everest?" Mallory replied, "Because it is there." What do you infer about Mallory from this quotation?

## Using the Encyclopedia to Prepare a Class Report

Research a person who has performed an important act of danger and daring and prepare a class report, answering the following questions:

1. What dangerous act did he or she perform?
2. Why was it important?
3. When did it happen?
4. How old was he or she at the time?
5. Why do you think he or she did it? For fame? For fortune? For knowledge? For religious or political convictions?

The easiest way to find out this information is probably to go to an encyclopedia, look up the person's name, and scan the article about him or her until you find what you want. Don't copy the phrases word for word from the encyclopedia. Instead, put the answers into your own words. Here are some suggestions for your research:

| | |
|---|---|
| Gonzalo Pizarro | Mohandas Gandhi |
| Martin Luther King, Jr. | Amelia Earhart |
| Leif Ericsson | Cleopatra |
| Mata Hari | Houdini |
| Louis Riel | Kosciuszko |

## SELECTION TWO

# A High Dive

The following story is fiction, which means that it did not really happen but was invented by the author. From looking at the title and illustrations, what dangerous or daring action do you think the story will relate? In other words, what do you think the *plot* of the story will be? (The term *plot*, when referring to stories, means the chain of events that makes up the action or main story line.) Traditionally, the *plot* of a piece of fiction follows four steps:

1. **Conflict.** The story begins with some problem or conflict. (If everything were going fine, there would be no movement, no real story to tell.)

2. **Complication.** Something happens to change and increase—to complicate—the problem.

3. **Climax.** Toward the end, the story reaches a climax, or turning point, a high point of interest or excitement that will determine how everything turns out.

4. **Resolution.** Soon after the climax, the conflict is resolved—either by being solved, for better or worse, or by being accepted or seen in a different way—and the story ends. Sometimes there is a happy ending and sometimes a sad one, depending on the author's view of reality and the point he or she wants to make. Often the French term *dénouement* is used in English instead of the word *resolution*.

Typical conflicts in fictional stories involve a struggle between a character and nature (a mountain to climb, a jungle to cross), between the main character and other characters (a detective against a criminal, a hero against evildoers), between a character and a social or economic situation, or between a character and himself or herself (a person who fights his or her own fear, ambition, ignorance, and so on). Sometimes there is more than one conflict in the same story. Take a guess about the following story. What type of conflict(s) do you think will occur in it?

_____

_____

## Prereading Exercise: Thinking Ahead and Predicting the Action

As you read, try to think ahead of the story. Don't worry about the words you don't understand. Simply follow the main steps of the plot and pick up clues from the context to help you predict what is going to happen next. The story will be interrupted at a few points and you will be asked some questions to guide you.

## *A High Dive*

The circus manager was worried. Attendances had been falling off and such people as did come—children they were, mostly—sat about listlessly, munching sweets or sucking ices, sometimes talking to each other without so much as glancing at the show. . . . What did people want? Something that was, in
5  his opinion, sillier and more pointless than the old jokes; not a bull's-eye on the target of humor, but an outer or even a near miss—something that brought in the element of futility and that could be laughed at as well as with; an unintentional joke against the joker.

The clowns were quick enough with their patter but it just didn't go down;
10  there was too much sense in their nonsense for an up-to-date audience, too

much articulateness. They would do better to talk gibberish perhaps. Now they must change their style, and find out what really did make people laugh, if people could be made to; but he, the manager, was over fifty and never good himself at making jokes, even the old-fashioned kind. What was this
15  word that everyone was using—"sophisticated"? The audiences were too sophisticated, even the children were: They seemed to have seen and heard all this before, even when they were too young to have seen and heard it.

"What shall we do?" he asked his wife. They were standing under the Big Top, which had just been put up, and wondering how many of the empty
20  seats would still be empty when they gave their first performance.

"I don't see what we can do about the comic side," she said. "It may come right by itself. Fashions change, all sorts of old things have returned to favor, like old-time dances. But there's something we could do."

"What's that?"
25  "Put on an act that's dangerous, really dangerous. Audiences are never bored by that. I know you don't like it, and no more do I, but when we had the Wall of Death—"

Her husband's big chest muscles twitched under his thin shirt.

---

**Prediction**   What is the conflict that begins the story? What possible solution does one of the characters offer? How can you tell that the other one doesn't like it? What do you think the "Wall of Death" is? Will the man and woman probably agree or disagree as they talk about it?

---

"You know what happened then."
30  "Yes, but it wasn't our fault; we were in the clear."

He shook his head.

"Those things upset everyone. I know the public came after it happened—they came in shoals.* They came to see the place where someone had been killed. But our people got the needle and didn't give a good performance for
35  I don't know how long. If you're proposing another Wall of Death I wouldn't stand for it—besides, where will you find a man to do it?—especially with a lion on his bike, which is the great attraction."

"But other turns are dangerous too, as well as dangerous looking. It's being dangerous that is the draw."
40  "Then what do you suggest?"

Before she had time to answer a man came up to them.

"I hope I don't butt in," he said, "but there's a man outside who wants to speak to you."

---

*shoals*   large groups, throngs, droves

"What about?"

45    "I think he's looking for a job."

"Bring him in," said the manager.

**Prediction**    What do you think is meant by the word *draw* in this context? What has happened to complicate the plot? What do you imagine the new character will propose?

The man appeared, led by his escort, who then went away. He was a tall, sandy-haired fellow with tawny leonine eyes and a straggling moustache. It wasn't easy to tell his age—he might have been about thirty-five. He pulled

50    off his old brown corduroy cap and waited.

"I hear you want to take a job with us," the manager said, while his wife tried to size up the newcomer. "We're pretty full up, you know. We don't take on strangers as a rule. Have you any references?"

"No, sir."

55    "Then I'm afraid we can't help you. But just for form's sake, what can you do?"

As if measuring its height the man cast up his eyes to the point where one of the two poles of the Big Top was embedded in the canvas.

"I can dive sixty feet into a tank eight feet long by four feet wide by four

60    feet deep." The manager stared at him.

"Can you now?" he said. "If so, you're the very man we want. Are you prepared to let us see you do it?"

"Yes," the man said.

"And would you do it with petrol burning on the water?"

65    "Yes."

"But have we got a tank?" the manager's wife asked.

"There's the old Mermaid's tank. It's just the thing. Get somebody to fetch it."

While the tank was being brought the stranger looked about him.

70    "Thinking better of it?" said the manager.

"No, sir," the man replied. "I was thinking I should want some bathing trunks."

"We can soon fix you up with those," the manager said. "I'll show you where to change."

75    Leaving the stranger somewhere out of sight, he came back to his wife.

"Do you think we ought to let him do it?" she asked.

"Well, it's his funeral. You wanted us to have a dangerous act, and now we've got it."

"Yes, I know, but . . ." The rest was drowned by the rattle of the trolley

80    bringing in the tank—a hollow, double cube like a sarcophagus. Mermaids

in low relief sported on its leaden flanks. Grunting and muttering to each other the men slid it into position, a few feet from the pole. Then a length of hosepipe was fastened to a faucet and soon they heard the sound of water swishing and gurgling in the tank.

85     "He's a long time changing," said the manager's wife.

"Perhaps he's looking for a place to hide his money," laughed her husband, and added, "I think we'll give the petrol a miss."

---

> **Prediction**   In what way do the manager and his wife seem to have changed their points of view? Why do you think this happened? What words or actions make you think that the stranger is not afraid? That he is poor? What do you predict will be the climax? Do you think it will bring success or tragedy? Might it be a solution to the problem that began this story?

---

At length the man emerged from behind a screen and slowly walked toward them. How tall he was, lanky and muscular. The hair on his body

90  stuck out as if it had been combed. Hands on hips he stood beside them, his skin pimpled by gooseflesh. A fit of yawning overtook him.

"How do I get up?" he asked.

The manager was surprised, and pointed to the ladder. "Unless you'd rather climb up, or be hauled up! You'll find a platform just below the top, to

95  give you a foothold."

He had started to go up the chromium-plated ladder when the manager's wife called after him: "Are you still sure you want to do it?"

"Quite sure, madam."

He was too tall to stand upright on the platform; the awning brushed his

100  head. Crouching and swaying forty feet above them he swung his arms as though to test the air's resistance. Then he pitched forward into space, unseen by the manager's wife, who looked the other way until she heard a splash and saw a thin sheet of bright water shooting up.

The man was standing breast-high in the tank. He swung himself over

105  the edge and crossed the ring toward them, his body dripping, his wet feet caked with sawdust, his tawny eyes a little bloodshot.

"Bravo!" said the manager, taking his shiny hand. "It's a first-rate act, that, and will put money in our pockets. What do you want for it, fifteen quid a week?"

110  The man shook his head. The water trickled onto his shoulders, oozed from his borrowed bathing suit and made runnels* down his sinewy thighs. A fine figure of a man: the women would like him.

"Well, twenty then." Still the man shook his head.

---

*runnel*  a small stream, brook, rivulet

"Let's make it twenty-five. That's the most we give anyone."

115    Except for the slow shaking of his head the man might not have heard. The circus-manager and his wife exchanged a rapid glance.

---

> **Prediction**   Were you right about the climax? Why do you think that the man is not responding? Do you predict that he will become a member of the circus or not? Why? How do you think the story will end?

---

"Look here," he said. "Taking into account the draw your act is likely to be, we're going to make you a special offer—thirty pounds a week. All right?"

Had the man understood? He put his finger in his mouth and went on shaking his head slowly, more to himself than at them, and seemingly uncon-

120    scious of the bargain that was being held out to him. When he still didn't answer, the knot of tension broke, and the manager said, in his ordinary, brisk voice, "Then I'm afraid we can't do business. But just as a matter of interest, tell us why you turned down our excellent offer."

The man drew a long breath and breaking his long silence said, "It's the

125    first time I done it and I didn't like it."

With that he turned on his heel and walked off unsteadily in the direction of the dressing room.

The circus-manager and his wife stared at each other.

"It was the first time he'd done it," she muttered. "The first time." Not

130    knowing what to say to him, whether to praise, blame, scold or sympathize, they waited for him to come back, but he didn't come.

"I'll go and see if he's all right," the circus-manager said. But in two minutes he was back again. "He's not there," he said. "He must have slipped out the other way, the crack-brained fellow."

**L. P. Hartley**

## Talking It Over

1. Were most of your predictions about the action correct? Did any part of the story surprise you?

2. By the way the younger man speaks, you can tell that he is not very well educated. What grammar mistake does he make toward the end of the story that shows you this?

3. Will the diver return? Explain your answer.

4. Why do you think the circus manager kept on making higher offers to the diver? What lesson does this teach us about bargaining? Do you think it is usually appropriate to bargain for a salary

or not? On which of the following occasions do you think it would be appropriate to bargain in North American society?

- purchasing food at the supermarket
- buying a new or used car
- arranging to sublet an apartment
- ordering dinner at a restaurant
- buying clothes at a department store
- buying second-hand furniture (or a used bicycle) that was advertised in the newspaper or on a bulletin board

## Understanding the Theme

Besides characters, plot, and setting, a story also has a *theme*: the general idea or main point of the story. An author combines the characters, plot, and setting in a particular way to show something. To find the theme of a story, you can ask yourself: Does the story express a particular opinion or belief? Perhaps it makes some statement about the meaning of courage or the true definition of love.

The preceding story deals with the need for making money and for taking risks and the danger that this sometimes involves for human life. But what exactly does it say about these subjects? Which of the following statements do you think expresses the theme of the story best? If you do not like any of them, write your own statement of the theme in the blanks provided.

1. No amount of money is worth the risk of losing a human life.
2. Only the person who takes a risk can judge how much it is worth.
3. It takes courage as well as skill to confront danger successfully.
4. _____

_____

_____

## Word Detective

Follow the clues to find the words and phrases in the article.

1. a hyphenated word in the first paragraph that refers to a part of an animal and means "an exact hit right in the center":

_____

2. an adjective used twice in the second paragraph; it begins with the letter *s* and means the opposite of simple or naive:

_____

3. a two-word phrase, used in the third paragraph and after, that means the large tent used for circuses:

_____

4. a noun used to describe the tank that is brought in toward the middle of the story; it begins with *s* and means "a coffin (box that holds a dead body for burial) used in ancient times":

_____

5. an *-ing* word that begins with *c* and is used to describe the way the diver stood at the top of the platform under the tent because he was too tall to stand up straight:

_____

6. a verb used in the second-to-last paragraph that means "to share the feelings (of someone)": _____

## Some Slang Used for Referring to Money

You can tell that this story takes place in Great Britain because the circus manager makes offers in pounds rather than in dollars. What slang word does he use to refer to pounds when he makes his first offer?

_____

Do you know the meaning of the slang words in the following sentences? They refer to money in Canada and in the United States.

1. You say the price is ten *bucks*. Why, that's outrageous!
2. I wouldn't give you *two bits* for that! Well . . . okay, for *six bits*, I'll take it.
3. Can you trust me until tomorrow? I don't have any *bread* on me now.
4. Let's go to a restaurant that accepts *plastic money*.

## SELECTION THREE

# The World We Lost

Do you ever have nightmares? What is your secret fear? Poisonous snakes? Earthquakes? Water? Fire? Everyone is afraid of something, and wild animals appear high on the list of horrors for many people. Farley Mowat, the world-famous Canadian writer and adventurer, shared this fear even though he accepted a job that meant living alone

in the far north for many months in direct contact with packs of wolves.
The Wildlife Service of the Canadian government hired him to investigate claims that hordes of blood-thirsty wolves were killing the arctic
caribou (large animals of the deer family). Much to his surprise, Mowat
discovered that the wolves were not savage killers, but cautious and
predictable animals that usually tried to stay out of people's way. He
gave names to the wolves he studied (Angeline, George, and so forth),
got to know them, and even became fond of them.

Later he wrote a book called *Never Cry Wolf* about his experiences.
It became a best-seller and was made into a popular movie that has
changed many people's ideas about wolves, although it has not done
much to stop the massive extermination campaigns against wolves in
certain parts of Canada and the United States. The following selection
is the last chapter of his book. It tells of an incident that seemed to be
very dangerous and that led the author to an important discovery, not
about the wolves but about himself. What do you think the title might
mean? See if your idea of it changes as you read the story.

## Prereading Exercise: Guessing the Meaning of New Words from Context

Read the following excerpts from the selection and choose the best
definition for each italicized word. Use the hints in parentheses to aid
you.

1. "In order to round out my study of wolf family life, I needed to
   know what the *den* was like inside—how deep it was, the diameter
   of the passage, the presence (if any) of a nest at the end of the *burrow*, and such related information." The *den* is the place where the
   wolves go to:

   a. hunt   b. sleep   c. die

   A *burrow* is:

   a. a pile of sticks and mud
   b. a young wolf or dog
   c. a hole dug by an animal

2. "The *Norseman* came over at about fifty feet. As it roared past, the
   plane waggled its wings gaily in salute, then lifted to skim the
   crest of the wolf *esker*, sending a blast of sand down the slope with
   its propeller wash." A *Norseman* is a type of:

   a. animal   b. wind   c. plane

   (*Hint:* The word *esker* is not well known even to English speakers,
   but the reader can use clues from the context: the word *crest*, your
   knowledge of where the man is going, what happens when the
   propeller gets near the esker.) An *esker* is:

   a. a ridge of sand   b. a small river   c. a kind of fruit tree

3. "My mouth and eyes were soon full of sand and I was beginning to suffer from *claustrophobia*, for the tunnel was just big enough to admit me." (*Hint: Phobia* is a term used in psychology to refer to a deep, irrational fear. If you remember that the word *for* means "because" when it starts a secondary clause, you will understand what fear is referred to by this word.) *Claustrophobia* is the unreasonable fear of:

   a. high, open places
   b. small, enclosed places
   c. wild animals

4. "Despite my close *familiarity* with the wolf family, this was the kind of situation where irrational but deeply ingrained *prejudices* completely overmaster reason and experience." In this context, *familiarity* means:

   a. similarity   b. hatred   c. acquaintance

   (*Hint:* If you break up the word *prejudice*, you get the prefix *pre-* meaning "before," and the root *jud*, which also appears in words such as *judge* and *judgment*.) *Prejudices* means:

   a. strong and warm emotions
   b. opinions formed with no basis in fact
   c. conclusions drawn from observation and action

5. "It seemed *inevitable* that the wolves <u>would</u> attack me, for even a *gopher* will make a fierce defense when he is cornered in his den." (*Hint:* The word *even* is your best clue to the meaning of both the italicized words.) *Inevitable* means:

   a. certain   b. highly unlikely   c. possible

   A *gopher* is an animal that is:

   a. large and dangerous
   b. small and defenseless
   c. similar to a wolf

6. "I was *appalled* at the realization of how easily I had forgotten, and how readily I had denied, all that the summer *sojourn* with the wolves had taught me about them . . . and about myself." *Appalled* means:

   a. pleased   b. shocked   c. relieved

   *Sojourn* means:

   a. reading   b. weather   c. stay

## The World We Lost

In order to round out my study of wolf family life, I needed to know what the den was like inside—how deep it was, the diameter of the passage, the presence (if any) of a nest at the end of the burrow, and such related information. For obvious reasons I had not been able to make the investigation

LENARD LEE RUE/MONKMEYER PRESS PHOTO SERVICE

Two baby wolves at the entrance to their den

5   while the den was occupied, and since that time I had been too busy with
other work to get around to it. Now, with time running out, I was in a hurry.

I trotted across country toward the den and I was within half a mile of it
when there was a thunderous roar behind me. It was so loud and unexpected
that I involuntarily flung myself down on the moss. The Norseman came over
10  at about fifty feet. As it roared past, the plane waggled its wings gaily in
salute, then lifted to skim the crest of the wolf esker, sending a blast of sand
down the slope with its propeller wash. I picked myself up and quieted my
thumping heart, thinking black thoughts about the humorist in the now rapidly
vanishing aircraft.

15  The den ridge was, as I had expected (and as the Norseman would have
made quite certain in any case), wolfless. Reaching the entrance to the burrow
I shed my heavy trousers, tunic, and sweater, and taking a flashlight (whose
batteries were very nearly dead) and measuring tape from my pack, I began
the difficult task of wiggling down the entrance tunnel.

20  The flashlight was so dim it cast only an orange glow—barely sufficient
to enable me to read the marks on the measuring tape. I squirmed onward,
descending at a forty-five-degree angle, for about eight feet. My mouth and
eyes were soon full of sand and I was beginning to suffer from claustrophobia,
for the tunnel was just big enough to admit me.

25  At the eight-foot mark the tunnel took a sharp upward bend and swung
to the left. I pointed the torch in the new direction and pressed the switch.

Four green lights in the murk ahead reflected back the dim torch beam.

In this case green was not my signal to advance. I froze where I was,
while my startled brain tried to digest the information that at least two wolves
30  were with me in the den.

Despite my close familiarity with the wolf family, this was the kind of situation where irrational but deeply ingrained prejudices completely overmaster reason and experience. To be honest, I was so frightened that paralysis gripped me. I had no weapon of any sort, and in my awkward posture

35 I could barely have gotten one hand free with which to ward off an attack. It seemed inevitable that the wolves *would* attack me, for even a gopher will make a fierce defense when he is cornered in his den.

The wolves did not even growl.

Save for the two faintly glowing pairs of eyes, they might not have been

40 there at all.

The paralysis began to ease and though it was a cold day, sweat broke out all over my body. In a fit of blind bravado, I shoved the torch forward as far as my arm would reach.

It gave just sufficient light for me to recognize Angeline and one of the

45 pups. They were scrunched hard against the back wall of the den; and they were as motionless as death.

The shock was wearing off by this time, and the instinct for self-preservation was regaining command. As quickly as I could I began wiggling back up the slanting tunnel, tense with the expectation that at any instant the

50 wolves would charge. But by the time I reached the entrance and had scrambled well clear of it, I had still not heard nor seen the slightest sign of movement from the wolves.

I sat down on a stone and shakily lit a cigarette, becoming aware as I did so that I was no longer frightened. Instead an irrational rage possessed

55 me. If I had had my rifle I believe I might have reacted in brute fury and tried to kill both wolves.

The cigarette burned down, and a wind began to blow out of the somber northern skies. I began to shiver again; this time from cold instead of rage. My anger was passing and I was limp in the aftermath. Mine had been the

60 fury of resentment born of fear: resentment against the beasts who had engendered naked terror in me and who, by so doing, had intolerably affronted my human ego.

I was appalled at the realization of how easily I had forgotten, and how readily I had denied, all that the summer sojourn with the wolves had taught

65 me about them . . . and about myself. I thought of Angeline and her pup cowering at the bottom of the den where they had taken refuge from the thundering apparition of the aircraft, and I was shamed.

Somewhere to the eastward a wolf howled; lightly, questioningly. I knew the voice, for I had heard it many times before. It was George, sounding the

70 wasteland for an echo from the missing members of his family. But for me it was a voice which spoke of the lost world which once was ours before we chose the alien role; a world which I had glimpsed and almost entered, . . . only to be excluded, at the end, by my own self.

**Farley Mowat**
*Never Cry Wolf*

# Filling in a Summary of the Plot

Fill in the blanks with appropriate words to complete the following summary of Farley Mowat's true story. For some blanks, several different words could be correct.

**THE WORLD WE LOST: A SUMMARY**

In the far north, the Canadian _____1 was

doing a study on _____2 and decided to go

inside the _____3. On his way there he was

_____4 by a low-flying

_____5. He took a _____6

to be able to see and a _____

_____7 to make measurements and entered.

As he went down the tight _____8, he began

to suffer from _____9. Suddenly he saw

ahead four green _____10, and he knew that

two _____11 were there with him. He felt

very _____12 and could not

_____13. Then he quickly

_____14 the burrow. Afterward, he no longer

felt frightened; instead he felt _____15 and

even wanted to _____16 the wolves. Later he

realized how easily he had _____17 all that
his study of the wolves had taught him, and he was

_____18. That day he made an important
discovery not about wolves but about

_____19.

# Understanding the Author's Purpose

Mowat's story is nonfiction, but it still has the same narrative elements that make up fiction stories: characters, setting, plot, and theme. What happened was true, but the author chose out of many true events certain ones to tell for a particular reason, to show a certain general idea (theme). Describe briefly in your own words the narrative elements of this story.

Setting: _____

Characters: _____

Plot: _____

What is the basic conflict? _____

_____

What is the climax of the action? _____

_____

*Theme:* (Think of the discovery the author makes at the end. Think of the title and how it relates to this discovery.)

_____

_____

## Talking It Over

1. Would you be afraid to study wild animals the way Mowat did or not? Would you be able to spend a summer completely alone, away from all human company? What character traits (qualities) must a person have to do these things?

2. Farley Mowat writes in a personal, down-to-earth style. He is not afraid to tell about his faults and his feelings. In your opinion, what does this indicate about his character?

3. At a dramatic point in his story, Mowat interjects a bit of humor. He says, "In this case green was not my signal to advance." What does he mean by this? The technique of using humor at a very serious moment is called *comic relief*. What do you think the purpose of this is?

4. How can you tell that Mowat has gotten to know the wolves as individuals and that he feels affection for them?

5. Have you ever seen wolves? Do you know of places other than Canada where they live?

6. In your opinion, should wolves be exterminated or not? Why?

## Solving Problems in Groups: Thinking Your Way Out of Danger

Many times the only way to get out of a dangerous spot is with your brain. Read over the following imaginary situations; then work together in small groups and try to figure out how you would escape from each of them. (If you give up, you can ask your teacher, who just might know the answer.)

**SITUATION A: THE WINDOWLESS PRISON**

While participating in a revolution against an unjust tyrant, you are caught and thrown into a prison cell that has a dirt floor, thick stone walls, and no windows. There is only a skylight, very high above, to provide light and air. To prevent escape, there are no tables or chairs, only a very small mattress on the floor. Just before you are locked in, a comrade whispers to you that it is possible to escape through the skylight by digging a hole in the floor. How can you do this?

**SITUATION B: THE CAVE OF THE TWO ROBOTS**

Having entered a time machine, you have been whisked one thousand years into the future to find yourself at the mercy of a superior civilization. These creatures of the future choose to amuse themselves by playing games with you. They set you in a cave that has two doors at the end of it: One leads back to the time machine that would transport you safely home, and the other leads to a pit filled with horrible monsters. There are also two robots in the cave. They know the secret of the doors. One always tells the truth and one always lies, and you do not know which is which. According to the rules of their game, you are allowed to ask one question to one of the robots. What question should you ask? How can you know which door to choose?

# CHAPTER 3

# Man and Woman

NINA HOWELL STARR/PHOTO RESEARCHERS, INC.

The eternal "battle of the sexes" continues to be a popular topic just as it has been down through the ages. This chapter begins with a discussion of how technology and tradition blend to aid romance in today's Japan. An analysis of the differences between men and women follows, comparing the two sexes with regard to sports, health, aggression, crime, child care, and brain structure, and drawing conclusions that may surprise you. The third selection is an essay written by a feminist with a good sense of humor. She expresses a number of serious opinions about marriage in an ironic and lighthearted style. The chapter then finishes with one man's view, written in poetry, of the transforming power of love.

## SELECTION ONE

# ▚ For Better or Worse, Arranged Marriages Still Thrive in Japan

What is the best way to find a husband or a wife? Should you let your family select a mate for you or should you date many people and try to "fall in love"? Many cultures have the tradition of arranged marriages. These are brought about by "matchmakers" who find and introduce possible candidates to a young person at the family's request and for a fee. What do you think of this practice? Judging by the title of the selection, do you think this tradition is popular in Japan? What does the first phrase of the title tell you about the author's point of view? In the article you will find out what the Japanese mean by being "wet" or "dry" when making a decision and how modern technology is aiding romance. Read for main ideas and see if you change some of your opinions about the best way to select a mate.

### Prereading Exercise: Distinguishing the General from the Specific

The following article is from the *Wall Street Journal*, a newspaper best known for its business and financial news. This, however, is a feature article, one that deals with a topic of general human interest. Like many feature articles, it alternates between *general* statements (large, broad ideas) and *specific* information (small points, details, statistics, particular cases, and examples that illustrate or support the general statements). Take three minutes to skim the selection. Then answer the following questions about its overall organization:

1. Does the article begin with the general or the specific? Why do
   you think it begins this way?

   _____

   _____

2. At what point does it change?

   _____

3. How does it end?

   _____

4. How could you briefly describe its organization?

   _____

   _____

## For Better or Worse, Arranged Marriages Still Thrive in Japan

"He was a banker," Toshiko says of the first young man her parents set her
up with. "He was *so-o-o-o-o* boring."

The second was an architect. He tried to impress her with his knowledge
of the historic hotel where they had coffee. "He was wrong on almost every
5   point," she sniffs.

The third, for some reason, "asked me a lot of questions about the French
revolution."

Seven more followed. She turned them all down. Just twenty-six, and
seeing on the sly a boyfriend from the wrong side of the tracks, Toshiko was
10   in no hurry to get married. With her Yale diploma, her colloquial English, and
her very modern outlook on life, this rich family's daughter from Tokyo could
almost pass for a rich family's daughter from Greenwich, Connecticut.

But Tokyo isn't Greenwich. Like most unmarried women here, Toshiko
(it's not her real name; her parents read this newspaper) still lives with her
15   mother and father. And like most parents here, they think that by the time a
young woman reaches her mid-twenties she ought to be married. About a
year ago, they began to pressure her to go through *omiai*, the ceremonial
first meeting in the traditional Japanese arranged marriage.

### Meet and Look

"It was such a drag to get up in the morning, because I knew at breakfast
20   we would have another fight about this," Toshiko says. "I did my first *omiai*
so I could have some peace at home."

These days lots of young Japanese do *omiai*, literally, "meet and look."
Many of them, unlike Toshiko, do so willingly. In today's prosperous and
increasingly conservative Japan, the traditional *omiai kekkon*, or arranged
25   marriage, is thriving.

But there is a difference. In the original *omiai*, the young Japanese couldn't reject the partner chosen by his parents and their *nakodo*, or middleman. After World War II, many Japanese abandoned the arranged marriage as part of their rush to adopt the more democratic ways of their American
30 conquerors. The Western *ren'ai kekkon*, or love marriage, came into vogue; Japanese began picking their own mates by dating and falling in love.

But the Western way was often found wanting in an important respect: It didn't necessarily produce a partner of the right economic, social, and educational qualifications. "Today's young people are quite calculating," says
35 Chieko Akiyama, a social commentator.

## No Strings
What seems to be happening now is a repetition of a familiar process in the country's history, the "Japanization" of an adopted foreign practice. The Western ideal of marrying for love is accommodated in a new *omiai* in which both parties are free to reject the match. "*Omiai* is evolving into a sort of stylized
40 introduction," Mrs. Akiyama says.

Many young Japanese now date in their early twenties, but with no thought of marriage. When they reach the age when society decrees they should wed—in the middle twenties for women, the late twenties for men—they increasingly turn to *omiai*. Some studies suggest that as many as 40 percent
45 of marriages each year are *omiai kekkon*. It's hard to be sure, say those who study the matter, because many Japanese couples, when polled, describe their marriage as a love match even if it was arranged.

These days, doing *omiai* often means going to a computer matching service rather than to a *nakodo*. The *nakodo* of tradition was an old woman
50 who knew all the kids in the neighborhood and went around trying to pair them off by speaking to parents; a successful match would bring her a wedding invitation and a gift of money. But Japanese today find it's less awkward to reject a proposed partner if the *nakodo* is a computer.

Japan has about five hundred computer matching services. Some big
55 companies, including Mitsubishi, run one for their employees. At a typical commercial service, an applicant pays $80 to $125 to have his or her personal data stored in the computer for two years and $200 or so more if a marriage results. The stored information includes some obvious items, like education and hobbies, and some not-so-obvious ones, like whether a person is the
60 oldest child. (First sons, and to some extent first daughters, face an obligation of caring for elderly parents.)

The customer also tells the computer service what he or she has in mind. "The men are all looking for good-looking women, and the women are all looking for men who can support them well," says a counselor at one service.
65 Whether generated by computer or *nakodo*, the introduction follows a ritual course. The couple, who have already seen each other's data and picture, arrive at a coffee shop or computer-service meeting room accom-

panied by their parents and the *nakodo* or a representative of the service. After a few minutes of pleasantries, the two are left to themselves. A recent
70    comedy movie had such a couple heading directly to one of Japan's "love hotels," which offer rooms by the hour; but ordinarily it takes love a good bit longer to flower, if it does at all.

And there still are those Japanese who consider love and marriage to be quite separate things. Here, in brief, are how three arranged marriages of
75    the past twenty-five years unfolded.

Japanese wedding banquet

## The Asamis

Munehiro Asami was a twenty-eight-year-old office worker at a machine-parts company. "I had a friend from childhood whose mother was very pushy," he says. "One day she stomped into my room and took a picture of me out of my picture album. She also left an *omiai* picture of a lady. I was to meet this
80    girl and I didn't want to go."

Neither did the woman. She was Reiko Ohtsuka, a twenty-three-year-old part-time office worker. She recalls how she "half jokingly" agreed to the meeting, then asked if it was too late to change her mind. It was.

But all was for the best, apparently. Mr. Asami warmly remembers the
85    ritual as "like being introduced to a cute girl by your friend." Miss Ohtsuka discovered that her worries about what to talk about were unfounded. "We dated for four months," she says, "fell in love, and got married."

## The Watanabes

In 1972 he was five years out of Tokyo University, Japan's Harvard. He was working for a big Tokyo bank. And, reflecting his heavy work schedule and a certain Japanese shyness, he had never had a date.

Mr. Watanabe—he doesn't want to be identified further—always intended to marry through *omiai*. "It's a good system," he says, because the partners don't waste time on someone who doesn't meet their specifications. It's also realistic, he adds: "In love marriages, the two look only at each other's good points: We calculate the bad as well."

Mr. Watanabe was looking for a wife who, first and foremost, "would get along well with my father." To that end, he asked for someone from his home prefecture of Yamanashi. He also wanted a wife who wouldn't have to support her parents. Being himself a second son, he could qualify for a woman who was also looking for a mate free of parental obligations.

Thus, after an introduction through his uncle, did Mr. Watanabe marry a second daughter from his home town in early 1973. They now have two children. "Everyone wants to get married through love, but not everyone can," Mr. Watanabe says.

The Japanese like to think they are "wet" (emotional) compared with "dry" (rational) Westerners. But Mr. Watanabe thinks that "when it comes to marriage, we Japanese are dry."

## The Azumas

Kikuko Azuma, who found her husband through *omiai* twenty-five years ago, says the custom is still "the shortest, most convenient way." She is recommending it to her twenty-two-year-old daughter.

Mrs. Azuma was only twenty and just out of junior college when she wed. But she was eager to study in the United States and by coincidence was introduced to a twenty-seven-year-old trading company executive about to be transferred to New York. He was from a well-to-do family, and Mrs. Azuma recalls being chauffeured to the *omiai* at an expensive Western restaurant. "I admired his social status," she says.

Then too, her own parents were having marital difficulties, and she feared that if they divorced she would seem a less desirable catch in a future *omiai*. So she had to move quickly, even though "at twenty I hadn't given much thought to getting married."

Did she love him? "Love and marriage are different," Mrs. Azuma replies firmly. "I think after you get married, love eventually emerges." Does her husband of twenty-five years agree? "I don't know," she says. "I don't really know him very well."

There is one other *omiai* success story to report. It is about Toshiko, the young sophisticate who opened this article. After coolly dismissing ten young men sent her way, she was intrigued by Number 11, a physician who had

worked in Africa. A friend says he was the first guy Toshiko had met whom she found "intellectually compatible" and who, more importantly, wasn't intim-
130    idated by her.

Toshiko herself isn't available for comment. She is in Fiji making wedding preparations.

**Urban C. Lehner**
*Wall Street Journal*

DAVID AUSTEN/STOCK, BOSTON

Japanese bride in traditional dress

# Recalling Information

Choose the best way of finishing each statement, based on what you have just read.

1. The literal translation of the Japanese word *omiai* is:
   a. ceremonial introduction
   b. meet and look
   c. computer wedding

2. After World War II, a new practice that came into fashion in Japan was:

   a. divorce   b. arranged marriage   c. love marriage

3. In order to use the new commercial services for *omiai*, a person must:

   a. pay money
   b. belong to a noble family
   c. go to a "love hotel"

4. Many Japanese do not want to marry:

   a. an oldest child   b. a youngest child   c. a middle child

5. The reason that this position in the family makes the person a less desirable marriage partner is that he or she:
   a. is usually very spoiled and arrogant
   b. does not inherit any money or property
   c. has to take care of his or her parents when they are older

6. In comparison with the time right after World War II, the practice of arranged marriages in Japan now seems to be:

   a. decreasing   b. increasing   c. about the same

## Finding Support for General Ideas

Find specific facts, statistics, and examples from the article to support the following general ideas.

1. "In today's prosperous and increasingly conservative Japan, the traditional *omiai kekkon*, or arranged marriage, is thriving."

   _____

   _____

   _____

2. "What seems to be happening now is a repetition of a familiar process in the country's history, the 'Japanization' of an adopted foreign practice."

   _____

   _____

   _____

3. "The Japanese like to think they are 'wet' (emotional) compared with 'dry' (rational) Westerners. But Mr. Watanabe thinks that 'when it comes to marriage, we Japanese are dry.'"

   _____

   _____

   _____

## Talking It Over

1. According to the article, at what age is a woman expected to marry in Japan? A man? Is it the same in your culture? What do you think is the ideal age to marry? Why?

2. What are some of the advantages of arranged marriages? What are some of the disadvantages?

3. Do you think that arranged marriages are more or less likely to end in divorce? Why?

4. Did reading the article give you any new information? Did it change your views on how to select a marriage partner? Explain.

(a)                                                                 (b)

## S E L E C T I O N   T W O

# ▇ The Sexes: Anatomy of a Difference

Are men stronger than women? _____

Are they better at sports? _____

Do women shoot guns as well as men do? _____

Will a woman ever win an important marathon race

(twenty-six miles)? _____

Which of the sexes commits more violent crimes? _____

Which one is more susceptible to disease? _____

Can men take care of babies as well as women can? _____

Can women be good engineers? _____

These are *controversial* questions, questions that cause a good deal of discussion because people tend to have differing opinions and strong emotions concerning them. Take a moment to think about them and write yes or no in the blanks. After you read the following article on sexual differences, look back at these questions to see if any of your views has changed. The article, taken from *Health Magazine*, is written in the form of commonly asked questions about male-female differences, with answers provided by the author, a popular writer on health and science topics.

## Prereading Exercise: Coping with Technical Terms

With a long article like this one, which uses a number of technical terms, your best strategy is to skim it, skipping over any words you don't understand. Then read it a second time and pay more attention to some of the terms—the ones that are used several times or that seem important for understanding the main ideas. Often you can figure these out from the context. Practice this skill with the following words taken from the reading.

1. *Sex hormones.* This is obviously an important term since it occurs many times and in many different parts of the article. It occurs first in Line 50. No definition is given, but you can tell from the context that it refers to substances or chemicals in the body, and you are told what they do. Look at Lines 50–55 and complete the following definition.

   *sex hormones:* substances that _____

   _____

2. *Testosterone.* This term is also used many times and appears first in Line 47. If you skip over it during the first reading, you will find that it is defined for you in Line 59. Look there now and write a definition.

   *testosterone:* _____

   _____

3. *Feedback.* This word is used only twice, but it is important for the understanding of a key idea: the relationship between testosterone and aggression. Like the words *program* and *programming*, *feedback* comes from the field of electronics but is now used in a broader way in general language. Read Lines 61–70 carefully; then write the best definition you can. (This may be hard, but it isn't impossible even if you know nothing about electronics.)

   *feedback:* _____

   _____

4. *Estrogen.* This term appears first in Line 100, where its definition can be guessed from the context. If you have understood terms 1 and 2, this should be easy.

*estrogen:* _____
_____

5. *Autism, hyperactivity, stuttering, dyslexia, aphasia.* All of these
   terms appear in one sentence in Lines 84–85, where two of them
   are defined. Why do you think the author did this when writing
   for an English-speaking audience? Why isn't it necessary to know
   all these terms in order to understand the basic point of the sentence? Scan the paragraph for the two definitions and write them
   below. Then write a general description that refers to all of them.

   1: _____

   2: _____

   *general description:* _____

6. *Chromosome, genes, immune system.* These three terms come from
   biology, and probably either you know all three or you don't know
   any of them. You need to understand them in order to grasp the
   idea presented in Lines 90–96, so this might be a time to go to the
   dictionary. If you look up the first term, you may be able to guess
   the others from a careful reading of the last sentence of the
   paragraph.

   *chromosome:* _____

   *gene:* _____

   *immune system:* _____

7. *Visual, spatial.* These two terms are first used together in hyphenated form in the third-to-the-last paragraph; they modify the word
   *abilities.* They are used in the last paragraphs in ways that hint at
   their meaning, but the best clues are right in the first three letters
   of each word.

   *visual and spatial abilities:* abilities to _____
   _____

# The Sexes: Anatomy of a Difference

How much do we really know about the differences between the sexes? Can
we separate nature (biology) from nurture (social training and expectations)?
Though there are no definite conclusions, science *has* come up with some
fascinating new answers to these and other age-old questions about *"la*
5  *différence."*

*Can a woman match—or beat—a man in any sport?*

If you're a woman and you want to challenge a man to a test of strength, your best bet would be either a contest to see who can do the most sit-ups, or leg wrestling (which works just like arm wrestling except that you lie on your back, hook ankles, and try to pull the other person over). Pound for pound, a woman can be as strong in the abdominal and leg muscles as a man because her relatively larger pelvis has plenty of room for muscle attachments. A woman's pelvis also gives her more leverage in leg wrestling.

Women's joints are more flexible and less tightly hinged than men's, so women get thrown about more in figure skating and ballet by men, whose upper-body strength is useful in lifting, holding, and throwing them. And in sports where strength is not a factor—skydiving, parachuting, sharpshooting—men and women perform and compete equally. Olympic rifle shooting has no separate categories for men and women; in fact, a woman, Margaret Murdoch, won the silver medal for rifle shooting in 1976.

*If women have such strong legs, how come the fastest runners are still men?*

In endurance events like running and long-distance swimming, women actually do very well. Grete Waitz beat 11,705 men in the 1982 New York City Marathon; only 124 men managed to beat her. In long-distance swimming, a woman's body fat becomes an advantage, providing both buoyancy and insulation against the cold. Women have traditionally done better than men in English Channel swimming, for instance.

To serve his greater muscle mass, a man has a larger heart and lungs, more oxygen-carrying hemoglobin in his blood, and a larger stroke volume. Muscles depend on oxygen to work; the more oxygen you can get to them, the more energy you have. And a man's cardiovascular system more than fills his oxygen needs.

Training increases stroke volume and cuts down body fat; Grete Waitz's levels in both, not to mention her pelvic width, are undoubtedly much closer to runner Alberto Salazar's than to mine. Nevertheless, in 1982 Salazar beat Waitz in the marathon by seventeen minutes, fifty-four seconds. The oxygen factor is probably the greatest male advantage, but the difference between men's and women's time has been getting smaller, and some experts think that the best women will one day equal the best men in events like marathons.

*OK, so the physical differences between men and women balance out. But are women as aggressive as men? Why is it usually men who commit violent crimes?*

In everything from dreams and fantasies to play and crime, males of all ages seem to be more aggressive than females. The difference is one of the few that has been generally accepted by experts, but nobody really knows exactly how aggression works. There is a clear correlation between male aggression and high testosterone levels; by far the majority of violent crimes, for instance, are committed by young men, whose testosterone levels are much higher than those of older men.

50    Sex hormones program our bodies to develop as male or female, and many researchers now think that hormones program our brains as well. For instance, the same part of the brain that regulates the production of sex hormones also regulates the basic patterns of *some* of our behavior in courtship and sex, aggression and nurturing—behavior, in short, in which men
55    and women act very differently.

The problem is that it isn't always clear which comes first, testosterone or the aggression. For example, it's been found that after a competition, a wrestler will have more testosterone in his bloodstream if he has won than if he has lost. Male hormone levels rise during a fight, as they do during sex,
60    but are they responsible for starting the fight in the first place?

What seems most likely is that there is a continuous feedback loop among hormones, the environment, and social programming, just as there's feedback between body and brain. Male violence against women, for instance, is fairly common in many societies. A man is more likely to respond to jealousy
65    by blaming his partner, getting angry, and using violence, but a woman is more likely to blame herself. The man's reaction could be connected to the fact that testosterone levels rise with desire, so the hormonal trigger for violence is ready to pull if other elements such as jealousy, frustration, or rejection are present. But not every man beats his wife; ultimately it's the
70    man, not the hormones, who's responsible.

Today, from the office to the tennis court, we expect women to be more aggressive than we did twenty years ago; not surprisingly, women have also been committing more—and more violent—crimes, although still far fewer than men.

75    *Why do women live longer than men?*

No one really knows. The difference is in the genes, and one suggestion has been that there was originally no evolutionary reason for men to live past the age when they are useful as hunters, while women, the social center of the group, remained useful for child care, housekeeping, and food gath-
80    ering even after their own childbearing years were over.

Men are much more vulnerable than women in a number of ways. Boy babies inherit more birth defects and suffer more birth traumas. In childhood, boys have more accidents, and they are far more likely than girls to suffer from autism, hyperactivity, stuttering, dyslexia (difficulty in reading), or aphasia
85    (the loss of the ability to use words as symbols). In young adulthood they are particularly prone to violent deaths, and in middle age they are more likely to develop digestive disorders and kidney disease. They remain more vulnerable to viral infections of all kinds, and if they *do* avoid all the risks and make it to old age, they generally still die sooner than their female peers.

90    What makes men so vulnerable? Boys may owe their susceptibility to diseases to the fact that they have only one X chromosome. The other, the Y, determines their sex and is the most basic difference between men and women. It contains genes which program for the production of testosterone and the other hormones which produce the male body. The X chromosome
95    includes genes that control the immune system; women, with two Xs, have a "backup" set of genes and, it may be, greater protection.

*Is there a maternal instinct that makes it more natural for a woman to mother than a man? Can men take care of babies?*

Unlike testosterone and male aggression, there is no clear correlation
100   between estrogen and the desire or ability to be a good mother. In fact, experiments on primates suggest that mothering is very much a learned activity. Monkeys and chimpanzees raised in isolation aren't very good at it.

Women are certainly physiologically designed and hormonally prepared to bear and nurse infants. They go through complex monthly hormonal cycles
105   which prepare their bodies for conception. During pregnancy their estrogen levels rise dramatically, then drop just before birth. Other hormones, *prolactin* and *oxytocin*, start milk production and release it in response to an infant's cry.

But adoptive mothers, who don't go through all these changes, still do a
110   very good job of mothering, while some biological mothers don't. And fathers who care for their babies and children report high levels of "maternal" feelings. All this suggests that maternal feelings in both sexes develop through closeness and caretaking rather than through biological programming.

*How come most of the engineers and computer experts are men?*

115   Women are, on the whole, more verbal than men. They are good at languages and verbal reasoning, while men tend to excel at tasks demanding visual-spatial abilities. In fact, along with aggression, these are the most commonly accepted differences between the sexes.

Words are tools for communicating with other people, especially infor-
120   mation about people. They are mainly social tools. Visual and spatial abilities are good for imagining and manipulating objects and for communicating information about them. Are these talents programmed into the brain? In some of the newest and most controversial research in neurophysiology, it has been suggested that when it comes to the brain, males are specialists
125   while women are generalists.

But no one knows what, if anything, this means in terms of the abilities of the two sexes. Engineering is both visual and spatial, and it's true that there are relatively few women engineers. But women become just as skilled as men at shooting a rifle or driving a car, tasks that involve visual-spatial
130   skills. They also do equally well at programming a computer, which is neither visual nor spatial. Women do, however, seem less likely to fall in love with

the objects themselves. We all know men for whom machines seem to be extensions of their identity. A woman is more likely to see her car, rifle, or computer as simply a tool—useful, but not in itself fascinating.

**Signe Hammer**
*Health Magazine*

## Reading Critically: Detecting a Bias

When writing about controversial topics, some authors try to be objective: to present information supporting both sides of the question without favoring either side. Most authors, however, have a *bias*, and in order to read critically you should learn to detect the bias. This means first determining which side of the question the author favors. The traditional viewpoint on the differences between men and women is that men are superior to women. It is also possible to have the opposite viewpoint—that women are superior to men—or that there is no important difference between the sexes. Answer the following questions about the bias of the author of the preceding article.

1. In your opinion, what is the author's bias?

   _____

2. On a separate piece of paper, make two lists, one of the good points the author mentions about men and one of the good points she mentions about women. What do you think of these lists? Should other points have been mentioned? Do you think the article is fair in its comparison of the physical traits of men and women? Why or why not?

   _____

   _____

   _____

   _____

3. What is your own personal bias regarding this question? Do you feel that you are completely objective?

   _____

   _____

   _____

## Separating Fact from Opinion

The difference between fact and opinion is not always clear, but some general rules can help you distinguish between them:

1. General statements (which could be verified in an encyclopedia or other reference book) about past or present events are usually facts; statements about the future are usually opinions, since the future by its nature is uncertain.

2. Statements that include the modals *may*, *might*, or *could*, or qualifiers such as *perhaps*, *maybe*, *possibly*, or *probably* are opinions.

3. Statements based on evidence (research, case studies, experiments, questionnaires) need to be evaluated. If they are based on only one person's research, they should be considered opinions. If they are based on a great deal of research and if most experts agree, then they can be considered facts.

4. If the statement concerns a controversial topic, it helps to know the author's bias. Statements that favor the opposite viewpoint are probably facts, since the author would not mention them unless he or she *had* to. Statements that favor his or her bias must be looked at very carefully and might well be opinions.

Tell whether each of the following statements based on the article is fact (F) or opinion (O). You might need to look at its context since the statements are not presented exactly as they appear in the text, so the line numbers are given.

_____ 1. A woman won the silver medal for rifle shooting in 1976. (Lines 18–20)

_____ 2. In endurance events such as running and long-distance swimming, women do very well. (Lines 22–23)

_____ 3. Men have greater muscle mass and larger hearts and lungs than women. (Lines 28–32)

_____ 4. The best women runners will one day equal the best men runners in events such as the marathon. (Lines 38–39)

_____ 5. Males are more aggressive than females. (Lines 43–49)

_____ 6. Sex hormones program our bodies to develop as male or female. (Lines 50–51).

_____ 7. Men's violent actions against women are related to the fact that testosterone levels rise with desire. (Lines 63–70)

_____ 8. Men commit more violent crimes than women. (Lines 71–74)

_____ 9. On the average, women live longer than men because in the past old women were more useful to the social group than old men. (Lines 76–80)

_____ 10. In general, men are more vulnerable to birth defects, disease, and accidents than women. (Lines 81–90)

_____ 11. Boys are more susceptible to disease than girls because they have only one X chromosome. (Lines 90–96)

_____ 12. Mothering is an activity that is learned, not inborn. (Lines 99–113)

_____ 13. Women are more verbal than men, while men are better than women at visual-spatial activities. (Lines 115–118)

_____ 14. There are very few women engineers. (Lines 127–128)

_____ 15. Women are just as good as men at driving a car. (Lines 128–130)

## Talking It Over

Discuss the following questions as a class or in small groups.

1. Are there some opinions expressed in the article that you do not agree with? Explain.

2. In your opinion, are men and women treated equally in society? Should they be?

3. Look back at the questions given before the article. Which ones would you answer differently now? Why?

4. Because of recent advances in technology, it is now possible to determine, with a fair degree of accuracy, the sex of a child before its conception. Do you think that this is a good thing? Should this technology be made available to everyone or not? Explain.

## Stories Behind Words: Mothering, Fathering, and the New "Ms."

Many people today feel that historically women have not been treated as well as men in many cultures. In the Western world, as recently as a hundred years ago, they were not allowed to vote in elections and were excluded from most professions. The attitude of favoring one sex over another (in this case, favoring the male) is called _sexism_, which is thought by many to be present in the very language we speak. For example, the verb _to mother_, used in the latter part of the article, generally means "to care for, protect" (for example, "That teacher _mothers_ all her students."); whereas the verb _to father_ usually means simply "to engender or originate" (for example, "He _fathered_ three sons."). Here the idea that women, not men, should take care of children is locked into our everyday speech.

  Feminists (people who fight for the rights of women) claim that there are examples of sexism in the vocabulary and even in the grammar of the English language. A common example is the use of the word _man_ or _mankind_ to refer to the whole human species: "_Man_ is the only tool-using animal. . . . The achievements of _mankind_ after the agricultural era began. . . ." Certain critics of the feminists have argued that this usage doesn't really matter because everyone knows that the words _man_ and _mankind_ also refer to women. Feminists, however, generally believe that this manner of speaking has created the idea that men have been the active participants in history—working, building, exploring, inventing—while women have sat quietly on the sidelines, helping them. Some people favor language reform and think that the words *people* or *humanity* should be used in these contexts. Others say, "Well, let's be honest! Men *have* been the active ones throughout history."

Similarly, now that women are present at professional and political meetings, certain terms, such as *Mr. Chairman*, have been called into question. What if the "chairman" is female? *Madame Chairman* and *chairperson* are now sometimes used, though certain groups still use *Mr. Chairman* even when speaking to a woman.

Another bone of contention has been the use of the titles that indicate the civil state (married or single) of a woman—*Miss* or *Mrs.*—while all men, regardless of civil state, are referred to as *Mr.* In order to equalize the situation, some women now use the title *Ms.* in front of their names.

Is sexism peculiar to the English language, or do such problems arise now in other languages because of the increasingly active role of women? Does any other language have an equivalent of *Ms.*? Should it? Are these important questions or simply petty complaints? What word would you use to refer to a woman leader at a meeting? To the human species, if you were writing a history book? One way or another, such questions as these need to be answered.

## SELECTION THREE

# ■■ I Want a Wife

What qualities are needed to be a perfect wife? Do our modern views on this subject differ greatly from those of our grandparents? The following selection talks about what a wife should be. Written by a contemporary American writer, this humorous essay has become quite popular, chiefly because of the author's clever use of *irony*, which is discussed in the following exercise. Pay attention to the author's style, or way of writing, and see if you can understand what makes it humorous and enjoyable to read.

### Prereading Exercise: Identifying an Ironic Tone

Everyone knows that a person's tone of voice can influence us a great deal. The sentence "Will you open the window?" can be said in a soft, pleasing way or with a harsh, demanding tone that makes us angry. We also speak of the *tone* of an essay, speech, or article. It might be formal or informal, serious or humorous, angry or playful. The important thing is that it is appropriate to the author's subject, audience, and purpose. For what kind of topic and audience do you think that an angry tone would be appropriate and effective? When would it be inappropriate? What about a formal tone?

The following essay is written in an *ironic tone*. This means that the author says something very different from (at times, even opposite to) what she means. *Irony* is a very common device, even in everyday conversation, and it usually has a humorous effect. For example, when it rains on the day of a school picnic, someone might say *ironically*, "What lovely weather!"

Take two minutes to skim the following essay for the main idea and the tone. Then answer the following questions.

1. At what point do you first notice that the tone seems ironic?

_____

2. What are some statements that seem to express something different from what the author really means?

_____

_____

_____

# I Want a Wife

I belong to that classification of people known as wives. I am a Wife. And, not altogether incidentally, I am a mother.

Not too long ago a male friend of mine appeared on the scene fresh from a recent divorce. He had one child, who is, of course, with his ex-wife. He
5 is obviously looking for another wife. As I thought about him while I was ironing one evening, it suddenly occurred to me that I, too, would like to have a wife. Why do I want a wife?

I would like to go back to school so that I can become economically independent, support myself, and, if need be, support those dependent upon
10 me. I want a wife who will work and send me to school. And while I am going to school I want a wife to take care of my children. I want a wife to keep track of the children's doctor and dentist appointments. And to keep track of mine, too. I want a wife to make sure my children eat properly and are kept clean. I want a wife who will wash the children's clothes and keep them
15 mended. I want a wife who is a good nurturant attendant to my children, who arranges for their schooling, makes sure that they have an adequate social life with their peers, takes them to the park, the zoo, etc. I want a wife who takes care of the children when they are sick, a wife who arranges to be around when the children need special care, because, of course, I cannot
20 miss classes at school. My wife must arrange to lose time at work and not lose the job. It may mean a small cut in my wife's income from time to time, but I guess I can tolerate that. Needless to say, my wife will arrange and pay for the care of the children while my wife is working.

I want a wife who will take care of my physical needs. I want a wife who
will keep my house clean. A wife who will pick up after me. I want a wife
who will keep my clothes clean, ironed, mended, replaced when need be,
and who will see to it that my personal things are kept in their proper place
so that I can find what I need the minute I need it. I want a wife who cooks
the meals, a wife who is a *good* cook. I want a wife who will plan the menus,
do the necessary grocery shopping, prepare the meals, serve them pleasantly, and then do the cleaning up while I do my studying. I want a wife who
will care for me when I am sick and sympathize with my pain and loss of
time from school. I want a wife to go along when our family takes a vacation
so that someone can continue to care for me and my children when I need
a rest and change of scene.

I want a wife who will not bother me with rambling complaints about a
wife's duties. But I want a wife who will listen to me when I feel the need to
explain a rather difficult point I have come across in my course of studies.
And I want a wife who will type my papers for me when I have written them.

I want a wife who will take care of the details of my social life. When my
wife and I are invited out by my friends, I want a wife who will take care of
the babysitting arrangements. When I meet people at school that I like and
want to entertain, I want a wife who will have the house clean, will prepare
a special meal, serve it to me and my friends, and not interrupt when I talk
about the things that interest me and my friends. I want a wife who will have
arranged that the children are fed and ready for bed before my guests arrive
so that the children do not bother us. I want a wife who takes care of the
needs of my guests so that they feel comfortable, who makes sure that they

have an ashtray, that they are passed the hors d'oeuvres, that they are offered
50  a second helping of the food, that their wine glasses are replenished when
necessary, that their coffee is served to them as they like it. And I want a
wife who knows that sometimes I need a night out by myself.

If, by chance, I find another person more suitable as a wife than the wife
I already have, I want the liberty to replace my present wife with another one.
55  Naturally, I will expect a fresh, new life: My wife will take the children and be
solely responsible for them so that I am left free.

When I am through with school and have a job, I want my wife to quit
working and remain at home so that my wife can more fully and completely
take care of a wife's duties.
60  My God, who *wouldn't* want a wife?

**Judy Syfers**

# Recalling Information

Put a + in front of the actions and attitudes that, according to the essay,
are part of being a wife. Put a 0 in front of those that, according to the
essay, would *not* be part of being a wife.

_____ 1. work and earn money so that her husband can go to school

_____ 2. keep track of doctor's and dentist's appointments for her
husband and children

_____ 3. lose time at her job if necessary so that she can care for the
children when they are sick

_____ 4. hire someone to clean the house, iron, and mend clothes so
that she can do well in her professional work

_____ 5. share with her husband the responsibility for cooking good
meals

_____ 6. take a vacation from time to time so that she can get away
from child care and have a change of scene

_____ 7. listen to her husband when he wants to talk and keep quiet
about the problems that are bothering her

_____ 8. entertain her husband's friends and make sure that the children do not bother them

_____ 9. have a night out by herself from time to time

_____ 10. allow her husband to leave and marry a younger woman if
he wants to

_____ 11. quit working and forget about her career when her husband
gets a job and wants her to stay home

## Recognizing the "Real" Point of View

As a class or in small groups, discuss the following questions.

1. What do you think is the *real* point of view of the author on the role of a wife? On a wife's attitude toward her career? On housework and child care? On entertaining friends? On getting a divorce?

2. If the author does not really believe that a wife should be the way she describes one in the essay, why does she describe her that way? Why doesn't she say directly what she means?

## Talking It Over

1. What do you think is the ideal arrangement for a couple when both work outside the home? Which household duties can be shared? Are certain chores the responsibility of the male? Of the female?

2. Are married people happier than single people?

3. Do you notice any differences between North American marriages and marriages in your culture?

4. What do you think of the "women's liberation" movement? Is there such a movement in your culture?

### SELECTION FOUR

# Oh, When I Was in Love with You

The English poet Alfred Edward Housman (1859–1936) expresses an opinion on love and its power to transform us in the following lyrical poem. (A lyrical poem is a short poem that expresses emotion.) Like many English poems, this one uses rhyme, the use of the same sounds at the end of the last words in certain lines (for example: *you / grew*, *brave / behave*). Read it aloud to enjoy the rhyme and rhythm and take care to pronounce the word *again* in the second stanza in the British (not American) way so that it will rhyme correctly.

# *Oh, When I Was in Love with You*

Oh, when I was in love with you,
    Then I was clean and brave,
And miles around the wonder grew
    How well I did behave.

5  And now the fancy passes by,
    And nothing will remain,
And miles around they'll say that I
    Am quite myself again.

**A. E. Housman**

## Talking It Over

1. In your opinion, what point of view does the poet have on love?

2. Do you think that love can transform a person? How? Is such a transformation permanent or temporary? Why?

3. Is there a regular pattern of rhyme in the poem? Why do you think the poet used rhyme? What effect does it have on a reader?

4. How would you describe the tone of the poem? Do you think a woman would use this tone when talking about love? Why or why not?

**A POPULAR SAYING**
A man chases a woman until she catches him.

# Mysteries Past and Present

Sleeping Buddha, Sichuan Province, China

What is the force that determines human destiny? Is it luck, divine providence, or simply "blind" chance? The first selection discusses what mathematicians who deal with probability theory think about this question in relation to those mysterious combinations of events called coincidences. After this, one of the classic puzzle stories of the English language focuses on a different sort of mystery: the complex motivations of the human heart. The final selection examines how the legendary figure of the dragon helped modern Chinese scholars to unravel an important mystery of their past.

## SELECTION ONE

# ■ Against All Odds

The dictionary defines a coincidence as "an accidental and remarkable occurrence of events in a way that suggests that one caused the other." By their very nature, coincidences seem rather mysterious. What causes them? Are they controlled by providence, fate, or destiny? Are some of them caused by ESP (extrasensory perception, the power of sending messages by thought)? Or do these events simply happen by chance? The following article tells us what mathematicians say about coincidences and also offers some less conventional explanations.

## Prereading Exercise: Anticipating the Reading

Have you ever experienced what seemed to be an amazing coincidence? Perhaps you were thinking of a friend whom you had not seen in ten years and just at that moment the phone rang—and it was a call from that same person! Or perhaps you were traveling in a foreign country and entered a café, only to find out through conversation that the owner is a relative of your former teacher!

In the space below, describe the most amazing coincidence that you know of from your own personal experience or from that of a friend.

_____

_____

_____

_____

_____

_____

Can you think of any rational way to explain this coincidence? Compare your story with those of your classmates. As a class, decide which coincidence seems the most "mysterious." Then see if the following article makes it seem less mysterious.

## Against All Odds

Just how coincidental is a coincidence? Scientists still don't know.

Several years ago, a Connecticut businessman named George D. Bryson was traveling by train from St. Louis to New York when he decided to make an unscheduled stop in Louisville, since he was in no hurry and had never
5 seen that city. At the Louisville train station, he asked for the name of the leading hotel and, accordingly, went to the Brown, where he was assigned room 307. After registering, he stepped over to the mail desk and inquired, just for fun, whether there was any mail waiting for him. The clerk handed over a letter addressed to "Mr. George D. Bryson, room 307."
10 By coincidence, it turned out the previous resident of the room had been another George D. Bryson, from Montreal, and the letter was for him.

An equally strange event happened to a Chester, Pennsylvania, man named John McCafferty, who was arrested in June 1949 as a vagrant. McCafferty insisted the police were wrong, claiming he had a home—at 714
15 McElvane Street. Tell it to the judge, the police said. McCafferty duly came before magistrate R. Robinson Lowry, who asked him, "Where did you get that address?"
"It's just an address," McCafferty replied.
"I'll say it is," responded the judge. "That's where I live. Ninety days."

"Well, against the odds, here we are—Fran, her ex, me, my ex, Dick, my ex's new, Phil, Fran's ex's new, Pearl, Fran's ex's ex, David, Fran's ex's ex's new. CHEERS!"

20    Similarly fascinating coincidences have intrigued scientists and nonscientists alike for many years. They come in all sizes and degrees of significance, and have been attributed to everything from chance, fate, acts of God, and ESP to simple mathematics and the hidden order of the universe.

For the mathematician, coincidences aren't mysterious at all and can be
25    explained by known laws of statistical probability. Such laws provide a way to estimate the chance that any event might occur, from the odds of a certain order of finish in a horse race to the likelihood that the second and third U.S. presidents (John Adams and Thomas Jefferson) would die on the same day—and that the day would be July 4, 1826, the fiftieth anniversary of the signing
30    of the Declaration of Independence. ("No language can exaggerate it—no reason account for it," mused a Washington, D.C., magazine at the time.)

Suppose, for example, you were at a party with twenty-two strangers and, while talking with one, discovered that you have the same birthday. A remarkable coincidence? Hardly. The odds are better than fifty-fifty that among a
35    group of twenty-three people chosen at random at least two will have identical birthdays.

In his book *Lady Luck*, the late Warren Weaver—who also related the George D. Bryson story—recalled mentioning these odds at a dinner meeting of high-ranking military officers. Many of the officers found it hard to believe.
40    Noticing that there were twenty-two people at the table, one proposed a test. In turn, each person stated his birthday: There was no duplication. Then the waitress spoke up. "Excuse me," she said, "but I'm the twenty-third person in the room and my birthday is May 17, just like the general's over there."

Much more astounding is the so-called small-world paradox. We all have
45    experienced the effects of this phenomenon, which can involve the most improbable-seeming chance encounters. While vacationing in Nepal, for instance, you might meet Joe Green from Dubuque who, it turns out, is married to the younger sister of your good friend Gertrude from Los Angeles. "Small world, isn't it?" you exclaim. Actually, sociologist Ithiel de Sola Pool
50    of MIT has demonstrated that the chances are ninety-nine in a hundred that any randomly selected American adult can be linked to any other randomly selected American adult by only two intermediates. Thus, if Smith and Jones are two persons in the United States picked at random, the chances are almost certain that Smith will know someone who knows someone who knows
55    Jones. This finding is based on the assumption that the "average" American knows about a thousand people well enough to recognize them on the street and greet them by name. But Pool has also shown that two hermits can be linked by seven intermediates at most, merely by assuming that each hermit knows one storekeeper (even hermits have to buy food).

60    The point, the mathematicians seem to be saying, is that even if the laws of probability show an event to be statistically *improbable*, that does not make it *impossible*. There's always that small chance.

Even if probability theory does account for unlikely coincidences, it does

nothing to decrease the profound sense of wonder experienced by someone
involved in such events. Moreover, certain coincidences depend on so many
peculiar variables that the chances of their occurring cannot be calculated.

Some coincidences have given rise to original theories on the part of
scientists who believe that probability can't explain everything. The pioneer
in this field was Carl Jung, who was fascinated by the subject and who
collected examples of rare coincidences all his life. Jung claimed in a 1952
essay that coincidences occur much more frequently than probability theories
would predict, and that many coincidences must therefore be the work of an
unknown force seeking to impose universal order.

Jung acknowledged that his theory might seem wildly illogical. But he
suggested that the fault may lie with our concept of logic rather than with the
theory.

Another theory about coincidences comes from research in crystallog-
raphy. British plant physiologist Rupert Sheldrake has proposed a new
hypothesis about the mystery of why compounds that are at first difficult to
crystallize somehow become easier to crystallize in laboratories all over the
world after the first successful crystallization is accomplished. The usual
explanation is that very small pieces of the first crystals are carried from
laboratory to laboratory on the hair and clothing of scientists, serving as
"seeds" that start the crystallization process in the new laboratory. Not so,
says Sheldrake. He believes that crystals—and, indeed, all objects—transmit
invisible forces that create what he calls morphogenetic fields, comparable
to radio transmissions. The field created by the first crystal, in his view, serves
as a code or pattern that influences the form and character of all later crystals
of that type. Sheldrake suggests that people are no exception to this scheme.
If true, each of us may transmit a field through which we unknowingly communicate knowledge and information to others, present and future, worldwide.

Of course, it's a long leap from such theories to real proof that coincidences are more than random occurrences. Still, they offer stimulus for the
belief that there are, indeed, "more things in heaven and earth, Horatio, than
are dreamt of in your philosophy." And as the scientific debate goes on, so
the coincidences continue to occur, providing puzzles to delight everyone.

**Richard Blodgett**

## Recalling Information

Choose the best way of finishing each statement, based on what you
have just read.

1. When George D. Bryson went to the mail desk of a Louisville hotel
   he had entered at random, he received:
   a. a letter from his wife
   b. a letter for a different George D. Bryson
   c. nothing at all

2. When a Pennsylvania man named McCafferty invented a false address in court, it turned out to be the address of:

   a. the judge
   b. his brother
   c. the mayor of the city

3. The amazing coincidence involving the second and third presidents of the United States is that they both:

   a. had the same name
   b. died on the same day
   c. signed the American Declaration of Independence

4. In general, mathematicians believe that coincidences can be explained by:

   a. the will of God
   b. mysterious unknown forces
   c. the laws of statistics

5. The odds that at a party of twenty-three strangers, two of them will have the same birthday are about:

   a. 1 in 365   b. 1 in 100   c. 1 in 2

6. The fact that Mr. Smith from California and Mr. Jones from New York meet on a trip and discover that Smith's doctor is a friend of Jones' aunt is:

   a. an amazing coincidence
   b. quite improbable
   c. not surprising

7. A pioneer in the field of explaining coincidences in nonmathematical ways was:

   a. William Shakespeare
   b. Carl Jung
   c. Ithiel de Sola Pool

8. The hypothesis that Sheldrake proposed to explain a mystery among crystallographers is that:

   a. tiny pieces of crystals are carried from laboratory to laboratory
   b. the laws of probability increase once a crystallization has been successful
   c. crystals and all objects transmit forces that create invisible fields

## Understanding Abbreviations

The abbreviation ESP is used in the article. Do you remember what it means? (If not, refer to the introduction.) Do you know the following abbreviations or can you guess them from context?

1. Someone tells you he has seen a mysterious UFO.

   _____

2. In Canada, robbers and other evildoers run when they hear that the RCMP are coming.

   _____

3. You are asked to hand in an assignment ASAP.

   _____

4. A friend invites you to a party but tells you it is BYO.

   _____

Notice that when you pronounce abbreviations you say each letter separately. In contrast, *acronyms*, such as *radar*, *scuba*, or *laser*, are made from abbreviations but are pronounced as words. Do you know what these acronyms mean and what their letters stand for?

## Talking It Over

1. Do you believe in ESP? Why or why not?
2. In your opinion, are most coincidences caused simply by chance, by fate, or by divine providence? Explain.
3. Do you think that Sheldrake's theory is a real possibility or just a crazy idea? Why?
4. The last paragraph contains a quotation from one of Shakespeare's most famous plays, *Hamlet*. Even if you do not know the play, what can you tell from the context of the paragraph about the meaning of the quotation?
5. The famous French biologist Louis Pasteur once said, "Chance favors the prepared mind." What do you think he meant by that?

## Reading Critically: Applying What You've Read

In 1963 the world was stunned when the president of the United States, John Fitzgerald Kennedy, was killed by an assassin's bullet. Later, many people pointed out what seemed to be mysterious similarities between his death and that of a former American president, Abraham Lincoln. Is there really some strange force of circumstance that unites the two men? After reading the article on coincidences, you probably have a better idea about which combinations of events can really be considered improbable. Read the following description of these "astonishing parallels." Decide which ones you consider to be really astonishing and which ones you think are simply ordinary coincidences and explain why.

**LINCOLN AND KENNEDY**

Two of the most tragic and dramatic deaths in American history, the assassinations of Presidents Abraham Lincoln and John Fitzgerald Kennedy, involve the following astonishing parallels:

1. Lincoln was elected president in 1860. Exactly one hundred years later, in 1960, Kennedy was elected president.
2. Both men were deeply involved in civil rights for blacks.
3. Both men were assassinated on a Friday, in the presence of their wives.
4. Each wife had lost a son while living in the White House.
5. Both men were killed by a bullet that entered the head from behind.
6. Lincoln was killed in Ford's Theater. Kennedy met his death while riding in a Lincoln convertible made by the Ford Motor Company.
7. Both men were succeeded by vice-presidents named Johnson who were southern Democrats and former senators.
8. Andrew Johnson (Lincoln's vice-president) was born in 1808. Lyndon Johnson was born in 1908, exactly one hundred years later.
9. The first name of Lincoln's private secretary was John; the last name of Kennedy's private secretary was Lincoln.
10. John Wilkes Booth (Lincoln's assassin) was born in 1839 (according to some sources). Lee Harvey Oswald (Kennedy's assassin) was born in 1939, one hundred years later.
11. Both assassins were Southerners who held extremist views.
12. Both assassins were murdered before they could be brought to trial.
13. Booth shot Lincoln in a theater and fled to a barn. Oswald shot Kennedy from a warehouse and fled to a theater.
14. The names Lincoln and Kennedy each have seven letters.

Your opinion: _____

_____

_____

_____

_____

_____

_____

_____

The dollar bill in the illustration, issued in Dallas only two weeks before JFK was killed there, is now known as the Kennedy assassination bill. Since Dallas is the location of the eleventh of the twelve Federal Reserve Bank districts, the bill bears the letter *K*, the eleventh letter of the alphabet, and the number 11 appears in each corner. The serial number begins with *K* and ends with *A*, standing for Kennedy Assassination. Eleven also stands for November, the eleventh month of the year; two 11s equal 22, the date of the tragedy. And the series number is 1963, the year the assassination occurred.

## SELECTION TWO

# The Lady or the Tiger

The following story, written by the American writer Frank Stockton (1834–1902), has been considered a classic "brainteaser" ever since it first appeared. Perhaps this is because it builds up to an intensely dramatic moment, a moment during which a single act will decide between life and death, between the most exquisite pleasure and the most horrifying pain. The story is presented as it was originally written, with no adaptation. The vocabulary is difficult, so you should *not* try to understand every word. Read for the main story line only.

## Prereading Exercise 1: Skimming

Since this story has a surprise ending, you will probably enjoy it more if you don't skim the whole selection in advance. Just look at the title and skim the first half; then answer the following questions about the three key narrative elements of *setting*, *character*, and *plot*.

1. What do you find out about the *setting* (the where and when) from the first paragraph?

   _____

2. Which of the *characters* is presented first?

   _____

Since the tone is playful and ironic, you might have to read over the first three paragraphs several times to understand the description of this character. Do you think he is kind or cruel? Humble or arrogant? What other qualities does he have?

_____

_____

3. It is obvious that in this story the setting and characterization are given first and the *plot* (action) comes later. By skimming over the first part and looking at the title, what can you guess about the plot?

_____

_____

## Prereading Exercise 2: Understanding Words and Phrases by Breaking Them Down

One skill that can help you guess the meanings of words better is breaking the words down into smaller parts. Practice this skill by writing definitions for the italicized words from the following sentences taken from the reading. Use the hints and the context to help you.

1. "In the very olden time, there lived a *semibarbaric* king, who was a man of exuberant fancy and of an authority so irresistible that, at his will, he turned his varied fancies into facts." (Lines 1–3) (*Hint:* What does the prefix *semi-* mean? If you know that *barbarous* and *barbaric* mean "not civilized, wild, rough," you should be able to combine these to get the meaning.)

   *semibarbaric:* _____

2. "He was greatly given to *self-communing*, and when he and himself agreed upon anything, the thing was done." (Lines 3–4) (*Hint:* Maybe you don't know *communing*, but what common word does it look like at the beginning?)

   *self-communing:* _____

3. "This vast amphitheater, with its encircling galleries, . . . was an agent of poetic justice in which crime was punished, or virtue rewarded, by the decrees of an *impartial* and *incorruptible* chance." (Lines 12–15) (*Hint:* Both words begin with prefixes that mean the same thing; both have smaller words—*partial* or *part* and *corrupt* in them.)

   *impartial:* _____

   *incorruptible:* _____

4. "He was subject to no guidance or influence but that of the *afore-mentioned* impartial and incorruptible chance." (lines 26–27)

*aforementioned:* _____

5. "The moment that the case of the criminal was thus decided, . . . great wails went up from the hired mourners posted on the outer rim of the arena, and the vast audience, with bowed heads and *downcast* hearts, wended slowly their *homeward* way, mourning greatly. . . ." (Lines 30–35)

*downcast:* _____

*homeward:* _____

6. "As is usual in such cases, she was the *apple of his eye* and was loved by him above all humanity." (Lines 67–69) (*Hint:* Here it is a phrase, not a word, you must break into smaller parts. When you do that, the phrase doesn't make any literal sense, but can you guess the meaning from the latter part of the sentence?)

*apple of his eye:* _____

7. "In *afteryears* such things became *commonplace* enough, but then they were, in no slight degree, novel and startling." (Lines 81–82)

*afteryears:* _____

*commonplace:* _____

## *The Lady or the Tiger?*

In the very olden time, there lived a semibarbaric king, who was a man of exuberant fancy and of an authority so irresistible that, at his will, he turned his varied fancies into facts. He was greatly given to self-communing, and when he and himself agreed upon anything, the thing was done. When
5   everything moved smoothly, his nature was bland and genial; but whenever there was a little hitch, he was blander and more genial still, for nothing pleased him so much as to make the crooked straight, and crush down uneven places.

Among his borrowed notions was that of the public arena, in which, by
10   exhibitions of manly and beastly valor, the minds of his subjects were refined and cultured.

But even here the exuberant and barbaric fancy asserted itself. This vast amphitheater, with its encircling galleries, its mysterious vault, and its unseen passages, was an agent of poetic justice in which crime was punished, or
15   virtue rewarded, by the decrees of an impartial and incorruptible chance.

When a subject was accused of a crime of sufficient importance to interest the king, public notice was given that on an appointed day the fate of the accused person would be decided in the king's arena.

When all the people had assembled in the galleries, and the king, surrounded by his court, sat high up on his throne of royal state on one side of the arena, he gave a signal, a door beneath him opened, and the accused subject stepped out into the amphitheater. Directly opposite him, on the other side of the enclosed space, were two doors, exactly alike and side by side. It was the duty and the privilege of the person on trial to walk directly to these doors and open one of them. He could open either door he pleased. He was subject to no guidance or influence but that of the aforementioned impartial and incorruptible chance. If he opened the one, there came out of it a hungry tiger, the fiercest and most cruel that could be procured, which immediately sprang upon him and tore him to pieces as a punishment for his guilt. The moment that the case of the criminal was thus decided, doleful iron bells were clanged, great wails went up from the hired mourners posted on the outer rim of the arena, and the vast audience, with bowed heads and downcast hearts, wended slowly their homeward way, mourning greatly that one so young and fair, or so old and respected, should have merited so dire a fate.

But if the accused person opened the other door, there came forth from it a lady, the most suitable to his years and station that His Majesty could select among his fair subjects; and to this lady he was immediately married, as a reward of his innocence. It mattered not that he might already possess a wife and family, or that his affections might be engaged upon an object of his own selection. The king allowed no such arrangements to interfere with his great scheme of punishment and reward. The exercises, as in the other instance, took place immediately, and in the arena. Another door opened beneath the king, and a priest, followed by a band of choristers, and dancing maidens blowing joyous airs on golden horns, advanced to where the pair stood side by side, and the wedding was promptly and cheerily solemnized. Then the gay brass bells rang forth their merry peals, and the people shouted glad hurrahs, and the innocent man, preceded by children strewing flowers on his path, led his bride to his home.

This was the king's semibarbaric method of administering justice. Its perfect fairness is obvious. The criminal could not know out of which door would come the lady. He opened either he pleased, without having the slightest ideas whether, in the next instant, he was to be devoured or married. On some occasions the tiger came out of one door, and on some, out of the other. The decisions were not only fair—they were positively decisive. The accused person was instantly punished if he found himself guilty, and if innocent, he was rewarded on the spot, whether he liked it or not. There was no escape from the judgments of the king's arena.

The institution was a very popular one. When the people gathered together on one of the great trial days, they never knew whether they were to witness a bloody slaughter or a hilarious wedding. This element of uncertainty lent

an interest to the occasion which it could not otherwise have attained. Thus the masses were entertained and pleased, and the thinking part of the community could bring no charge of unfairness against his plan; for did not the
65    accused person have the whole matter in his own hands?

The semibarbaric king had a daughter as blooming as his most rosy fancies, and with a soul as fervent and imperious as his own. As is usual in such cases, she was the apple of his eye and was loved by him above all humanity. Among his courtiers was a young man of that fineness of blood
70    and lowness of station common to the heroes of romance who love royal maidens. This royal maiden was well satisfied with her lover, for he was handsome and brave to a degree unsurpassed in all this kingdom, and she loved him with an ardor that had enough of barbarism in it to make it exceedingly warm and strong. This love affair moved on happily for many months,
75    until one day, the king happened to discover its existence. He did not hesitate or waver in regard to his duty. The youth was immediately cast into prison, and a day was appointed for his trial in the king's arena. This, of course, was an especially important occasion, and His Majesty, as well as all the people, was greatly interested in the workings and development of this trial. Never
80    before had such a case occurred—never before had a subject dared to love the daughter of a king. In afteryears such things became commonplace enough, but then they were, in no slight degree, novel and startling.

The tiger cages of the kingdom were searched for the most savage and relentless beasts, from which the fiercest monster might be selected for the
85    arena, and the ranks of maiden youth and beauty throughout the land were carefully surveyed by competent judges, in order that the young man might have a fitting bride in case fate did not determine for him a different destiny. Of course, everybody knew that the deed with which the accused was charged had been done. He had loved the princess, and neither he, she,
90    nor anyone else thought of denying the fact. But the king would not think of allowing any fact of this kind to interfere with the workings of the court of judgment, in which he took such great delight and satisfaction. No matter how the affair turned out, the youth would be disposed of, and the king would take pleasure in watching the course of events which would determine
95    whether or not the young man had done wrong in allowing himself to love the princess.

The appointed day arrived. From far and near the people gathered and thronged the great galleries of the arena, while crowds, unable to gain admittance, massed themselves against its outside walls. The king and his court
100    were in their places, opposite the twin doors—those fateful portals, so terrible in their similarity!

All was ready. The signal was given. A door beneath the royal party opened, and the lover of the princess walked into the arena. Tall, beautiful, fair, his appearance was greeted with a low hum of admiration and anxiety.

105 Half the audience had not known so grand a youth had lived among them. No wonder the princess loved him! What a terrible thing for him to be there!

As the youth advanced into the arena, he turned, as the custom was, to bow to the king. But he did not think at all of that royal personage; his eyes were fixed upon the princess, who sat to the right of her father. Had it not

110 been for the barbarism in her nature, it is probable that lady would not have been there. But her intense and fervid soul would not allow her to be absent on an occasion in which she was so terribly interested. From the moment that the decree had gone forth that her lover would decide his fate in the king's arena, she had thought of nothing, night or day, but this great event

115 and the various subjects connected with it. Possessed of more power, influence, and force of character than anyone who had ever before been interested in such a case, she had done what no other person had done—she had possessed herself of the secret of the doors. She knew in which of the two rooms behind those doors stood the cage of the tiger, with its open front,

120 and in which waited the lady. Through these thick doors, heavily curtained with skins on the inside, it was impossible that any noise or suggestion should come from within to the person who should approach to raise the latch of one of them. But gold and the power of a woman's will had brought the secret to the princess.

125 Not only did she know in which room stood the lady, ready to emerge, all blushing and radiant, should her door be opened, but she knew who the lady was. It was one of the fairest and loveliest of the damsels of the court who had been selected as the reward if the accused youth should be proved innocent of the crime of aspiring to one so far above him; and the princess

130 hated her. Often had she seen, or imagined that she had seen, this fair creature throwing glances of admiration upon the person of her lover, and sometimes she thought these glances were perceived and even returned. Now and then she had seen them talking together. It was but for a moment or two, but much can be said in a brief space. It may have been on most

135 unimportant topics, but how could she know that? The girl was lovely, but she had dared to raise her eyes to the loved one of the princess, and, with all the intensity of the savage blood transmitted to her through long lines of wholly barbaric ancestors, she hated the woman who blushed and trembled behind the silent door.

140 When her lover turned and looked at her, his eye met hers as she sat there paler and whiter than anyone in the vast ocean of anxious faces about her, he saw, by that power of quick perception which is given to those whose souls are one, that she knew behind which door crouched the tiger, and behind which stood the lady. He had expected her to know it. He understood

145 her nature, and his soul was assured that she would never rest until she had made plain to herself this thing, hidden to all other lookers-on, even to the king. The only hope for the youth in which there was any element of certainty

was based upon the success of the princess in discovering the mystery, and the moment he looked upon her he saw she had succeeded.

150     Then it was that his quick and anxious glance asked the question, "Which?" It was as plain to her as if he shouted it from where he stood. There was not an instant to be lost. The question was asked in a flash; it must be answered in another.

    Her right arm lay on the cushioned parapet before her. She raised her
155 hand, and made a slight, quick movement toward the right. No one but her lover saw her. Every eye but his was fixed on the man in the arena.

    He turned, and with a firm and rapid step he walked across the empty space. Every heart stopped beating, every breath was held, every eye was fixed immovably upon that man. Without the slightest hesitation, he went to
160 the door on the right and opened it.

    Now, the point of the story is this: Did the tiger come out of that door, or did the lady?

    The more we reflect upon this question, the harder it is to answer. It involves a study of the human heart which leads us through roundabout
165 pathways of passion, out of which it is difficult to find our way. Think of it, fair reader, not as if the decision of the question depended upon yourself, but upon that hot-blooded, semibarbaric princess, her soul at a white heat beneath the combined fires of despair and jealousy. She had lost him, but who should have him?

170     How often, in her waking hours and in her dreams, had she started in wild horror and covered her face with her hands as she thought of her lover opening the door on the other side of which waited the cruel fangs of the tiger!

    But how much oftener had she seen him at the other door! How in her
175 grievous reveries had she gnashed her teeth and torn her hair when she saw his start of rapturous delight as he opened the door of the lady! How her soul had burned in agony when she had seen him rush to meet that woman, with her flushing cheek and sparkling eye of triumph; when she had seen him lead her forth, his whole frame kindled with the joy of recovered
180 life; when she had heard the glad shouts from the multitude, and the wild ringing of the happy bells; when she had seen the priest, with his joyous followers, advance to the couple, and make them man and wife before her very eyes; and when she had seen them walk away together upon their path of flowers, followed by the tremendous shouts of the hilarious multitude, in
185 which her one despairing shriek was lost and drowned!

    Would it not be better for him to die at once, and go to wait for her in the blessed regions of semibarbaric futurity?

    And yet, that awful tiger, those shrieks, that blood!

    Her decision had been indicated in an instant, but it had been made after
190 days and nights of anguished deliberation. She had known she would be

asked, she had decided what she would answer, and without the slightest hesitation, she had moved her hand to the right.

The question of her decision is one not to be lightly considered, and it is not for me to presume to set up myself as the one person able to answer it. So I leave it with all of you: Which came out of the opened door—the lady or the tiger?

195

**Frank R. Stockton**

## Talking It Over

1. What do you think of the king's method of administering justice? The author states that by it the minds of the people were "refined and cultured" and that "its perfect fairness is obvious." Does he really mean this or is he being ironic? Explain.

2. In your opinion, are there some advantages to living in a kingdom like the one described? Do you think that most of the king's subjects probably lead fairly happy lives or not? Why?

3. Do any leaders in the world today have characters and governments similar to this king's? Explain.

4. How would you describe the character of the princess? Is she like her father or not?

## Identifying Support for Hypotheses

What do you think was behind the door—the lady or the tiger? Why? Some parts of the story (certain words, phrases) support one hypothesis and some support the other.

Check either "lady" or "tiger" for each of the following statements to show which hypothesis it supports. Be prepared to explain your choice. (If you think a statement supports neither or both, put a 0 in front of each or check both.)

1. "The semibarbaric king had a daughter as blooming as his most rosy fancies, *and with a soul as fervent and imperious as his own.*"

    _____ lady     _____ tiger

2. "This royal maiden *was well satisfied with her lover,* for he was handsome and brave to a degree unsurpassed in all this kingdom, and *she loved him with an ardor that had enough of barbarism in it to make it exceedingly warm and strong.*"

    _____ lady     _____ tiger

3. "It was one of the *fairest and loveliest* of damsels of the court who had been selected as the reward of the accused youth, . . . *and the princess hated her.*"

   _____ lady    _____ tiger

4. "*Often had she seen*, or imagined that she had seen, *this fair creature throwing glances of admiration upon the person of her lover, and sometimes* she thought *these glances were perceived and even returned.*"

   _____ lady    _____ tiger

5. "When her lover turned and looked at her, and his eye met hers as she sat there *paler and whiter* than anyone in the vast ocean of anxious faces. . . ."

   _____ lady    _____ tiger

6. "*He understood her nature, and his soul was assured that she would never rest until she had made plain to herself this thing, hidden to all other lookers-on. . . .*"

   _____ lady    _____ tiger

7. "*Without the slightest hesitation,* he went to the door on the right and opened it."

   _____ lady    _____ tiger

8. "But *how much oftener* had she seen him at the other door! How in her grievous reveries had she *gnashed her teeth and torn her hair when she saw his start of rapturous delight* as he opened the door of the lady!"

   _____ lady    _____ tiger

## Formulating a Line of Argument: The Lady or the Tiger?

Discuss the central question of the story in small groups and try to reach a unanimous decision (one agreed on by everybody) about whether the princess chose the lady or the tiger. Use some of the quotations in the preceding exercise or find others of your own to support your position. After twenty minutes, one member of each group should report the decision to the class and present the main argument(s) or reason(s) for the choice. If the decision was not unanimous, the statistics should also be presented (for example: tiger: 3 to 2, or lady: 4 to 1). After the reports from all the groups, determine which way the class as a whole answered the question.

# It All Started with Dragon Bones

Does anybody believe in dragons? We think of them as mythical, fire-breathing beasts that exist only in the pages of storybooks. But even though they don't really exist, can they affect us? Can they influence our knowledge and our history? The title of the selection suggests that something important began with the bones of these legendary reptiles. Without even reading the selection, how can you tell that this important event relates to Chinese culture? Read to find out how myths can influence history.

## Prereading Exercise: Reading to Answer Specific Questions

Although the article contains many words you might not know, you should be able to understand the main ideas if you simply keep going. Skim the article to find out which sections relate to the following key questions.

1. What importance did dragons have in Chinese cultural and religious traditions?

   Section: _____

2. Why did Chinese scholars at the beginning of the twentieth century start to have many doubts about their ancient traditions of history and language?

   Section: _____

3. How did the mood of self-doubt among scholars combine with the interest in "dragon bones" to produce objective evidence of the ancient origins of the Chinese language?

   Section: _____

## It All Started with Dragon Bones

The beginning of the twentieth century was a low point in Chinese history. Drought, famine, and disease troubled the common people. Opium addiction spread, and the government was powerless to stop it, for British guns protected the drug importers. Because of economic dominance, China was
5  forced to bow before the superior weaponry and technology of countries it had once considered inferior.

RAPHO/PHOTO RESEARCHERS, INC.

Street scene in northern Hunan Province

Even worse, a cultural tradition three thousand years old was falling apart beneath the impact of Western scientific thought, further demoralizing Chinese intellectuals. Chinese writers published articles claiming that their own people were inherently incapable of operating foreign machines, let alone inventing new ones. A mood of self-doubt, of dissatisfaction with old wisdom, extended into every branch of study.

Pushed by Occidental standards for scientific proof, Chinese historians studied their ancient records with increased skepticism. Were the stirring histories of the earliest dynasties Yin and Chou only legends? Were there enough hard facts to prove that Confucius really lived? Some Western scholars even cast doubt on the foundation stone of Chinese culture, its written language, by suggesting that Chinese characters had been imported from the Middle East in ages long past.

Then something happened to restore confidence in ancient tradition. A small coincidence struck a spark that would later become a light brilliant enough to illuminate the dim reaches of Chinese history. Here, then, is the story of this coincidence.

The farmers around the village of Hsiao T'un in northern Hunan Province sometimes earned extra money from a most unusual crop: pieces of bone turned up by the plow or by heavy rain. It was well known then that a dragon sheds its bones as a snake sheds its skin. Dragons have always played a starring role in Chinese folklore, religion, and philosophy.

To the common mind, dragons are generally good creatures (unlike the Western dragon, which is pictured as an evil monster in league with the devil)

R.C. HIRSCH/O.M.D.

"Dragon bones"

associated with rain, rivers, and mists, and with the emperor. Taoism, a native Chinese religion, later developed a complex mythology featuring the dragon as a mythical force of cosmic power who appears for a moment to fill man with awe, then disappears into the mist. The Buddhist sect called Ch'an in
35   China and better known in the West by its Japanese name, Zen, elevates the dragon to a philosophical symbol for the flash of Truth that comes to enlighten the thinker. Traditional healers believed that ground-up dragon bones could cure women's diseases, dysentery, and malaria, as well as a number of other maladies.
40      The farmers of Hsiao T'un could not be sure the bones they found came from dragons. Some had strange symbols scratched on them. Crosses and straight and curved lines could be deciphered, and even sketchy pictures. Might dragon bones carry these marks? Probably not. But the pharmacies in Peking wanted dragon bones, and the farmers needed money, so they
45   scraped off the peculiar markings and sent the bones to Peking.
         Fortunately, one farmer did not scrape well, and a piece of marked bone was sold by a Peking pharmacist to a scholar who was ill. Imagine the sick man's astonishment when he recognized, on an object he was about to grind up for medicinal broth, a written message from China's mythical past!
50      The year was 1899. Tantalized by the mysterious "dragon bone" hieroglyphics, a small group of Chinese scholars collected quantities of inscribed bones from the fields around Hsiao T'un. Five years passed before enough symbols could be deciphered to reveal the true nature of the "dragon bones."
         They were a record of a people who called themselves Shang, and ruled
55   lands in the area some four thousand years ago. Here was objective proof for the existence of a dynasty called "Yin" (about 1766–1122 B.C.) by its Chou conquerors, part of a heroic epoch of Chinese history, described until then only in semilegendary histories.

The objects embedded in the fields of Hsiao T'un came not from dragons
60 but from turtles and cattle. Shang kings sought to learn the future through
their diviners, who inscribed royal questions on a carefully scraped and pol-
ished bone. The inscribed oracle shells and bones were partially drilled in
prescribed patterns. Heat was applied, and the course of the resulting cracks,
determined by ancestral spirits, indicated answers to their questions.
65      Shang oracle bones provide intriguing glimpses of life in China four thousand years ago. Kings then yearned to know the results of military campaigns
and hunting expeditions. They asked spirits to forecast the weather, the sex
of unborn children, the outcome of diseases bothering the royal family. Yet
Shang oracle bones raise more questions than they answer. Like a tiny
70 flashlight played over a dark room filled with unknown objects, they give us
a fragmented understanding of the Shang people.

**Raymond Chang and Margaret Scrogin Chang**
*Speaking of Chinese*

## Recalling Information

The following statements relate to the three questions you were asked
to focus on in the prereading exercise. Write T (true) or F (false) in front
of each statement. Correct false statements to make them true.

_____ 1. At the beginning of the twentieth century, China found itself
humiliated and controlled militarily and economically by cultures it had once considered unimportant.

_____ 2. Chinese writers of this time paid no attention to Western scientific thought and maintained that the ancient wisdom of
their culture was superior.

_____ 3. Some Western scholars even suggested that the Chinese written language had been invented by the British.

_____ 4. Just as in Western tradition, the Chinese dragon has always
been portrayed as an evil monster in league with the devil.

_____ 5. In the Chinese Buddhist sect called Ch'an (known as Zen in
Japan), the dragon was a symbol for the flash of Truth that
enlightens a person.

_____ 6. The farmers from the village of Hsiao T'un used to scrape off
the strange symbols from the bones because they didn't want
people to know the origins of the Chinese language.

_____ 7. Fortunately, a scholar in Peking bought a bone for medicine
and recognized a symbol that had not been scraped off.

_____ 8. The bones provided proof that the Chinese language was about
a thousand years old.

_____  9. In reality, the "dragon bones" were from cattle and turtles.

_____  10. These bones had been used in ages past in special rituals for the purpose of answering questions about the future.

## Talking It Over

1. In Lines 20–21, the authors mention "a small coincidence" that was eventually to provide an important key to Chinese history. What is this coincidence?

2. Do you think that the origins of the Chinese language would have been discovered some day even without this coincidence? Why or why not? Do you believe that this coincidence occurred simply by chance?

3. Have you heard of any other legends or mysteries from the past that people used to laugh at but that were later discovered to be true?

## Stories Behind Words: Words with Origins in Mythology

The article describes some Chinese scholars as being "*tantalized* by the mysterious dragon bone hieroglyphics." *Tantalized* is one of many English words that have their origins in myths and legends of the past (in this case, Greek and Roman ones). The meaning of the verb *tantalize* is a very particular one: "to promise or show something desirable to a person and then take it away; to tease by arousing hope." Many (but not all) English dictionaries give you a brief indication of a word's origins in brackets before or after the explanation of the meaning. For *tantalize* the following explanation is given: [>Tantalus]. This means that you should look up the name *Tantalus* to find out the word's origins, and if you do, you will find out that in Greek mythology, Tantalus was a king who was punished in the lower world with eternal hunger and thirst; he was put up to his chin in water that always moved away when he tried to drink it and with fruit on branches above him placed just a little bit out of his reach. Can you see why his name was changed into a verb meaning "to tease or torment by arousing desire"?

Another example is the word *siren*, familiar to us as the mechanical device that makes such an alarming sound when police cars, ambulances, or fire engines approach. This word also has its origins in Greek mythology. The traveler Odysseus (Ulysses to the Romans) made his men plug their ears so that they wouldn't hear the dangerous voices of the *sirens*, creatures who were half bird and half woman and who lured sailors to their deaths on sharp rocks. So the word came to be associated both with a loud sound and with danger! Of course, it also has another meaning when referring to a woman, and this one is also related to the legend. Similarly, when someone speaks of a "*jovial* mood" or a "*her-*

BETTMANN ARCHIVE

In Greek mythology, Tantalus was punished
by having to suffer eternal hunger and thirst
while food and water were in sight.

*culean* effort," he or she is using words with origins in mythology. Look
these words up to find their meaning and relationship to myths.

Many common words, such as the names for the days of the week
and the months of the year, also come from mythology. *Wednesday*
derives from the ancient Norse king of the gods, Woden, and *Thursday*
was originally *Thor's day*, in honor of Thor, the god of thunder. Do you
know which of the days of the week was named in honor of a Roman
god? There is also a planet named for him. Another one of the planets
is named for the Roman god of war because it is red, and one of the
months is named for him too. Can you guess which one? In fact, all the
planets, except the one we live on, bear names that come from Roman
mythology, including the planet that is farthest away from the sun and
for that reason was called after the Roman god of the dead. This god
has also given his name to one of the chemical elements. Do you know
what his name is? Several other elements have names that come from
mythology, too.

It seems that myths and legends live on in the English language. Is
this true in other languages, too? Are the days of the week, the months,
the planets, and the chemical elements named for mythological gods in
the language of your native culture? Does it also contain words and
expressions derived from the ancient beliefs of your ancestors?

## Finding Out More About Mysterious Phenomena

Work with one or two other members of your class to prepare a brief report about one of the following unsolved mysteries. Each person should use a different source (book or magazine article). You should discuss in class beforehand how to find the information in the library. The first person will explain what the phenomenon is; then the others will read in turn a small section about it from their book or article.

1. the Yeti, or Abominable Snowman
2. UFOs
3. the Loch Ness monster
4. werewolves
5. the Lost Continent of Atlantis
6. ESP
7. the Bermuda Triangle
8. firewalkers
9. Count Dracula
10. The *Llorona* of Mexico
11. black holes

## Answering Riddles

A riddle is a minimystery or little puzzle in the form of a question asked in such a way that it requires some cleverness to answer it. Often you must look at the whole question in a manner that is not at first obvious. Riddles are popular in most cultures and are often humorous. Some are silly and some are sophisticated, but they can all be fun if you are in the mood to relax and play with words and ideas. Sometimes they relate to current events or famous people in the news. Read the following riddles and try to answer them. They all refer to letters of the alphabet and to the dictionary. The answer is given for the first one; the answers to the others are listed in an appendix at the end of this book. Tell which answer corresponds to each of the riddles.

**EXAMPLE**    I occur once in every minute, twice in every moment but not once in a hundred thousand years. What am I?

**The letter *m*.**

**RIDDLES**

_____ 1. Why is the letter *e* lazy?

_____ 2. What is the end of everything?

_____ 3. What begins with a *t*, ends with a *t*, and has *t* in it?

_____ 4. Why is an island like the letter *t*?

_____ 5. What four letters frighten a thief?

_____ 6. Which is easier to spell, seventeen or eighteen?

_____ 7. Why is *smiles* the longest word in the dictionary?

_____ 8. Where does Thursday come before Wednesday?

_____ 9. What's the definition of *minimum*?

**C H A P T E R 5**

# Transitions

ARVIND GARG/PHOTO RESEARCHERS, INC.

Individuals, groups, and nations are constantly going through changes, or transitions, to which they must adjust. The first selection deals with the different stages of life—youth, career, family life, old age—and how individuals adjust and prepare financially for each stage. The second selection presents a different type of transition: the changes that people in the Third World go through when they find themselves confronted for the first time with the modern urban environment. The chapter concludes with a selection on the "human waves" that are at present changing the make-up of world populations.

## SELECTION ONE

# Life Cycle Planning

Psychologists have given a great deal of attention in recent years to the different stages of life—such as youth, young adulthood, middle age, old age, etc.—and the need for people to prepare themselves for transitions from one stage to another. In *The Lifetime Book of Money Management* Grace Weinstein focuses on the financial aspects of the life cycle. In the following excerpt from this book, you'll see how three Americans of different ages are spending their money. You'll also encounter an outline that gives you an idea of how a typical American should be planning before the transition to each new stage in his or her life in order to be financially responsible.

### Prereading Exercise: Relating Vocabulary to an Idea

Words and expressions relating to money are important in the following selection. Working as a class or in groups, discuss the meaning of these words and expressions and arrange them from those indicating the *largest amount of money* to those indicating the *smallest*. (In some cases the exact order may be a matter of opinion.)

| | | |
|---|---|---|
| affluence | *Most $$* | _____ |
| go into debt | | _____ |
| the Depression | | _____ |
| economic boom | | _____ |
| frugality | | _____ |
| prosperous | | _____ |
| struggle to make ends meet | | _____ |
| buy on credit | | _____ |
| make investments | *Least $$* | _____ |

BARBARA RIOS/PHOTO RESEARCHERS, INC.

In general, young Americans today are not afraid to go into debt because they feel tomorrow's dollars are worth less and less. Older Americans, however, may be extremely reluctant to buy on credit and likely to save as much money as possible.

Now that you understand the financial terms in the box, read the selection to see how they fit into the different stages of the life cycle.

## *Life Cycle Planning*

- Sherry is 23 and engaged to be married. She has grown up in a society shaped by affluence and molded by inflation. Sherry, as a result, shares some attitudes and expectations common to her peers: She'll start married life in an apartment, but she'll have a home of her own, because that's what people do. She'll go into debt to buy that home, and to acquire other possessions as well, because that's also what people do. Why pay cash today, after all, when tomorrow's dollars will be worth less and less?

- Rob is Sherry's father. At 47, he is doing well with his own accounting firm. His early years were shaped by his parents' experience of the Depression, but his own youth was lived in the economic boom that followed World War II. He thinks his parents' frugality excessive, but can't quite accept the free-spending ways of his children's generation. Rob is, in fact, somewhat concerned about his own approaching retirement. He's afraid continually rising prices will make it increasingly difficult to live on a limited income.

- Fred is 74 and recently retired. He married and became a father during the Great Depression of the 1930s, at a time when he was grateful for a civil service desk job. His whole life has been shaped by the memories of those years: of his father losing a prosperous business, of neighbors out of work, of his own struggles to make ends meet and raise a growing family. The children are long since grown, and Fred and his wife, Trudy, have been financially comfortable for quite a few

years. But old memories are hard to shed. Fred is still reluctant to buy
on credit, still scrupulous in keeping track of expenditures. He suspects
it's simply too late to change.

The traditional life sequence—school, job, marriage, childrearing, back
to being a couple as children leave the nest, back to being alone as one
spouse dies—has its counterpart in monetary terms: Income rises gradually
from young adulthood through the child-rearing years, remains relatively
stable from the middle years until retirement and in widowhood. Outgoing
income, in the same sequence, starts low, rises for the setting-up-house-
keeping expenses of early marriage, declines briefly, rises sharply with the
arrival of children and still more sharply with the college years, and falls off
abruptly as children leave the nest.

But this neat sequence is no longer universal. Young adults marry later,
or not at all. Married couples often defer parenthood, and one in ten married
couples do not have children at all. Four in ten marriages dissolve long before
widowhood. The divorced remarry, form new families, and face the expenses
of those new families against the backdrop of continuing expense for the
existing family. All these changes reshape the face of society. They also affect
the financial planning of the people involved.

Check the following chart to see what financial tasks people face at
different ages and stages of their lives. See where you fit in the cycle.

## Financial Planning Throughout the Life Cycle
## Ages 13–17

1.  Learn to budget through handling an allowance.
2.  Develop financial understanding by working for pay.
3.  Begin to think about future career options.

## Ages 18–24

1.  Establish household.
2.  Train for career.
3.  Identify long-range goals.
4.  Begin to attain financial independence.
5.  Start a savings program.
6.  Establish a credit identity.
7.  Begin to invest.
8.  Purchase insurance.
9.  Develop a financial record-keeping system.

## Ages 25–40

1.  Provide for childbearing and child-rearing costs.
2.  Provide for expanding housing needs.
3.  Expand career goals.

60    4. Manage increased need for credit.

5. Invest for capital growth.

6. Build an education fund for children.

7. Expand insurance to meet expanding needs.

8. Write a will; name guardian for children.

65    9. Involve every member of the household in financial management.

**Ages 41–54**

1. Continue career development.

2. Diversify investments.

3. Provide greater income for growing needs.

4. Continue to build education funds, provide education for children.

70    5. Begin to develop estate plan.

6. Explore retirement goals.

7. Review and revise will as necessary.

**Ages 55-64**

1. Evaluate and update retirement plans.

2. Concentrate on income-producing investments.

75    3. Review insurance and reduce coverage where not needed.

4. Decide where to live in retirement.

5. Meet responsibilities for aging parents.

6. Review estate plan.

**Ages 65 and over**

1. Reevaluate budget to meet retirement needs.

80    2. Investigate part-time employment and/or volunteer work for retirement.

3. Review will.

4. Write a letter of instructions to accompany will.

5. Share financial management and household management tasks with spouse.

**Grace W. Weinstein**
*The Lifetime Book of Money Management*

# Completing a Comparison of Attitudes and Their Causes

Fill in the blanks to complete the comparison of the three different financial attitudes given as examples. In the first blank put the name and age of the appropriate person; in the second, a cause of his or her attitude toward money; and in the third, a description or explanation of the cause.

**SHERRY, 23**        **ROB, 47 (SHERRY'S FATHER)**        **FRED, 74**

1. _____ is the most frugal and does not like to buy on credit. In part this attitude is due to memories of the _____ when _____ .

2. _____ is the most free-spending and does not hesitate to go into debt. In part this attitude is due to _____ which means that _____ .

3. _____ is in between the two others, not spending money too easily, but not wanting to go into debt either. In part this attitude is due to the youthful experience of _____ that followed after _____ .

## Analyzing an Outline

The outline (chart) given at the end of the selection shows what financial tasks North Americans face at different stages of life. Without looking back at the excerpt, write down in Column A which stage you recall as corresponding to each of the following tasks.

13–17, 18–24, 25–40, 41–54, 55–64, 65 and over

|  | A | B |
|---|---|---|
| 1. Explore retirement goals: | ____ | ____ |
| 2. Establish a credit identity: | ____ | ____ |
| 3. Write a will: | ____ | ____ |
| 4. Share financial management and household management tasks with spouse: | ____ | ____ |
| 5. Start a savings program: | ____ | ____ |
| 6. Develop financial understanding by working for pay: | ____ | ____ |
| 7. Decide where to live in retirement: | ____ | ____ |
| 8. Build an education fund for children: | ____ | ____ |
| 9. Begin to develop an estate plan: | ____ | ____ |
| 10. Begin to think about future career options: | ____ | ____ |

Scan the outline and write the stage given there in Column B. Compare the two columns. In general, did you remember the tasks as corresponding to *earlier* or *later* stages? Now think back over each task. Try to explain why the author suggests the stages listed in Column B.

## Vocabulary Analysis: The Suffix *-hood*

Several words ending in *-hood* are used for different stages of the life cycle: *motherhood, fatherhood, childhood,* for example. By thinking about the meaning of these words, what can you infer about the meaning of the suffix *-hood*? Scan the article for three other words ending in *-hood*, write them down, and explain their meanings. Then guess at the meanings of the two other words listed as 4 and 5 and try using each one in a sentence.

1. _____    meaning: _____

2. _____    meaning: _____

3. _____    meaning: _____

4. *nationhood*    sentence: _____

5. *selfhood*    sentence: _____

## Talking It Over

1. According to the selection, what is the traditional life sequence of North Americans? How does this relate to income and expenditures?

2. What does the author mean when she says that children "leave the nest"? How does this affect the household's finances?

3. Is the life sequence in your culture similar or different? Explain.

4. What are some of the recent changes in life sequence that are reshaping "the face of society"? Are these changes occurring in your culture too? Why or why not?

5. In general, psychologists say that planning ahead helps people to make a good transition from one stage of life to another. What examples of planning ahead do you see in the financial planning outline?

6. Were there any examples or suggestions in the selection that surprised you? Do you agree or disagree with the ideas presented there about money and how to spend it? Explain.

SELECTION TWO

# Conversations in Malaysia

The following selection is taken from the book *Among the Believers: An Islamic Journey* by V. S. Naipaul, one of the most renowned writers of English of our times. It is his interview of Shafi, a young Muslim man in Kuala Lumpur, the capital city of Malaysia. Shafi used to live in a village and finds that life in the big city is very different. Think for a moment about what it would be like to move from a very small village to a modern city. What aspects of the urban lifestyle do you imagine would appeal to him? Which aspects would disturb him or cause him trouble? As you read, try to understand Shafi's point of view. At the same time, notice what elements in his background would give him this point of view and ask yourself if your reactions would be similar to or different from his.

## Prereading Exercise: Taking Note of the Change of Speakers

Although the title uses the word *conversation*, the following selection is really an *interview*. In what way is an interview different from a conversation? While reading either of these, it is important to take note of which person is speaking in each section as you read. How can you tell when the speaker changes? Sometimes the author tells you directly. Sometimes you get clues from the punctuation, the paragraph divisions, or simply the context. Sometimes the people speaking have different styles of speech. V. S. Naipaul speaks perfect English, for example, while Shafi makes certain grammar mistakes. In an interview, which person would you expect to ask more questions: the interviewer or the person being interviewed? Would this always be true?

Skim the selection and note each time the speaker changes. Be prepared to explain how you know in each case. Then complete this statement by circling the correct number: In "Conversations in Malaysia," the number of "paragraphs" spoken by Shafi is: 9  14  18  25.

## Conversations in Malaysia

Shafi worked for the Muslim cause. He didn't wear Arab clothes. But he understood the young men who did. Shafi had come to Kuala Lumpur from a village in the north. The disturbance of the move was still with him.

Shafi said: "When I was in the village the atmosphere is entirely different.
5  You come out of the village. You see all the bright lights, you begin to sense the materialistic civilization around you. And I forgot about my religion and my commitments—in the sense that you had to pray. But not to the extent of going out and doing nasty things like taking girls and drinking and gambling and drugs. I didn't lose my faith. I simply forgot to pray, forgot responsibilities.
10  Just losing myself. I got nothing firm in my framework. I just floating around and didn't know my direction."

I said, "Where did you live when you came to Kuala Lumpur?"

He didn't give a straight answer. At this early stage in our conversation concreteness didn't come easily to him. He said, "I was living in a suburb

PAUL CONKLIN/MONKMEYER PRESS PHOTO SERVICE

Rural Malaysia, rice fields

15  where I am exposed to materialistic civilization to which I had never been
exposed before. Boys and girls can go out together. You are free from family
control. You are free from society who normally criticize you in a village when
you do something bad. You take a goat, a cow, a buffalo—somewhere where
the goat is being tied up all the time—and you release that goat in a bunch
20  of other animals: The goat would just roam anywhere he want to go without
any strings."

"Is that bad for the goat?"

"I think the goat would be very happy to roam free. But for me I don't
think that would be good. If goat had brains, I would want to say, 'Why do
25  you want to roam about when you are tied and being fed by your master
and looked after? Why do you want to roam about?'"

I said, "But I want to roam about."

"What do you mean by being free? Freedom for me is not something that
you can roam anywhere you want. Freedom must be within the definition of
30  a certain framework. Because I don't think we are able to run around and
get everything. That freedom means nothing. You must really frame yourself
where you want to go and what you want to do."

"But didn't you know what you wanted to do when you came to Kuala
Lumpur?"

35  "The primary aim was education. That was a framework. But the conflict
of this freedom and the primary aim is there, and I consider this is the problem
I faced and many of my friends face."

"Other people in other countries face the same problem."

Shafi said, "Do they face the same restrictions of family life as I do?"

40  "What restrictions?"

"Religious restrictions. You have that frame with you. Religious tradition, family life, the society, the village community. Then you come into the city, where people are running, people are free. The values contradict.

"You see, in the village where I was brought up we have the bare minimum.
45 We have rice to eat, house to live. We didn't go begging. In the city you can buy a lunch at ten dollars (Malaysian dollars, $2.20 to the American). Or in a stall you can have a lunch for fifty cents. That excess of nine-fifty which the city dwellers spend will be spent by us on other purposes. To us, with our framework and tradition and religion, that is excessiveness.

50 "Sometimes my wife feels that we should go back to the village, and I also feel the same. Not running away from the modern world, but trying to live a simpler, more meaningful life than coming to the city, where you have lots of waste and lots of things that is not real probably. You are not honest to yourself if you can spend fifty cents and keep yourself from hunger, but
55 instead spend ten dollars.

"I will tell you about waste. Recently the government built a skating rink. After three months they demolished it because a highway going to be built over it. They are building big roads and highways across the villages. And whose lorries are passing by to collect the produce of the poor and to dump
60 the products that is manufactured by the rich at an exorbitant price—colour TVs, refrigerators, air conditioners, transistor radios?"

"Don't people want those things?"

"In the end they are going to use the colour TVs—which the people enjoy—to advertise products to draw people into wasteful living."

65 "Village life—wouldn't you say it is dull for most people?"

"The village? It's simple. It's devoid of—what shall I say?—wastefulness. You shouldn't waste. You don't have to rush for things. My point about going back to the *kampong* is to stay with the community and not to run away from development. The society is well knit. If someone passed away there is an
70 alarm in the *kampong*, where most of us would know who passed away and when he is going to be buried, what is the cause of death, and what happened to the next of kin—are they around? It's not polluted in the village. Physical pollution, mental, social."

"Social pollution?"

75 "Something that contradicts our customs and traditions. A man cannot walk with a woman who doesn't belong to his family in the *kampong*. It is forbidden."

"Why is it wrong?"

"The very essence of human respect and dignity comes from an hon-
80 ourable relationship of man and woman. You must have a law to protect the unit of your society. You need your family to be protected. When the girls come from the villages to Kuala Lumpur they don't want to be protected by the law."

**V. S. Naipaul**
*Among the Believers: An Islamic Journey*

## Finding Support for Main Ideas

The main purpose of the selection is to present Shafi's point of view concerning his transition from village to city life. Check the statement in each group that expresses a main idea Shafi communicates. (Remember: You are looking for Shafi's ideas, not those of the author.) Then find at least two examples in the reading that support or illustrate each of these main ideas.

_____ 1. City life is better than village life because it gives more freedom.

_____ City life is not as good as village life because it lacks structure.

_____ 2. People in the city are wasteful.

_____ People in the village are dull.

_____ 3. The city offers many wonderful products—color TVs, refrigerators, and so on—that improve people's lives.

_____ The village (*kampong*) offers a sense of community that improves people's lives.

## Paraphrasing What You've Read

Explain the following opinions taken from the selection in a clear and concise manner and in your own words.

1. "He didn't give a straight answer. At this early stage in our conversation concreteness didn't come easily to him."

_____

_____

_____

_____

2. "You take a goat, a cow, a buffalo—somewhere where the goat is being tied up all the time—and you release that goat in a bunch of other animals: The goat would just roam anywhere he want to go without any strings."

_____

_____

_____

_____

3. "In the end they are going to use the colour TVs—which the people enjoy—to advertise products to draw people into wasteful living."

_____

_____

_____

_____

4. "It's not polluted in the village. Physical pollution, mental, social."

_____

_____

_____

_____

## Talking It Over

1. In your opinion, why does Shafi have problems in adjusting to city life?
2. Do you agree with Shafi's ideas about the city and the village or not? In which place would you live more happily? Explain.
3. When Shafi gives an example of the excesses of city life, he talks about the difference between a lunch of ten dollars and one of fifty cents. He speaks as if the nine dollars and fifty cents were simply thrown away and would not benefit anyone in any way. What might an urban person argue in defense of the ten-dollar lunch?

## Interviewing a Classmate

Select a partner and interview each other about some important transition that you each have made (for example, a move from one country to another, a change of lifestyle, a change of job, a marriage). Before you start, decide on four or five questions. Try to focus on how the other person's point of view has changed or is changing because of the transition. Take notes and be prepared to hand them in or read them to the class.

## Some Differences Between British and American English

Most people learn either the British or American form of English. Canadians speak in their own style, which contains some elements in common with each of the others. Could you tell which type was being used by the author and the young man he interviewed in Malaysia? Two words show us immediately that they are using the British form of English: *lorries* in Line 59 and *honourable* in Lines 79–80. Americans do not use the word *lorry*, and many of them would not even know what it means; instead they say *truck*. *Honourable* would be spelled *honorable*—without the *u*—by an American.

How good are you at spotting differences in vocabulary and spelling between the two types of English? Do you know which of the two types has retained the longer, more old-fashioned way of spelling certain words and which one now spells them in a shorter way?

Test your skill at making this distinction by guessing which of the words in the following pairs is American and which is British.

| **VOCABULARY** | **SPELLING** |
|---|---|
| 1. subway/underground | 1. programme/program |
| 2. (electric) flex/cord | 2. cheque/check |
| 3. stove/cooker | 3. color/colour |
| 4. (car) hood/bonnet | 4. catalogue/catalog |
| 5. flashlight/torch | 5. behavior/behaviour |

## SELECTION THREE

# Human Waves

While our own crises and those of our families or of our generation concern us in a dramatic and personal way, there are also larger transitions, which affect the whole world. One of these is the mass migration or movement of people to new regions. Can you think of three different reasons why large numbers of people are leaving the lands of their birth and moving to other areas or countries?

1. _____

2. _____

3. _____

Which of these do you think is the most common?

What problems does it cause and for whom? The following article examines those and other questions relating to current trends in human migration and population.

## Prereading Exercise: Guessing the Meaning of New Words from Context

Use the context and the hints provided in parentheses to make up definitions for the italicized words taken from the article.

1. "When the problem of worldwide population growth is mentioned, attention is almost always focused on *fertility* rates." (Lines 1–2) (*Hint:* This noun [here used as an adjective] is related to the adjective *fertile*, which means "productive, capable of having children.")

   *fertility:* _____

2. ". . . some are illegal migrants who enter a country *surreptitiously* and lead *guarded* lives for fear of *apprehension*." (Lines 22–23) (*Hint:* Adverbs often answer the question *how*? How would people with no legal papers enter?)

   *surreptitiously:* _____

   (*Hint:* The verb *guard* means to "watch over, protect." What do you think the related adjective means?)

   *guarded:* _____

   (*Hint:* Remember that *comprehension* means "a grasping or catching hold of an idea [in the sense of understanding it].")

   *apprehension:* _____

3. "Some half a million Colombians may be living *clandestinely* in Venezuela." (Lines 32–33) (*Hint:* The paragraph is talking about *illegal* immigrants. The sentence expresses uncertainty—they *may* be living there—which is due in part to *how* they are living.)

   *clandestinely:* _____

4. "Does a nation have a right to determine its own *demographic* and cultural characters?" (Lines 69–70) (*Hint:* demo- is a prefix from Greek meaning "people" and is used in such words as *democracy*. The second part contains the word *graph*, which should be familiar to you.)

   *demographic:* _____

## Human Waves

When the problem of worldwide population growth is mentioned, attention is almost always focused on fertility rates. Yet another side of the population problem is causing growing concern—the movement across national borders of millions of people in search of a better life. People have always dreamed
5  of moving to greener pastures, but never in history have migration levels been as high as those of today.

   In 1940, 65 percent of the people on the earth lived in developing countries; today the number approaches 75 percent of the 4.6 billion world population. In a short seventeen years it will surpass 80 percent or some 6.1
10  billion people. Increasingly, residents of the poorest nations are making the decision to move across international borders in an attempt to improve their lives. But with the appearance of nation-states and political barriers, migration has become subject to control. To people facing the prospect of staggering

BUDD GRAY/STOCK, BOSTON

Refugees from El Salvador to whom the Lutheran Church in
the United States has given sanctuary—they do not have legal
documents, so are wearing handkerchiefs to protect their
identities. Thousands of refugees fleeing problems in Central
America have gone to the United States in search of a better
life.

poverty at home, the spectacular advances in communications and trans-
15  portation have made the possibly dire consequences of migration seem less
risky than staying put. This is becoming evident all over the planet as people
move from Mexico and Central America to the United States; from Guinea
to the Ivory Coast; from Colombia to Venezuela; even from such small islands
as Saint Vincent and Saint Lucia to Barbados. Some are legal migrants whose
20  decision to move results from considerable discussion and thought; some
13 million are refugees forced to abandon their homelands for political reasons; some are illegal migrants who enter a country surreptitiously and lead
guarded lives for fear of apprehension. The effects of these movements
across borders are awesome.
25      When Third World countries exhibit rapid industrial growth, as some OPEC
nations have in recent years, they attract residents from less fortunate neighboring states. Thus in Kuwait and the United Arab Emirates, 75 to 80 percent
of the population are immigrants—temporary residents who are not citizens
and probably will never become citizens. Illegal immigrants from such impov-
30  erished countries as Colombia and Ghana have moved in great numbers to
Venezuela and Nigeria. The recent forced departure of Ghanaians from
Nigeria uncovered hundreds of thousands of illegal migrants. Some half a
million Colombians may be living clandestinely in Venezuela. About 25 percent of the population of the Ivory Coast are foreigners, many having migrated
35  from Upper Volta and other African countries.
        What happens when the economic bubble bursts and there is no longer
any employment for foreign workers, when there is not even enough work
for the native-born citizens of the country? Nigeria has provided one answer

with its sudden mass expulsion of Ghanaians. The arbitrary and cyclical
40    nature of economic differences between countries is pointed up by Ghana's
expulsion in 1969 of all aliens without residential permits, forcing some
200,000 persons, mostly Nigerians, to leave.

In the United States there is increasing concern with immigration issues
involving refugees and both legal and illegal immigrants. Since the mid-1970s
45    we have accepted well over 100,000 refugees every year, and given the
unstable political situation in many regions of the world, one can only speculate as to the demands in future years. Since 1980, legal immigrants to the
United States have averaged more than 600,000 per year. To that we must
add the untold hundreds of thousands of clandestine immigrants who enter
50    the country without legal documents. Their number is simply not known. Some
illegal immigrants return home each year so that estimates of net illegal
migration vary from as low as 100,000 to upward of 500,000 per year. In
particular, the number of clandestine entrants across the two-thousand-mile
border between the United States and Mexico is increasing as economic and
55    political conditions grow worse in parts of Latin America.

Does an independent nation have the right to block immigration or to
expel recent and not-so-recent immigrants if their presence is perceived as
jeopardizing the economic well-being of the native inhabitants?

In the United States more than one million apprehensions of those
60    engaged in illegal entry occur each year. These people are sent back to their
home countries, but many return again and again. . . .

Many in the United States feel that the increase in number should come
to an end and be followed by an era of zero population growth at perhaps
275 or 300 million. Even with our very low fertility the population will, if
65    immigration continues at recent rates, approach 350 million within a hundred
years and will still be growing. Furthermore, the existing culture of the nation
will be altered by the increasing proportion of immigrants and their descen-
dants in the population. Thus ethical considerations are raised that go far
beyond the matter of competition for jobs. Does a nation have a right to
70    determine its own demographic and cultural characters?

The problems are not limited to countries with a long history of receiving
immigrants. Tiny Belize, with a population of fewer than 150,000 people and
independent of Great Britain only since September 1981, is faced with massive refugee and immigrant movements from El Salvador, Guatemala, and
75    Nicaragua. Some inhabitants worry that their English-speaking country will
lose its own culture and become Hispanic through immigration. Barbados,
population 250,000 with fertility below replacement, is concerned about current immigration from neighboring, poorer islands; some Barbadians are
worried that their nation's culture will be changed by the incursion of East
80    Indians. Such agonizing issues face many nations. Is it proper for a nation
to insist that its culture remain as it is? If the answer is yes, is this a subtle
new form of racism or is it a laudable expression of cultural identity?

**Leon F. Bouvier**

## Scanning for Statistics to Support Generalizations

Scan the article to find the statistics (numbers and percentages) that relate to the following points of information. Write them in the blanks provided. On the basis of these statistics, complete the generalizations correctly.

1.  The number of immigrants accepted by the United States each year:

    _____

    This figure is (more / less) than the number of illegal immigrants who are apprehended and sent back to their own countries.

2.  The percentage of the world population living in developing (Third World) countries now and in the past:

    _____

    This percentage seems to be (increasing / decreasing).

3.  The percentage of immigrants who reside in some of the wealthy Arab states and who probably will never be citizens:

    _____

    These states seem to have one of the (highest / lowest) percentages of immigrants in their populations.

## Sentence Blocking for Better Understanding

Long, complex sentences contain several ideas and are often hard to understand at first glance. Sometimes they also contain unfamiliar vocabulary. Figuring out the relationships between the ideas, though, can help you to understand the vocabulary. It certainly helps you to grasp the whole meaning. One way of doing this is by sentence blocking.

To block out a long, complex sentence, follow these steps (a sentence from the selection is used to illustrate):

"To people facing the prospect of staggering poverty at home, the spectacular advances in communications and transportation have made the possibly dire consequences of migration seem less risky than staying put."

1.  Find the main idea (clause), the one that *does not* start with any connecting word (such as a conjunction, preposition, or transition). Copy the sentence on a piece of paper and put a block or rectangle around the simple subject and the simple verb. If there is an object of the verb, block out the object, too. Now what you have in blocks is this:

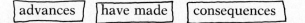

advances  |  have made  |  consequences

2. Now block out the modifiers that are needed to make some sense of the idea, skipping the ones you don't know.

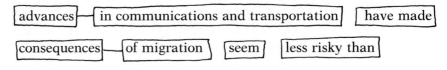

3. Block out whatever else you need to complete the main idea. Try to guess from the context the meaning of key words or idioms. *Staying put* is contrasted with another word by the comparative expression *than*. This usually indicates that its meaning is the opposite of or at least very different from that word. What do you think it means? Now try to put in your own words the main idea of the sentence:

_____

_____

4. Go back to the secondary or subordinate ideas (clauses or phrases). In this case there is one, separated by a comma from the rest of the sentence. How is it related to the main idea? Are the words *staggering* and *dire* needed to understand the general meaning? Add this secondary idea to the main idea to express the meaning of the sentence briefly in your own words.

_____

_____

_____

_____

In small groups or as a class, block out the following sentences from the article. Do not use a dictionary. Finish with a brief, clear paraphrase of the general meaning of each sentence. Compare these with your class.

1. "The arbitrary and cyclical nature of economic differences between countries is pointed up by Ghana's expulsion in 1969 of all aliens without residential permits, forcing some 200,000 persons, mostly Nigerians, to leave." (Lines 39–42)

_____

_____

_____

2. "Since the mid-1970s we have accepted well over 100,000 refugees every year, and given the unstable political situation in many regions of the world, one can only speculate as to the demands in future years." (Lines 44–47)

3. "Does an independent nation have the right to block immigration or to expel recent and not-so-recent immigrants if their presence is perceived as jeopardizing the economic well-being of the native inhabitants?" (Lines 56–58)

## Talking It Over

1. What countries in the world have large numbers of illegal immigrants at present?
2. What kinds of lives do you imagine that these people lead?
3. A law went into effect in November of 1986 granting amnesty to undocumented aliens who could prove they entered the United States before January 1, 1982. Should the law make a distinction between those who have just arrived and those who came before 1982? Explain your opinion.
4. Why are people in certain small countries concerned about the large number of refugees entering their country?
5. The last two paragraphs of the article end with questions. Questions such as these, which are used without the expectation of getting an answer, are called *rhetorical questions*. Why do you think an author uses them? Are these questions at the end of the paragraphs different or do they ask the same thing?
6. How would you answer the question at the end of the reading?

## Discussion

The Universal Declaration of Human Rights adopted by the United Nations General Assembly in 1948 states: "Everyone has the right to leave any country including his own and to return to that country." Is this actually observed in the world today? Should it be? Read the following proposition and decide if you agree with it or not, or if you agree perhaps with only part of it. Be prepared to explain your opinion to the class or to a small group, according to your teacher's instructions.

**PROPOSITION:**   Everyone should have the right to leave any country and to go to live in any country he or she chooses, without fear of penalties or imprisonment.

# Stories Behind Words: Counting Worlds and Measuring Development

In the article, the terms *developing* and *Third World* seem to be used as synonyms to refer to certain countries. Which countries are these? Why do they belong to a "Third World"? One explanation of the popular use of this term is that the press in democratic nations tends to divide the world in two: (1) the free (capitalist) world and (2) the totalitarian (communist) world. The press in communist countries makes a similar division but with different terms: (1) the socialist world and (2) the imperialistic world. In both cases, a section of the world does not quite fit into either category, and so the term *Third World* has come to be used.

It is interesting to note that the newspapers of a given country tend to use complimentary, flattering words such as *free* or *socialist* to describe themselves and *pejorative* or *derogatory* (negative, unflattering) words to describe those countries that have different politics: *totalitarian* or *imperialistic*. Vocabulary often reflects the attitude of the speaker, and the very same character trait can be described in a flattering or in a pejorative way, depending on the viewpoint of the speaker. For example, someone might refer to a man who spends all his evenings and weekends working at his job as an *industrious person* or a *hard worker*. A person with a different viewpoint might refer to the same man as a *workaholic*, a term that implies that the man is addicted to work as an alcoholic is addicted to alcohol. The compliment has become a criticism.

Can you recognize pejorative words in English? Would you rather have someone call you *thin* or *skinny*? *Lazy* or *easygoing*? *Proud* or *arrogant*? *Stingy* or *frugal*? Can you think of any other traits that can be described in both a flattering and a pejorative way?

The countries now referred to as *developing* used to be referred to as *underdeveloped* until this was officially changed and the new term substituted a couple of decades ago. Why do you think it was changed? Do you think it was a good idea to change it? How are these countries referred to in the language of your culture?

# The Mind

PETER MENZEL

Many scientists today speak of the mind as the "new frontier," the single most dynamic and productive area of research. Psychologists have been studying people with an extraordinary ability for remembering or memorizing and have recently come up with some amazing results, discussed in the first selection. A look at the actual physical repository of the mind, the human brain, is presented next, with a description of some of the electrical and chemical aspects of its functions. Then the classic American writer of horror stories, Edgar Allan Poe, gives us an inside look at the disordered and diseased mind of a madman who seems to possess a strange rationality. The final selection is a timed reading about artificial brains—computers.

## SELECTION ONE

# A Memory for All Seasonings

Memory is one of the most important functions of the mind. Without our memories, we would have no identity, no individuality. The following article is about a *mnemonist*, a person with an extraordinary power to remember things or people. The title includes a *pun*, a form of humor based on a play on words. The usual phrase to describe something constant and dependable is "for all seasons"; here the phrase is changed to "for all *seasonings*." (*Seasonings* is another word for spices, such as salt, pepper, and curry.) What hint does this give you about the mnemonist? (Early in the article you will find out.)

## Prereading Exercise: Anticipating the Reading

Before beginning to read an article, it's helpful to try to anticipate what it will be about and determine what associations you have with the topic.

1. When you think of a person with an extraordinary memory, what is the first question that comes to your mind?

   _____

2. Is there something practical you might learn from this reading?

   _____

3. What is the earliest distinct event in your life that you can remember?

   _____

   _____

4. Approximately how old were you when it occurred? _____

Compare your first memory with those of your classmates. When you read the article, you will find out how these memories compare with the earliest memory of the mnemonist. You may also learn the answers to your questions about memory.

## A Memory for All Seasonings

One evening two years ago, Peter Polson, a member of the psychology department at the University of Colorado, took his son and daughter to dinner at Bananas, a fashionable restaurant in Boulder. When the waiter took their orders, Polson noticed that the young man didn't write anything down. He
5 just listened, made small talk, told them that his name was John Conrad, and left. Polson didn't think this was exceptional: There were, after all, only three of them at the table. Yet he found himself watching Conrad closely when he returned to take the orders at a nearby table of eight. Again the waiter listened, chatted, and wrote nothing down. When he brought Polson
10 and his children their dinners, the professor couldn't resist introducing himself and telling Conrad that he'd been observing him.

The young man was pleased. He wanted customers to notice that, unlike other waiters, he didn't use a pen and paper. Sometimes, when they did notice, they left him quite a large tip. He had once handled a table of nineteen
15 complete dinner orders without a single error. At Bananas, a party of nineteen (a bill of roughly $200) would normally leave the waiter a $35 tip. They had left Conrad $85.

Polson was impressed enough to ask the waiter whether he would like to come to the university's psychology lab and let them run some tests on
20 him. Anders Ericsson, a young Swedish psychologist recently involved in memory research, would be joining the university faculty soon, and Polson thought that he would be interested in exploring memory methods with the waiter. Conrad said he would be glad to cooperate. He was always on the lookout for ways to increase his income, and Polson told him he would receive
25 $5 an hour to be a guinea pig.

Conrad, of course, was not the first person with an extraordinary memory to attract attention from researchers. Alexander R. Luria, the distinguished Soviet psychologist, studied a Russian newspaper reporter named Shereshevskii for many years and wrote about him in *The Mind of a Mnemonist*
30 (Basic Books, 1968). Luria says that Shereshevskii was able to hear a series of fifty words spoken once and recite them back in perfect order fifteen years later. Another famous example of extraordinary memory, the conductor Arturo Toscanini, was known to have memorized every note for every instrument in 250 symphonies and 100 operas.

35 For decades the common belief among psychologists was that memory was a fixed quantity; an exceptional memory, or a poor one, was something with which a person was born.

This point of view has come under attack in recent years; expert memory is no longer universally considered the exclusive gift of the genius, or the abnormal. "People with astonishing memory for pictures, musical scores, chess positions, business transactions, dramatic scripts, or faces are by no means unique," wrote Cornell psychologist Ulric Neisser in *Memory Observed* (1981). "They may not even be very rare." Some university researchers, including Polson and Ericsson, go a step further than Neisser. They believe that there are no physiological differences at all between the memory of a Shereshevskii or a Toscanini and that of the average person. The only real difference, they believe, is that Toscanini trained his memory, exercised it regularly, and wanted to improve it.

Like many people with his capacity to remember, Toscanini may also have used memory tricks called mnemonics. Shereshevskii, for example, employed a technique known as *loci*. As soon as he heard a series of words, he mentally "distributed" them along Gorky Street in Moscow. If one of the words was "orange," he might visualize a man stepping on an orange at a precise location on the familiar street. Later, in order to retrieve "orange," he would take an imaginary walk down Gorky Street and see the image from which it could easily be recalled. Did the waiter at Bananas have such a system? What was his secret?

John Conrad would be the subject of Anders Ericsson's second in-depth study of the machinations of memory. As a research associate at Carnegie-Mellon University in Pittsburgh, Ericsson had spent the previous three years working with William Chase on an extensive study of Steve Faloon, an under-graduate whose memory and intellectual skills were considered average.

BRIAN PAYNE

John Conrad

When Ericsson and Chase began testing Faloon, he could remember no more than seven random digits after hearing them spoken once. According to generally accepted research, almost everyone is capable of storing five to nine random digits in short-term memory. After twenty months of working with Chase and Ericsson, Faloon could memorize and retrieve eighty digits.

"The important thing about our testing Faloon is that researchers usually study experts," Chase says. "We studied a novice and watched him grow into an expert. Initially, we were just running tests to see whether his digit span could be expanded. For four days he could not go beyond seven digits. On the fifth day he discovered his mnemonic system and then began to improve rapidly."

Faloon's intellectual abilities didn't change, the researchers say. Nor did the storage capacity of his short-term memory. Chase and Ericsson believe that short-term memory is a more or less fixed quantity. It reaches saturation quickly, and to overcome its limitations one must learn to link new data with material that is permanently stored in long-term memory. Once the associations have been made, the short-term memory is free to absorb new information. Shereshevskii transferred material from short-term to long-term memory by placing words along Gorky Street in Moscow. Faloon's hobby was long-distance running, and he discovered that he could break down a spoken list of eighty digits into units of three or four and associate most of these with running times.

To Faloon, a series like 4, 0, 1, 2 would translate as four minutes, one and two-tenths seconds, or "near a four-minute mile"; 2, 1, 4, 7 would be encoded as two hours fourteen minutes seven seconds, or "an excellent marathon time." When running didn't provide the link to his long-term memory, ages and dates did; 1, 9, 4, 4 is not relevant to running, but it is "near the end of World War II."

Chase and Ericsson see individual differences in memory performance as resulting from previous experience and mental training. "In sum," they write, "adult memory performance can be adequately described by a single model of memory."

Not every student of psychology agrees with Chase and Ericsson, of course. "I'm very suspicious of saying that everyone has the same kind of memory," says Matthew Erdelyi, a psychologist at Brooklyn College. "In my research," he says, "I find that people have very different memory levels. They can all improve, but some levels remain high and some remain low. There are dramatic individual differences."

It is unlikely that there will be any agreement among psychologists on the conclusions that they have thus far drawn from their research. The debate about exceptional memory will continue. But in the meantime it is interesting to look deeper into the mind of a contemporary mnemonist.

Ericsson and Polson, both of whom have tested Conrad over the past two years, believe that there is nothing intellectually outstanding about him.

When they began testing Conrad's memory, his digit scan was normal: about seven numbers. His grades in college were average.

Conrad himself says that he is unexceptional mentally, but he has compared his earliest memories with others' and has found that he can recall things that many people can't. His first distinct memory is of lying on his back and raising his legs so that his mother could change his diapers. As a high-school student he didn't take notes in class—he says he preferred watching the girls take notes—and he has never made a list in his life. "By never writing down a list of things to do, and letting it think for me," he says, "I've forced my memory to improve."

Conrad does believe that his powers of observation, including his ability to listen, are keener than most people's. Memory, he says, is just one part of the whole process of observation. "I'm not extraordinary, but sometimes people make me feel that way. I watch them and realize how many of them have disorganized minds and memories and that makes me feel unusual. A good memory is nothing more than an organized one."

One of the first things Conrad observed at Bananas was that the headwaiter, his boss, was "a very unpleasant woman." He disliked being her subordinate, and he wanted her job. The only way he could get it was by being a superior waiter. He stayed up nights trying to figure out how to do this; the idea of memorizing orders eventually came to him. Within a year he was the headwaiter.

"One of the most interesting things we've found," says Ericsson, "is that just trying to memorize things does not insure that your memory will improve. It's the active decision to get better and the number of hours you push yourself to improve that make the difference. Motivation is much more important than innate ability."

Conrad began his memory training by trying to memorize the orders for a table of two, then progressed to memorizing larger orders.

He starts by associating the entree with the customer's face. He might see a large, heavy-set man and hear "I'd like a big Boulder Steak." Sometimes, Peter Polson says, "John thinks a person looks like a turkey and that customer orders a turkey sandwich. Then it's easy."

In memorizing how long meat should be cooked, the different salad dressings, and starches, Conrad relies on patterns of repetition and variation. "John breaks things up into chunks of four," Ericsson says. "If he hears 'rare, rare, medium, well-done,' he instantly sees a pattern in their relationship. Sometimes he makes a mental graph. An easy progression—rare, medium-rare, medium, well-done—would take the shape of a steadily ascending line on his graph. A more difficult order—medium, well-done, rare, medium—would resemble a mountain range."

The simplest part of Conrad's system is his encoding of salad dressings. He uses letters: *B* for blue cheese; *H* for the house dressing; *O* for oil and vinegar; *F* for French; *T* for Thousand Island. A series of orders, always

arranged according to entree, might spell a word, like *B-O-O-T*, or a near-word, like *B-O-O-F*, or make a phonetic pattern: *F-O-F-O*. As Ericsson says, Conrad remembers orders, regardless of their size, in chunks of four. This is similar to the way Faloon stores digits, and it seems to support Chase and
155   Ericsson's contention that short-term memory is limited and that people are most comfortable working with small units of information.

One of the most intriguing things about Conrad is the number of ways he can associate material. Another is the speed with which he is able to call it up from memory. Ericsson and Polson have also tested him with animals,
160   units of time, flowers, and metals. At first, his recall was slow and uncertain. But with relatively little practice, he could retrieve these "orders" almost as quickly as he could food.

"The difference between someone like John, who has a trained memory, and the average person," says Ericsson, "is that he can encode material in
165   his memory fast and effortlessly. It's similar to the way you can understand English when you hear it spoken. In our tests in the lab, he just gets better and faster." "What John Conrad has," says Polson, "is not unlike an athletic skill. With two or three hundred hours of practice, you can develop these skills in the same way you can learn to play tennis."

**Stephen Singular**

# Study Skills: Underlining and Marginal Glossing

Memorizing is necessary when you review for a test. John Conrad spoke of the importance of having an organized mind in developing one's memory. In this textbook, four skills will be presented that can help you to organize materials for study: underlining, marginal glossing, study mapping, and outlining. This section will deal with underlining and glossing.

### Underlining

Before underlining, you should have read the material once. Then skim the reading, underlining key words and phrases that relate to main ideas and important statistics or examples that support them. Do not underline entire sentences. Underline only about 20 to 30 percent of the material. Many students underline with felt pens, often using one color for main concepts and a different color for statistics and examples.

### Marginal Glossing

Marginal glossing is another way to organize material for study. In this case, a marginal gloss is a note in the margin of your book summarizing the material next to it. When you study, these notes stand out and remind you of other points as well. This saves time because you do not reread everything, only the brief notes.

Here are the first eight paragraphs from a "Memory for All Seasonings" with underlining and marginal glosses done for the first four paragraphs. Look over the four paragraphs that have been marked. Then finish the remaining paragraphs by underlining and glossing them yourself. Afterward, compare what you have done with your classmates. Choose the best work by selecting the shortest one that includes all main points. (If you cannot write in your textbook, make a photocopy of the pages. Ask your instructor for help with any difficulties.) Afterward, you should find that the first part of the comprehension quiz is quite easy.

## A Memory for All Seasonings

One evening two years ago, Peter Polson, a member of the psychology department at the University of Colorado, took his son and daughter to dinner at Bananas, a fashionable restaurant in Boulder. When the waiter took their orders, Polson noticed that the young man didn't write anything down. He
5   just listened, made small talk, told them that his name was John Conrad, and left. Polson didn't think this was exceptional: There were, after all, only three of them at the table. Yet he found himself watching Conrad closely when he returned to take the orders at a nearby table of eight. Again the waiter listened, chatted, and wrote nothing down. When he brought Polson
10   and his children their dinners, the professor couldn't resist introducing himself and telling Conrad that he'd been observing him.

*Peter Polson, from University Colo. Psy. Dept., saw a waiter at Bananas Restaurant with an amazing memory. The waiter was John Conrad.*

    The young man was pleased. He wanted customers to notice that, unlike other waiters, he didn't use a pen and paper. Sometimes, when they did notice, they left him quite a large tip. He had once handled a table of nineteen
15   complete dinner orders without a single error. At Bananas, a party of nineteen (a bill of roughly $200) would normally leave the waiter a $35 tip. They had left Conrad $85.

*Conrad did not write his orders. He memorized all of them.*

    Polson was impressed enough to ask the waiter whether he would like to come to the university's psychology lab and let them run some tests on
20   him. Anders Ericsson, a young Swedish psychologist recently involved in memory research, would be joining the university faculty soon, and Polson thought that he would be interested in exploring memory methods with the waiter. Conrad said he would be glad to cooperate. He was always on the lookout for ways to increase his income, and Polson told him he would receive
25   $5 an hour to be a guinea pig.

*Polson invited Conrad to come to the lab for further memory study. Anders Ericsson, from Sweden, would be there. Conrad agreed to go for $5 an hour.*

    Conrad, of course, was not the first person with an extraordinary memory to attract attention from researchers. Alexander R. Luria, the distinguished Soviet psychologist, studied a Russian newspaper reporter named Shereshevskii for many years and wrote about him in *The Mind of a Mnemonist*
30   (Basic Books, 1968). Luria says that Shereshevskii was able to hear a series of fifty words spoken once and recite them back in perfect order fifteen years later. Another famous example of extraordinary memory, the conductor Arturo

*Other people with amazing memories include a Russian reporter named Shereshevskii and the conductor Arturo Toscanini.*

Toscanini, was known to have memorized every note for every instrument in 250 symphonies and 100 operas.

35    For decades the common belief among psychologists was that memory was a fixed quantity; an exceptional memory, or a poor one, was something with which a person was born.

This point of view has come under attack in recent years; expert memory is no longer universally considered the exclusive gift of the genius, or the
40    abnormal. "People with astonishing memory for pictures, musical scores, chess positions, business transactions, dramatic scripts, or faces are by no means unique," wrote Cornell psychologist Ulric Neisser in *Memory Observed* (1981). "They may not even be very rare." Some university researchers, including Polson and Ericsson, go a step further than Neisser. They believe
45    that there are no physiological differences at all between the memory of a Shereshevskii or a Toscanini and that of the average person. The only real difference, they believe, is that Toscanini trained his memory, exercised it regularly, and wanted to improve it.

Like many people with his capacity to remember, Toscanini may also
50    have used memory tricks called mnemonics. Shereshevskii, for example, employed a technique known as *loci*. As soon as he heard a series of words, he mentally "distributed" them along Gorky Street in Moscow. If one of the words was "orange," he might visualize a man stepping on an orange at a precise location on the familiar street. Later, in order to retrieve "orange," he
55    would take an imaginary walk down Gorky Street and see the image from which it could easily be recalled. Did the waiter at Bananas have such a system? What was his secret?

John Conrad would be the subject of Anders Ericsson's second in-depth study of the machinations of memory. As a research associate at Carnegie-
60    Mellon University in Pittsburgh, Ericsson had spent the previous three years working with William Chase on an extensive study of Steve Faloon, an under-graduate whose memory and intellectual skills were considered average. When Ericsson and Chase began testing Faloon, he could remember no more than seven random digits after hearing them spoken once. According
65    to generally accepted research, almost everyone is capable of storing five to nine random digits in short-term memory. After twenty months of working with Chase and Ericsson, Faloon could memorize and retrieve eighty digits.

# Comprehension Quiz

Choose the best way of finishing each statement, based on what you have just read.

1. The psychology professor discovered John Conrad's incredible ability to memorize:

   a. in school

   b. on a test

   c. in a restaurant

2. Conrad agreed to let the professor study his memory because:

   a. Conrad was interested in psychology
   b. Conrad wanted to increase his income
   c. Conrad needed to improve his memory

3. The famous Russian mnemonist Shereshevskii used a memory trick called *loci* to remember objects by:

   a. associating them with events in Russian history
   b. imagining them placed along a street in Moscow
   c. picturing each one in his mind in a different color

4. The memory trick used by Steve Faloon was the association of certain numbers with:

   a. running times            c. both of the above
   b. important dates           d. none of the above

5. Conrad had been:

   a. a gifted student
   b. a below-average student
   c. an average student

6. Part of Conrad's motivation for developing memory tricks to aid him as a waiter was:

   a. his desire to get his boss's job
   b. his great admiration for the headwaiter
   c. his fear of not finding any work

7. Imagine that four customers have requested that their steaks be cooked in the following way: well-done, medium, medium-rare, rare. According to John Conrad's "mental graph" technique, this order would be remembered as:

   a. a steadily ascending line      c. a mountain range
   b. a steadily descending line

8. From this article a careful reader should infer that:

   a. everyone has about the same memory capacity and can develop a superior memory through practice and motivation
   b. a good or bad memory is an ability that a person is born with and cannot change to any great degree
   c. there is still no conclusive evidence as to whether outstanding memories are inborn or developed

# Applying Concepts from the Reading

Several different mnemonic systems (memory tricks) are described in the reading. Working by yourself or in small groups, show that you have understood these tricks by applying them to the following situations. (A list of the systems with line references is given in case you want to review them.)

**Mnemonic Systems Mentioned in Article**

a. *loci* (imagining objects in a familiar place), used by Shereshevskii, Lines 50–56

b. number association, used by Steve Faloon, Lines 81-90

c. physical appearance association, used by John Conrad, Lines 136–139

d. mental graph or picture, used by Conrad, Lines 140–147

e. word or sound pattern association, used by Conrad, Lines 148–153

**SITUATION 1**   You want to remember the names of all the psychologists mentioned in this article: Polson, Ericsson, Luria, Neisser, Chase. How would you do this using word or sound pattern association?

**SITUATION 2**   You want to remember to buy the following items at the grocery store: apples, milk, rice, pepper, salad dressing, and olives. How would you do this, using *loci*? How would you do it using word or sound pattern association? Which system would be better for you?

**SITUATION 3**   You have just a minute or two to look at the alphabetical list of exam grades and want to remember the grades of seven of your friends. What kind of mental graph would you picture in your mind to remember them in the following order: A, D, A, D, B, C, B?

**SITUATION 4**   You want to remember the combinations for the locks you use for your bicycle, your school locker, and your gym locker: 0915, 1220, 1492. How could you do this, using number association? Can you think of any other way of doing it?

**SITUATION 5**   You are at a dinner party and want to remember the names of the four other guests: a very tall lady named Mrs. Stemski; a large, heavy-set man named Mr. Barnes; a cheerful young woman with a big smile named Miss Rich; and a sad-looking young man named Mr. Winter. How could you use physical appearance association to remember their names?

# Talking It Over

1. In what other professions, besides that of a waiter, is it useful to have a good memory? Why?

2. Do you know or have you heard of any people (besides those mentioned in the article) who have extraordinary memories?

3. What techniques, other than those mentioned in the preceding exercise, are sometimes used to aid memory?

4. Are there some situations in life when it is important to develop the ability to forget rather than to remember? If so, how can this be done? Explain.

## Finding Support for or Against a Hypothesis

As the article points out, some psychologists today believe that extraordinary memories are simply the result of development through hard work and the application of a system. According to them, an average person could achieve a superior memory if he or she tried hard enough. Find evidence from the article to support this hypothesis. Then find evidence from the article that goes against this hypothesis. What is your opinion of this controversial question?

## SELECTION TWO

# ▐▀ Under the Skull

While psychologists are learning a great deal about memory and other functions of the human mind through clinical studies, biologists and neurophysiologists are using experiments, dissection, and high technology to penetrate its mysteries. Did you know that a particular section of the brain controls laughing? This was discovered by accident in 1955 during an operation. When one part of his brain was touched, the patient immediately broke out into wild laughter, completely amazing the doctor, who had certainly not expected his surgery to be so entertaining!

There is also a chemical related to the use of obscene words. People who suffer from Gilles de la Tourette's disease lack this chemical and find themselves, to their great embarrassment, shouting out foul language even at good friends. Fortunately, this syndrome is now controlled by medication containing the important chemical. These examples show that scientists have discovered a great deal about our mental functioning, though they still have a long way to go. Nigel Calder, a noted British scientist and writer, presents some basic facts about the brain in this excerpt from his book *The Mind of Man*.

## Prereading Exercise: Anticipating the Reading

Thinking ahead about the contents of an article can help you focus on the important points. What do you already know about the human brain? Fill out the following description as well as you can, using the drawings to help you.

Color: _____     Weight: _____

Consistency: _____

Major sections: _____

_____

Number and types of cells: _____

_____

Method of transmitting its messages: _____

_____

As you read the excerpt from Calder's book, see what new information you can learn about these aspects of the brain.

## *Under the Skull*

The "face barrier" is a perpetual problem for anyone to overcome who tries to imagine the brain at work. The brain seems almost like an abstract theory, even though it lies only a few millimetres behind the eyebrows. Yet it is the more durable embodiment of human and individual nature, while the face is
5   just a kind of cinema screen across which flicker the projections of the brain's activities.

Even when exposed, the human brain is not very impressive to look at. Greyish in colour and with the consistency of soft cheese, it fits snugly inside the top of the skull. It weighs about as much as a dictionary of moderate
10   size. But this lump of tissue, your brain or mine, is the most intricate and powerful of all the works of nature known to us. It is a machine millions of times more complex than the mightiest computers now built; furthermore, it is a machine that is conscious of its own existence. Here, and nowhere else, we presume, are generated the thoughts and feelings, dreams and creative
15   actions that are the essence of human life; it is the organ of the mind of man.

Like all other parts of the body, and all plants and animals, the brain consists of cells, little units of life normally visible only under the microscope. There are many billions of cells in the brain. The ones most directly involved in mental and other processes are the neurons, nervelike cells that come in
20   many shapes and sizes and have vast numbers of connections. The others are glia, or "flue" cells. If the cells were as big as grains of sand, they would fill a large truck. This great mass of cells is bewildering for those who try to trace its organisation and connections, but it is certainly not without pattern. The cells are arranged neatly in layers, which plainly has something to say
25   about how the brain operates. Furthermore, the overall sculpture of the brain is far from meaningless.

The most obvious part of the human brain consists of the two cerebral hemispheres on the top. The hemispheres are separated by a fissure running from front to back, but they are reconnected by thick cables of fibres lying
30   towards the centre of the brain. Message-carrying fibres also fill much of the volume of the hemispheres, leaving most of the work of the brain to be done in the outermost three millimetres. This is the cerebral cortex, to which I shall refer as "the roof of the brain." It is very crumpled; if it were ironed flat, it would form a sheet about half a metre square.

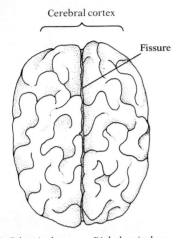

Cerebral cortex

Fissure

Left hemisphere        Right hemisphere

View from the top. The wrinkled surface of the two cerebral hemispheres, the cortex, is much greater than the cortex of any comparable animal brain.

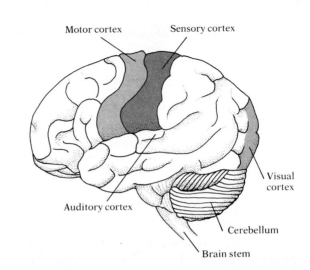

Motor cortex        Sensory cortex

Visual cortex

Auditory cortex

Cerebellum

Brain stem

Left hemisphere. This hemisphere, in the great majority of cases, is responsible for language. It also contains regions responsible for vision, the senses, and movement on the right side of the body.

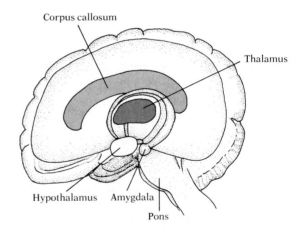

Corpus callosum

Thalamus

Hypothalamus    Amygdala

Pons

Right hemisphere. The connection between the hemispheres is the *corpus callosom*. The *thalamus* and *hypothalamus* both contain many nuclei dealing with specific functions of body and brain (such as emotions, regulation of body temperature, and secretions of the pituitary glands).

35    The upper components of the brain grow outwards from a stem. The central part of the brain, closest to the top of the brain stem, is the hub of communications for the whole brain, with busy traffic of information flowing in all directions. It also has a specialised role in the expression of drives and emotions. The brain stem itself runs down to connect with the cables of the
40    spinal cord, from which radiates the tracery of nerves that carry signals to and from all parts of the body. The important sense organs, including those of sight, hearing, and smell, have more direct access to the higher parts of the brain. At the back of the brain there is an additional component, the cerebellum, or "little brain," which is dedicated to learning and reconstructing
45    skilled movements.

The brain is an electrical machine. That much is evident from the EEG [electroencephalograph] recorded at its outer surface, and disturbances due to epilepsy and other malfunctions appear in the wavy traces of the pen recorders. The technique was pioneered in the 1920s by Hans Berger of the University of Jena. Apart from other obvious uses in studies of sleeping, waking, and excitement, the EEG recorded at the scalp remains rather disappointing. After half a century, it still tells us little about how the normal human brain works, although, with modern techniques, it is possible to detect the arrival of signals in particular regions of the brain.

The intricate electric business of the brain is transacted by impulses within individual brain cells which "fire" intermittently. These can be detected only with very fine probes, or microelectrodes, inserted right into the brain. An understanding of the ever-changing patterns of electrical activity comes with the simultaneous tracing of connections and influences involving many individual cells, but in very few parts of the brain has this tracing been done thoroughly.

The brain is also a chemical machine. The discovery that chemicals are involved in nerve action outside the brain was made at about the same time as that of the EEG. In 1921 Otto Loewi of the University of Graz showed that material produced when a nerve stopped the action of one frog's heart could be used to stop the heart of another frog. The identification of chemical agents within the brain has been a slow business. But it is now abundantly clear that one brain cell influences the action of another not by direct electrical

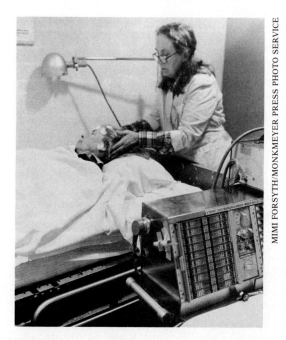

MIMI FORSYTH/MONKMEYER PRESS PHOTO SERVICE

An EEG examination

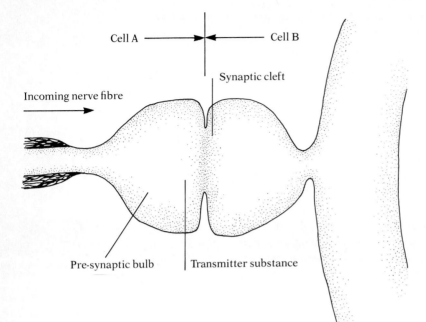

Cell A ⟶ ← Cell B

Synaptic cleft

Incoming nerve fibre ⟶

Pre-synaptic bulb | Transmitter substance

The link, or synapse, between one brain cell
and another. A signal travels from left to right
by the release of a transmitter substance.

connection but by releasing a "transmitter" substance into a narrow gap that
70  separates them.

Different cells use different transmitters with fairly awkward names: Noradrenalin, serotonin, dopamine, GABA, and acetylcholine are all now thought
to figure as brain transmitters. One recent benefit of the studies of transmitters
has been the introduction of dopa, a drug related to dopamine, as a treatment
75  for many cases of Parkinson's disease. This brain disorder, which causes
loss of muscular control and was known to our forefathers as the shaking
palsy, is found sometimes to involve shortages of dopamine in an important
mass of cells deep in the brain.

**Nigel Calder**

## Study Skills: Study Mapping

In the first section of this chapter, you were instructed to underline and
gloss the important points in part of an article to help you review it.
Another way to organize information for study is to make a study map.

Study mapping is a method of taking notes. It is unique in that an
entire article or even a chapter of a textbook is mapped on just one
page. To make a map, you must select the major and minor points of
the article or chapter. Then arrange them in graph form. Students who
enjoy drafting, charts, or symbols tend to like mapping. No exact method

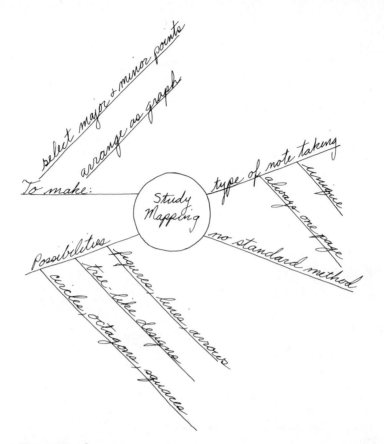

How-to-study map

of map making is standard. Figures or shapes, lines, and arrows can be used. Some students prefer treelike designs for their maps; others use circles, octagons, or squares.

Like underlining, mapping should be done after the first reading. A study map of the preceding paragraph appears at the top of this page.

Look at the incomplete study map for "Under the Skull" shown on the next page. Working as a class or in small groups, finish the map. Compare your work afterward with your classmates'. Did you add too much information? Too little? Refer to your map if you need help as you work on the comprehension quiz.

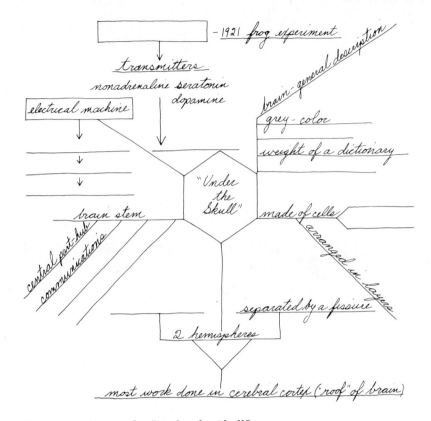


- 1921 *frog experiment*

*transmitters*
*nonadrenaline seratonin*
*dopamine*

*electrical machine*

*brain stem*

*central part-hub*
*communications*

"Under the Skull"

*brain - general description*

*grey - color*

*weight of a dictionary*

*made of cells*

*arranged in layers*

*separated by a fissure*

*2 hemispheres*

*most work done in cerebral cortex ("roof" of brain)*

How-to-study map for "Under the Skull"

## Comprehension Quiz

Choose the best way of finishing each statement, based on what you have just read.

1. The brain has the consistency of:

   a. soft cheese   b. hard wood   c. dry cotton

2. The cells of the brain most directly involved in mental processes are:

   a. glia   b. "flue" cells   c. neurons

3. The two large hemispheres of the brain are separated by:

   a. thick cables of fibres
   b. a fissure running between them
   c. the crumpled cerebral cortex

4. The cerebellum, or "little brain," specializes in:

   a. the expression of drives and emotions
   b. sending signals to and from all parts of the body
   c. learning and reconstructing skilled movements

5. The EEG demonstrates that the brain is an electrical machine by:
   a. measuring intelligence with electrical energy
   b. drawing a map of the mind's functions
   c. recording disturbances with a wavy line

6. In 1921, Otto Loewi stopped the heart of a frog with a substance produced in a different frog when a nerve had stopped its heart. This experiment was important because it showed that:
   a. one brain cell influences the action of another by direct electrical connection
   b. the brain is a chemical machine and depends in part on chemicals to send its messages
   c. the impulses that "fire" within individual cells can be detected by very fine probes

7. Transmitters such as noradrenalin and dopamine are substances that:
   a. cure many diseases, such as measles and the common cold
   b. act as a bridge to carry messages from one cell to another
   c. are related to the brain's action in a way that is still not understood

## Paraphrasing Complex Ideas

Show that you have understood the following excerpts from the article by rephrasing the ideas in simpler words.

1. "The 'face barrier' is a perpetual problem for anyone to overcome who tries to imagine the brain at work."

   _____

   _____

   _____

2. "The cells are arranged neatly in layers, which plainly has something to say about how the brain operates."

   _____

   _____

   _____

3. "The central part of the brain, closest to the top of the brain stem, is the hub of communications for the whole brain, with busy traffic of information flowing in all directions."

   _____

   _____

   _____

## Talking It Over

1. What examples can you give from the introduction and the article to show that research into the brain has benefited humanity?

2. What new facts did you learn about the human brain from the article? Did you learn anything that surprised you? Explain.

3. Do you think there is any danger in scientists' continued research into the brain's functions? Why or why not?

4. There are many common expressions related to the brain in English. Would you rather that someone called you *brainy* or *scatterbrained*? Why? What does it mean if someone says to you that he or she has just had a *brainstorm*? If someone complains about the *brain drain* that is affecting certain countries?

## Some Small Differences Between British and North American English

Calder states that there are "many billions of cells in the brain." Exactly what does this author mean by the word *billion*: 1,000,000,000 or 1,000,000,000,000? Here we see a difference between usage in Great Britain and in the United States and Canada. Nigel Calder is British, and so he actually means a million millions (the second figure), whereas a North American means a thousand millions (the first figure) when he or she says a *billion*.

All languages that have spread over a large geographic area show differences from one region to another, but in written English, these are surprisingly small. Examples of these are in the spelling of the following words taken from the selection. How would a North American spell them?

1. organisation _____

2. specialised _____

3. fibre _____

4. metre _____

5. colour _____

## SELECTION THREE

# The Tell-Tale Heart

It is not only science that brings us a better understanding of the human mind: Throughout the ages writers of fiction have examined the mind also. The famous American poet and short-story writer Edgar Allan Poe was born in Boston, Massachusetts, in 1809. He died forty years later after a stormy but productive life that included wild sprees of drinking and gambling and numerous love affairs as well as a great deal of serious writing in journalism and literature. His works are still popular today, and several have served as the basis for modern plays and movies. He is best known for his tales of horror, such as "The Tell-Tale Heart."

The story is told from the point of view of a madman who commits a terrible crime. Many psychologists and criminologists have felt that Poe describes with great accuracy the inner workings of a severely disordered mind. What do you know, from reading or from personal contact, about madness (insanity)? List some of the characteristics of the thinking, perception, or speech of a person that show he or she is insane.

_____

_____

_____

Watch for examples of these in the story.

## Prereading Exercise: Reading Nineteenth-Century English

Some words and expressions that Poe uses in the story are now archaic (no longer used or quite uncommon in modern English). Most English-speaking readers would not be familiar with them. However, they would have little trouble following the story because the context provides many clues, so it is not necessary to understand every word.

Many great American and English writers lived in the nineteenth century; to read nineteenth-century English, simply skip words or expressions you do not understand and then go back and reread after you see more of the context. Practice this technique in the following exercise. Read the selections from Poe's story and select the modern word or expression that best fits the context to replace the old-fashioned one in italics.

1. "How, then, am I mad? *Hearken*! and observe how healthily—how calmly I can tell you the whole story." (Lines 5–6)

   a. Speak!  b. Listen!  c. Go away!

2. "It is impossible to say how first the idea entered my brain, but once conceived, it haunted me day and night. *Object* there was none. Passion there was none. . . . For his gold I had no desire." (Lines 7–10)

   a. fear  b. purpose  c. argument

3. "Now this is the point. You *fancy* me mad. Madmen know nothing. But you should have seen <u>me</u>." (Lines 15–16)

   a. like  b. imagine  c. offend

4. "Presently I heard a slight groan, and I knew it was the groan of mortal terror. It was not a groan of pain or of grief—oh, no!—it was the low stifled sound that arises from the bottom of the soul. . . . I knew the sound well. Many a night . . . it has welled up from my own *bosom*. . . ." (Lines 55–59)

   a. house   b. chest   c. table

5. "I knew what the old man felt, and pitied him. . . . His fears had been ever since growing upon him. . . . He had been saying to himself—'It is nothing but the wind in the chimney. . . .' Yes, he had been trying to comfort himself with these suppositions: but he had found all *in vain*. All in vain; because Death . . . had stalked with his black shadow before him, and enveloped the victim." (Lines 60–68)

   a. useless   b. successful   c. harmful

6. "But, for many minutes, the heart beat on with a muffled sound. This, however, did not *vex* me; it would not be heard through the wall. *At length* it ceased. The old man was dead." (Lines 99-101).

   *vex:*  a. delight   b. confuse   c. irritate

   *at length:*  a. soon   b. finally   c. in a moment

7. "I took my visitors all over the house. I *bade* them search—search well." (Lines 124–125)

   a. finished   b. directed   c. refused

8. "They sat, and while I answered cheerily, they chatted of familiar things. But, *ere long*, I felt myself getting pale and wished them gone." (Lines 131–132)

   a. after many hours        c. with too much time
   b. in a short while

## The Tell-Tale Heart

True—nervous—very, very dreadfully nervous I had been and am; but why *will* you say that I am mad? The disease had sharpened my senses—not destroyed—not dulled them. Above all was the sense of hearing acute. I heard all things in the heaven and in the earth. I heard many things in hell.
5    How, then, am I mad? Hearken! and observe how healthily—how calmly I can tell you the whole story.

It is impossible to say how first the idea entered my brain; but once conceived, it haunted me day and night. Object there was none. Passion there was none. I loved the old man. He had never wronged me. He had
10   never given me insult. For his gold I had no desire. I think it was his eye! Yes, it was this! He had the eye of a vulture—a pale blue eye, with a film over it. Whenever it fell upon me, my blood ran cold; and so by degrees—very gradually—I made up my mind to take the life of the old man, and thus rid myself of the eye forever.

Scenes from the animated version of "The Tell-Tale Heart," based on the short story by
Edgar Allan Poe

15    Now this is the point. You fancy me mad. Madmen know nothing. But you
should have seen *me*. You should have seen how wisely I proceeded—with
what caution—with what foresight—with what dissimulation I went to work!
I was never kinder to the old man than during the whole week before I killed
him. And every night, about midnight, I turned the latch of his door and opened
20   it—oh, so gently! And then, when I had made an opening sufficient for my
head, I put in a dark lantern, all closed, closed, so that no light shone out,
and then I thrust in my head. Oh, you would have laughed to see how
cunningly I thrust it in! I moved it slowly—very slowly, so that I might not
disturb the old man's sleep. It took me an hour to place my whole head within
25   the opening so far that I could see him as he lay upon his bed. Ha!—would
a madman have been so wise as this? And then, when my head was well
in the room, I undid the lantern cautiously—oh so cautiously—cautiously (for
the hinges creaked)—I undid it just so much that a single thin ray fell upon
the vulture eye. And this I did for seven long nights—every night just at
30   midnight—but I found the eye always closed; and so it was impossible to do
the work; for it was not the old man who vexed me, but his Evil Eye. And
every morning, when the day broke, I went boldly into the chamber, and
spoke courageously to him, calling him by name in a hearty tone, and inquiring
how he had passed the night. So you see he would have been a very profound
35   old man, indeed, to suspect that every night, just at twelve, I looked in upon
him while he slept.
    Upon the eighth night I was more than usually cautious in opening the
door. A watch's minute hand moves more quickly than did mine. Never before
that night, had I *felt* the extent of my own powers—of my sagacity. I could
40   scarcely contain my feelings of triumph. To think that there I was, opening
the door, little by little, and he not even to dream of my secret deeds or
thoughts. I fairly chuckled at the idea; and perhaps he heard me; for he
moved on the bed suddenly, as if startled. Now you may think that I drew
back—but no. His room was as black as pitch with the thick darkness (for

45 the shutters were close fastened, through fear of robbers), and so I knew that he could not see the opening of the door, and I kept pushing it on steadily, steadily.

I had my head in, and was about to open the lantern, when my thumb slipped upon the tin fastening, and the old man sprang up in bed, crying
50 out—"Who's there?"

I kept quite still and said nothing. For a whole hour I did not move a muscle, and in the meantime I did not hear him lie down. He was still sitting up in the bed listening;—just as I have done, night after night, hearkening to the death watches in the wall.

55 Presently I heard a slight groan, and I knew it was the groan of mortal terror. It was not a groan of pain or of grief—oh, no!—it was the low stifled sound that arises from the bottom of the soul. I knew the sound well. Many a night, just at midnight, when all the world slept, it has welled up from my own bosom, deepening, with its dreadful echo, the terrors that distracted me.
60 I say I knew it well. I knew what the old man felt, and pitied him, although I chuckled at heart. I knew that he had been lying awake ever since the first slight noise, when he had turned in the bed. His fears had been ever since growing upon him. He had been trying to fancy them causeless, but could not. He had been saying to himself—"It is nothing but the wind in the
65 chimney—it is only a mouse crossing the floor." Yes, he had been trying to comfort himself with these suppositions: but he had found all in vain. *All in vain*; because Death, in approaching him had stalked with his black shadow before him, and enveloped the victim. And it was the mournful influence of the unperceived shadow that caused him to feel—although he neither saw
70 nor heard—to *feel* the presence of my head within the room.

When I had waited a long time, very patiently, without hearing him lie down, I resolved to open a little—a very, very little crevice in the lantern. So I opened it—you cannot imagine how stealthily, stealthily—until, at length a single dim ray, like the thread of the spider, shot from out the crevice and
75 fell full upon the vulture eye.

It was open—wide, wide open—and I grew furious as I gazed upon it. I saw it with perfect distinctness—all a dull blue with a hideous veil over it that chilled the very marrow in my bones; but I could see nothing else of the old man's face or person: for I had directed the ray, as if by instinct, precisely
80 upon the damned spot.

And have I not told you that what you mistake for madness is but over-acuteness of the senses?—now, I say, there came to my ears a low, dull, quick sound, such as a watch makes when enveloped in cotton. I knew *that* sound well, too. It was the beating of the old man's heart. It increased my
85 fury, as the beating of a drum stimulates the soldier into courage.

But even yet I refrained and kept still. I scarcely breathed. I held the lantern motionless. I tried how steadily I could maintain the ray upon the eye. Meantime the hellish tattoo of the heart increased. It grew quicker and quicker, and louder and louder every instant. The old man's terror *must* have been

90   extreme! It grew louder, I say, louder every moment—do you mark me well?
I have told you that I am nervous: so I am. And now at the dead hour of the
night, amid the dreadful silence of that old house, so strange a noise as this
excited me to uncontrollable terror. Yet, for some minutes longer I refrained
and stood still. But the beating grew louder, louder! I thought the heart must
95   burst. And now a new anxiety seized me—the sound would be heard by a
neighbor! The old man's hour had come! With a loud yell, I threw open the
lantern and leaped into the room. He shrieked once—once only. In an instant
I dragged him to the floor, and pulled the heavy bed over him. I then smiled
gaily, to find the deed so far done. But, for many minutes, the heart beat on
100   with a muffled sound. This, however, did not vex me; it would not be heard
through the wall. At length it ceased. The old man was dead. I removed the
bed and examined the corpse. Yes, he was stone, stone dead. I placed my
hand upon the heart and held it there many minutes. There was no pulsation.
He was stone dead. His eye would trouble me no more.

105   If you still think me mad, you will think so no longer when I describe the
wise precautions I took for the concealment of the body. The night waned,
and I worked hastily, but in silence. First of all I dismembered the corpse. I
cut off the head and the arms and the legs.

I then took up three planks from the flooring of the chamber, and deposited
110   all between the scantlings. I then replaced the boards so cleverly, so cunningly, that no human eye—not even *his*—could have detected anything
wrong. There was nothing to wash out—no stain of any kind—no blood-spot
whatever. I had been too wary for that. A tub had caught all—ha! ha!

When I had made an end of these labors, it was four o'clock—still dark
115   as midnight. As the bell sounded the hour, there came a knocking at the
street door. I went down to open it with a light heart,—for what had I *now*
to fear? There entered three men, who introduced themselves, with perfect
suavity, as officers of the police. A shriek had been heard by a neighbor
during the night; suspicion of foul play had been aroused; information had
120   been lodged at the police office, and they (the officers) had been deputed to
search the premises.

I smiled,—for *what* had I to fear? I bade the gentlemen welcome. The
shriek, I said, was my own in a dream. The old man, I mentioned, was absent
in the country. I took my visitors all over the house. I bade them search—
125   search *well*. I led them, at length, to *his* chamber. I showed them his treasures,
secure, undisturbed. In the enthusiasm of my confidence, I brought chairs
into the room, and desired them *here* to rest from their fatigues, while I myself,
in the wild audacity of my perfect triumph, placed my own seat upon the very
spot beneath which reposed the corpse of the victim.

130   The officers were satisfied. My *manner* had convinced them. I was sin-
gularly at ease. They sat, and while I answered cheerily, they chatted of
familiar things. But, ere long, I felt myself getting pale and wished them gone.
My head ached, and I fancied a ringing in my ears: but still they sat and still
chatted. The ringing became more distinct:—it continued and became more

135  distinct: I talked more freely to get rid of the feeling: but it continued and
gained definiteness—until, at length, I found that the noise was *not* within
my ears.

No doubt I now grew *very* pale;—but I talked more fluently, and with a
heightened voice. Yet the sound increased—and what could I do? It was *a*
140  *low, dull, quick sound—much such a sound as a watch makes when envel-*
*oped in cotton*. I gasped for breath—and yet the officers heard it not. I talked
more quickly—more vehemently; but the noise steadily increased. I arose
and argued about trifles, in a high key and with violent gesticulations; but
the noise steadily increased. Why *would* they not be gone? I paced the floor
145  to and fro with heavy strides, as if excited to fury by the observations of the
men—but the noise steadily increased. Oh God! what *could* I do? I foamed—
I raved—I swore! I swung the chair upon which I had been sitting, and grated
it upon the boards, but the noise arose over all and continually increased. It
grew louder—louder—*louder*! And still the men chatted pleasantly, and
150  smiled. Was it possible they heard not? Almighty God!—no, no! They
heard!—they suspected!—they *knew*!—they were making a mockery of my
horror!—this I thought, and this I think. But anything was better than this
agony! Anything was more tolerable than this derision! I could bear those
hypocritical smiles no longer! I felt that I must scream or die! and now—
155  again!—hark! louder! louder! louder! *louder*!

"Villains!" I shrieked, "dissemble no more! I admit the deed!—tear up the
planks! here, here!—it is the beating of his hideous heart!"

**Edgar Allan Poe**

## Recalling Information

Choose the best way of finishing each statement, based on what you
have just read.

1. The narrator believes that he suffers from acute nervousness that
   has:
   a. destroyed the power of his senses
   b. increased the power of his senses
   c. driven him mad

2. The motive for the murder was:
   a. a strong desire for the victim's money
   b. an intense hatred for the victim
   c. a dislike of the victim's eye

3. During the week before he killed him, the narrator's manner
   toward the old man was very:
   a. kind   b. angry   c. indifferent

4. Each night just at midnight, he thrust into the old man's room a:
   a. black cat   b. chain   c. lantern

5. On the eighth night, the old man awakened because of a noise and then:

   a. went right back to sleep    c. sat up waiting in terror
   b. began to shriek for help

6. After a while, the murderer heard a sound that increased his fury and that he thought was:

   a. a watch enveloped in cotton
   b. the neighbors coming to enter the house
   c. the beating of his victim's heart

7. The murderer disposed of the old man's body by putting it:

   a. in the garden   b. under the floor   c. into the chimney

8. At four in the morning three police officers arrived because neighbors had complained of:

   a. the lights   b. some knocking   c. a shriek

9. The officers found out the truth because:

   a. the murderer confessed
   b. they heard a strange sound
   c. there was a bloodstain on the floor

## Talking It Over

1. Give three statements the narrator makes to prove he is sane. Then show how the author indicates to us that these claims are not true.

2. We are not told what relationship the murderer had to the old man or why they lived together. What did you imagine about this?

3. To whom do you think the murderer is telling this story and for what reason?

4. Have you heard of people who believe in the "evil eye"? According to this belief, you can suffer bad luck or illness if you are looked at by someone who has this power. What do you think is the origin of this belief? Why do you think the narrator of the story was so disturbed by the old man's eye?

5. Various interpretations have been given to explain the loud beating that the narrator hears during the police visit. Do you agree with any of the following interpretations?

   a. It is simply a clock or other normal sound that seems louder to him because of his guilt.
   b. It is really the beating of his *own* heart, which becomes stronger as he gets more and more nervous.
   c. It is the old man's ghost taking revenge on him.

   Or do you have some other interpretation? Explain.

6. What do you think causes madness? What should be done with people who are insane?

## Identifying Elements That Create a Feeling of Horror

Edgar Allan Poe is considered a master of the horror story. Have you ever read a horror story or seen a horror movie that really frightened you? Many people in North America seem to enjoy being frightened in this way. Are horror stories popular in your culture as well?

This story and several others by Poe have been recorded. If you can get one of these recordings, listen to it in class. If you cannot get a recording, your teacher and a few volunteers from the class should read aloud some sections. After listening to them, try to explain how tone of voice increases the feeling of terror.

Most horror stories include certain elements commonly used to provoke terror. Can you think of some of these? Listen to the story or look through it and make a list of these elements. Then compare your lists. Why do you think that these elements are frightening?

## Making a Summary from a Different Point of View

What really happened when the three police officers came to search the narrator's house? What did he do or say to make them so suspicious that they stayed to chat with him? The events are presented from *his* point of view, but we must read "between the lines" in order to see what really happened. We must take into account his character and pinpoint the places in which he describes events incorrectly. Working as a class or in small groups, make a summary of what really occurred in the form of a brief *police report* from the point of view of the three officers.

## TIMED READING

# Are Computers Alive?

You have been practicing study skills for times when you must study a text thoroughly, perhaps to prepare for an exam or interview. Sometimes, however, you have only a small amount of time and you must read something quickly. In this and several of the remaining chapters, there will be a timed reading to give you a chance to practice reading rapidly for main ideas. A quiz at the end of each timed reading will test your comprehension.

The following selection discusses what many people view as the most recent extension of the human mind: the computer. Is it simply a tool or can we speak of it as an intelligent being that "thinks"? Read the selection to find out the author's point of view on this question. Try to finish the reading and quiz in six minutes. (*Hint:* Looking at the quiz first will help you focus on the reading.)

## Are Computers Alive?

The topic of *thought* is one area of psychology, and many observers have considered this aspect in connection with robots and computers: Some of the old worries about AI (artificial intelligence) were closely linked to the question of whether computers could think. The first massive electronic com-

5  puters, capable of rapid (if often unreliable) computation and little or no creative activity, were soon dubbed "electronic brains." A reaction to this terminology quickly followed: To put them in their place, computers were called "high-speed idiots," an effort to protect human vanity. In such a climate the possibility of computers actually being alive was rarely considered: It was

10  bad enough that computers might be capable of thought. But not everyone realized the implications of the *high-speed idiot* tag. It has not been pointed out often enough that even the human idiot is one of the most intelligent life forms on earth. If the early computers were even that intelligent, it was already a remarkable state of affairs.

15      One consequence of speculation about the possibility of computer thought was that we were forced to examine with new care the idea of thought in general. It soon became clear that we were not sure what we meant by such terms as *thought* and *thinking*. We tend to assume that human beings think, some more than others, though we often call people *thoughtless* or *unthink-*

20  *ing*. Dreams cause a problem, partly because they usually happen outside our control. They are obviously some type of mental experience, but are they a type of thinking? And the question of nonhuman life forms adds further problems. Many of us would maintain that some of the higher animals— dogs, cats, apes, and so on—are capable of at least basic thought, but what

25  about fish and insects? It is certainly true that the higher mammals show complex brain activity when tested with the appropriate equipment. If thinking is demonstrated by evident electrical activity in the brain, then many animal species are capable of thought. Once we have formulated clear ideas on what thought is in biological creatures, it will be easier to discuss the question

30  of thought in artifacts. And what is true of thought is also true of the many other mental processes. One of the immense benefits of AI research is that we are being forced to scrutinize, with new rigor, the working of the human mind.

    It is already clear that machines have superior mental abilities to many

35  life forms. No fern or oak tree can play chess as well as even the simplest digital computer; nor can frogs weld car bodies as well as robots. The three-fingered mechanical manipulator is cleverer in some ways than the three-toed sloth. It seems that, viewed in terms of intellect, the computer should

be set well above plants and most animals. Only the higher animals can, it
seems, compete with computers with regard to intellect—and even then with
diminishing success. (Examples of this are in the games of backgammon
and chess. Some of the world's best players are now computers.)

**Geoff Simons**

## Comprehension Quiz

Choose the best way of finishing each statement, based on what you
have just read.

1. The first electronic computers were:
   a. slow and reliable
   b. creative and accurate
   c. large and fast

2. The author feels that by calling these early computers "high-speed
   idiots," people were really implying that computers:
   a. would never be capable of thought
   b. were already somewhat intelligent
   c. can never work as rapidly as people

3. The author believes that such words as *thought* and *thinking*:
   a. are terms that are not clear and will never be exactly defined
   b. might come to be better understood because of research into
      artificial intelligence and computers
   c. have precise biological meanings that refer only to human
      mental processes

4. In the author's view, mental activities are characteristic of:
   a. all plants and animals
   b. some animals
   c. human beings alone

5. The author's opinion regarding the possibility of machines thinking seems to be that:
   a. there are already machines that think
   b. this is somewhat possible
   c. this is totally improbable

**CHAPTER 7**

# Working

HAZEL HANKIN/STOCK, BOSTON

From the moment they finish school to the day they retire, most people spend about a third of their lives working. Whether these hours bring them pleasure and fulfillment or boredom and frustration depends on many factors (besides the most obvious one of salary). Some of these factors are explored in the first selection, an excerpt from an economics textbook that describes modern experiments in work management. The second selection discusses a topic that has been getting more and more attention lately: honesty and integrity in the working world, or business ethics. The last selection is a description of the qualities needed to be a good manager, written by a businessman with many years of experience.

## SELECTION ONE

# The Quality of Work in America

More than fifty years ago the famous comic actor Charlie Chaplin appeared in a movie called *Modern Times*, which presented the modern factory worker in a series of comical situations. In one scene he was shown trying desperately to keep in time with a rapid assembly line on which his job consisted of turning two bolts with a pair of pliers. After a while, dazed with boredom and frustration, he began running around trying to turn anything that looked like those bolts—including two buttons on the blouse of a rather large lady who happened to pass by! Beneath the humor there seemed to be a sad and serious message: a picture of the modern worker, reduced and humiliated, a servant to the machine. Has this dire prediction come true? What is it like to work on an assembly line or in an office in North America today? The following excerpt from a textbook titled *Economics: Principles and Applications* discusses this important question.

## Prereading Exercise: Anticipating the Reading

Work. Think about it for a moment.

1. What conditions do you need to get enjoyment out of work?

   _____

   _____

2. What conditions make you frustrated and unhappy when you work?

   _____

   _____

3. What changes do you think need to be made in factories to motivate workers and make them more content?

_____

_____

Compare your answers with those of your classmates. Then see how these compare to the contents of the selection.

## Defining Key Words and Expressions from Context

Write your own definitions or explanations of the italicized words or expressions in the following excerpts from the selection. Use the hints to aid you.

1. "It lists two job characteristics that seem particularly unpleasant to many people: (1) situations involving *repetitive operations* performed according to *set procedures*. . . ."

   (*Hint:* You probably know the verbs *repeat* and *proceed*, which should help you with the related words.)

   _____

   _____

2. "Even if one has a job of responsibility and freedom, the pleasure from this activity can be severely undermined if the worker knows that the product is worthless, unimportant, or *shoddy*."

   (*Hint:* You must use logic here and guess what other quality in a product, besides the two listed, would undermine a worker's pleasure.)

   _____

   _____

3. "Large-scale *bureaucracies* dominate business, government, and universities. All rely on organizational procedures for accomplishing their tasks."

   (*Hint:* It is derived from the French word *bureau*, meaning "office.")

   _____

   _____

4. "The traditional view of management is based on the 'boss system,' which relies on the *carrot and stick* to motivate employees—the carrot of wages and the stick of dismissal."

   (*Hint:* In olden days, many machines were powered by donkeys that walked in a circle with a carrot suspended from a stick on

their heads so that they would keep going forward trying to eat it.
When this did not work, they were hit from behind with a stick.)

_____

_____

5. "The Imperial Chemical Industries of Great Britain had factory
   workers with low *morale*—as indicated by five *walkouts* in one
   week!"

   (*Hint:* The end punctuation tells you that the situation is emotional, and you can figure out *walkouts* by breaking the word
   apart.)

   _____

   _____

## *The Quality of Work in America*

When college students anticipate future employment, they often imagine
many things: high status, stimulation, good income, prestige, responsibility,
and some freedom. They seek meaning and enjoyment in their work. In this
section we investigate the quality of work available in America.

5   The U.S. Department of Labor has developed a set of job descriptions to
help guide people into employment that appeals to them. This *Dictionary of
Occupational Titles* describes the training and education required for each
occupation, the physical abilities and aptitudes required, and working conditions. It lists two job characteristics that seem particularly unpleasant to
10  many people: (1) situations involving repetitive operations performed according to set procedures, and (2) situations allowing no room for independent
action or judgment.

Unfortunately, almost 22 percent of all jobs in the United States have both
these characteristics. Forty percent have one of them. Among the occupa-
15  tions with both are farm laborers, dishwashers, and auto assemblers. The
latter job is widely considered one of the worst occupations in the United
States. The reason is probably best stated by an auto worker interviewed by
Studs Terkel. Phil Stallings, a spot welder, describes his job:

   I stand in one spot two or three feet in area, all night. The only time
20   a person stops is when the line stops. We do about thirty-two jobs per
   car, per unit. Forty-eight units an hour, eight hours a day. Thirty-two
   times forty-eight times eight. Figure it out. That's how many times I
   push that button.

   The noise, oh, it's tremendous. You open your mouth and you are
25   liable to get a mouth full of sparks. (*Shows his arms.*) That's a burn,
   these are burns. You don't compete against the noise. You go to yell
   and at the same time you are straining to maneuver the gun to where
   you have to weld. . . . I don't understand how come more guys don't

Charlie Chaplin in *Modern Times*

flip. Because you are nothing more than a machine when you hit this
30  type of thing. They give better care to that machine than they will give
to you. They'll have more respect, give more attention to that machine.
And you know this. Somehow you get the feeling that the machine is
better than you are.*

Independent of working conditions, other factors may undermine the
35  rewards of work. Even if one has a job of responsibility and freedom, the
pleasure from this activity can be severely undermined if the worker knows
that the product is worthless, unimportant, or shoddy. Psychologist Abraham
Maslow once observed that he did not think he could feel self-esteem if he
worked in a factory producing chewing gum or shoddy furniture. To get
40  rewards from work, one must be doing something one feels is important: To
do an idiotic task very well is not a real accomplishment.

Being a professional does not necessarily solve the problem. Management specialist Peter Drucker has observed that many people see themselves
as professionals but in fact are merely upgraded skilled workers. Rather than
45  work as professionals they work as staff, dependent upon some higher author-
ities who determine to a large extent the pace and quality of their work.
According to Drucker, this explains why so many highly educated young
people are unhappy in their jobs. And they have few places to turn. Large-
scale bureaucracies dominate business, government, and universities. All
50  rely on organizational procedures for accomplishing their tasks. By their very
presence, these procedures reduce independence and freedom on the job.

---

*Studs Terkel, *Working* (New York: Avon, 1975), pp. 159–160.

## Two Theories of Management

Major developments in management theory in the past two decades reflect worker desires for job satisfaction. The traditional view of management is based on the "boss system," which relies on the carrot and stick to motivate
55    employees—the carrot of wages and the stick of dismissal. This is sometimes called the *Theory X approach to management*. It is based on the proposition that people hate to work and will do so only if threatened in some way. It holds that people wish to avoid responsibility, have little ambition, and will work effectively only under strict and continuous supervision.

60    Another approach to management is based on a different conception of human motivation. This view, called *Theory Y*, is based on the notion that most workers want to like their work. They will seek responsibility and job satisfaction. This is an integral part of Peter Drucker's theory that defines "the guidelines by which management can encourage the achieving worker,
65    make his efforts productive, provide him constant feedback, and allow for the constant learning that transcends the immediate jobs." Workers are motivated by the carrot of material reward *combined* with an opportunity for personal development. As workers become more affluent and money becomes relatively less important to them, it is likely that there will be incentives for private
70    business corporations to meet these other needs.

Experiments indicate that business firms benefit by improving the work experience because satisfied workers are more productive. Evidence suggests that meeting the higher needs of workers can increase productivity by as much as 40 percent. Consider the following cases:

75    1. Texas Instruments, Inc. experimented with improved working conditions for 600 women who assembled electronic instruments. The workers derived more satisfaction from their work, and assembly time per unit decreased from 138 to 132 hours. Absenteeism, labor turnover, and complaints also declined.

80    2. Nob Fabrikker of Norway wanted to improve simple repetitive jobs. In a one-year experiment, production rates increased 22 percent, and worker absenteeism fell.

3. The Imperial Chemical Industries of Great Britain had factory workers with low morale—as indicated by five walkouts in one week! Changes
85    giving workers more autonomy and variety on their jobs resulted in a 20 percent increase in production and a 30 percent cut in supervision.

4. Monsanto Chemical's textile division reported that its attempts at job improvement resulted in workers making 50 percent more instruments and a 50 percent reduction in the number of supervisors. An agricultural
90    division of Monsanto reported a 75 percent increase in productivity after four months of a job-improvement program.

5. Corning Glass Works abandoned an assembly line technique for electrical hotplates in favor of workers assembling the entire product. A worker

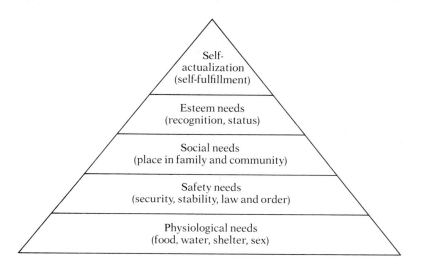

When people have their basic needs satisfied (food, water, shelter, sex), they can begin to think of other things to fulfill their life expectations. Well-known psychologist Abraham Maslow has developed a "Hierarchy of Human Needs" pyramid, in which he categorizes the steps to "self-fulfillment." At which stages of the pyramid do working and job satisfaction fit in? What are the most important requirements for a job? Is self-esteem directly connected with the type of job one has or are other things in life more important?

reported, "I feel like a human being. You know what you have to do and you push to do it." The firm reported that absenteeism fell from 8 to 1 percent, and rejected products dropped from 23 to 1 percent.

These results seem to support the Theory Y approach to management: Ordinary workers may have higher motivations than Theory X gives them credit for.

Workers have ways of registering their unhappiness with work. Absenteeism, carelessness, labor turnover, walkouts, and outright sabotage all raise the costs of production. Each can be reduced through efforts to improve the job design. Unfortunately, there are no clear formulas to show how to meet these needs. The small number of firms redesigning jobs makes the entire process very experimental.

### The Volvo Experiment

As workers become more educated and their career expectations rise, they are less willing to work on noisy, dirty, and mind-numbing assembly lines. Volvo's auto plant in Kalmar, Sweden, was designed to improve working conditions by eliminating the assembly line. Volvo adopted a flexible pro-

110  duction technique that allows work teams to take responsibility for a large
area of production—for example, door assembly or electric wiring. The workers can switch jobs within their groups and can organize production as they
like; they can have some responsibility, variety, and creativity that is impossible on an ordinary automobile assembly line.

115      Worker morale is reported to be high in the Kalmar plant, and production
costs are only $7.74 per auto higher than at conventional Volvo plants. This
production technique has been widely studied, but U.S., French, and Italian
auto makers don't believe it can be adapted to large-scale plants. Volvo's
Kalmar plant turns out 60,000 units a day, whereas General Motors' Lords-
120  town plant can produce 400,000. Although the Volvo design may not be
appropriate for other firms, it shows that it is possible to redesign the work
place and still turn a profit.

**David W. Rasmussen and Charles T. Haworth**

# Study Skills: Outlining

Underlining, marginal glossing, and study mapping can help you select
and organize your material. Another important tool for students is the
outline.

An outline is a word graph, a method of describing in visual form
the relationships between ideas. When you write an outline for your
own use—for an essay exam, for a report, or for general study purposes—
the form is not important. However, outlining for formal purposes—for
example, for a course assignment or for a research proposal—requires
that you follow certain conventions. Generally, you use roman numerals
for the main ideas and capital letters for points to be included under
these; you then use arabic numerals and finally small letters for further
details. Here is an incomplete outline of the article you just read. Read
the way the first part of the selection has been outlined. Use it as a
guide. Then fill in the outline of the rest of the article, beginning with
II. After you have finished, compare your outline with those of your
classmates and make any necessary changes. Use your corrected outline
to help you with the exercises that follow.

"THE QUALITY OF WORK IN AMERICA"

I.  U.S. Department of Labor *Dictionary of Occupational Titles*

   A. Describes training, education, aptitude for jobs
   B. Classifies two undesirable characteristics of work
      1. Repetitive tasks with set procedures
      2. Situations with no room for independence
   C. Twenty-two percent of jobs in U.S. have both characteristics
      (example: quotation from auto worker on assembly line)

II.  Other factors that undermine the rewards of work

    A.  Product is worthless, _____

        _____

    B.  Professionals are _____

        _____

    C.  Large-scale bureaucracies _____

        _____

III.  Two theories of management

    A.  _____

        1.  _____

        2.  _____

    B.  _____

        1.  _____

        2.  _____

IV.  _____

    A.  Five examples

        1.  Texas Instruments, Inc.:  _____

          _____

        2.  Nob Fabrikker of Norway:  _____

          _____

        3.  _____

          _____

        4.  Monsanto Chemical's textile division:  _____

          _____

        5.  _____

          _____

    B.  Results support _____

        _____

V.  Volvo experiment

    A.  _____

        _____

    B.  _____

        _____

# Comprehension Quiz

Choose the best way of finishing each statement, based on what you have just read.

1. The U.S. Department of Labor has developed a set of job descriptions to help people find appealing jobs. This resource is entitled:
   a. *Finding Work in America*
   b. *American Job Directory*
   c. *Dictionary of Occupational Titles*
   d. *Dictionary of Trades and Professions*

2. According to this article, two job characteristics that most people seem to dislike are:
   a. low pay and short hours
   b. few supervisors and crowded offices
   c. no seniority or incentive program
   d. repetitive operations and little independence

3. According to management specialist Peter Drucker, many highly educated young people who are called professionals are unhappy in their jobs because:
   a. they have too much responsibility and stress
   b. they must determine their own pace and the quality of their work
   c. large bureaucracies control their actions
   d. necessary procedures are usually absent

4. Theory X, the traditional view of management, is based on the following philosophy:
   a. people enjoy the challenge of work and respond to supportive staff
   b. workers are very ambitious and want to be promoted
   c. people hate to work and will do so only when threatened
   d. since each individual is different, generalizations are inaccurate

5. According to Theory Y, it is *not* true that:
   a. workers want to like their work
   b. workers will seek responsibility and job satisfaction
   c. workers are motivated by money combined with opportunity for personal development
   d. workers need strict and constant supervision

6. Evidence suggests that when companies improve working conditions and give their workers more responsibility, they get:
   a. increased production
   b. improved employee morale
   c. reduced absenteeism and labor turnover
   d. all of the above

7. It is believed that the flexible production technique of Volvo's auto plant in Sweden cannot be used in many plants in other countries because:

a. it works only in a cold climate
b. most other plants are much bigger
c. the Swedish have the best work teams
d. the production costs are higher

## Linking Supporting Material to Main Ideas

Read the following examples, quotations, and statistics from the selection "The Quality of Work in America." Then tell what main idea or ideas each one supports or illustrates.

1. The Imperial Chemical Industries of Great Britain achieved a 20 percent increase in production by giving workers more variety and autonomy in their work.

   _____

   _____

2. Phil Stallings, a spot welder, described his job on the assembly line in the following words: "We do about thirty-two jobs per car, per unit. Forty-eight units an hour, eight hours a day. Thirty-two times forty-eight times eight. Figure it out. That's how many times I push that button."

   _____

   _____

3. The Volvo auto plant in Kalmar, Sweden, replaced the assembly line with work teams that have responsibility for a large area of production and found that worker morale improved.

   _____

   _____

4. "Absenteeism, carelessness, labor turnover, walkouts, and outright sabotage all raise the costs of production."

   _____

   _____

5. Abraham Maslow once said that he did not think he could feel self-esteem if he worked in a factory producing chewing gum or shoddy furniture.

   _____

   _____

6. A worker at Corning Glass Works reported his feelings about his company's change from the assembly line to the method of each

worker assembling the entire product: "I feel like a human being. You know what you have to do and you push to do it."

_____

_____

## Using an Outline for a Brief Oral Summary

Using your outline as a guide, talk for about half a minute on one of the following topics:

1. working on an assembly line
2. what people want and need from their jobs
3. two different theories of management

"I had a terrible dream. Someone offered me a job."

## SELECTION TWO

# ▦ Why Ethics?

In the past five to ten years, a new course has appeared on the curriculum of most American business schools: Business Ethics. No one knows exactly why this change has taken place. Perhaps the chief reason is the growing conviction expressed in the title of a recent book on the subject by Robert C. Solomon and Kristine Hanson, *It's Good Business*. One of the goals stated on the book jacket is to show "how ethics is the key to

improved performance in business—for your company and yourself."
Before reading the following excerpt from the book, answer these questions: Do you think that ethics is important in business today? Why?

_____

_____

_____

## Prereading Exercise: Relating Vocabulary to Ideas

Because the book *It's Good Business* is often used in business seminars,
the authors employ a number of colloquial and slang expressions. Some
of these are listed below as "Key Vocabulary." Working with your class,
discuss what each expression means. Then decide which of the three
main ideas from the excerpt you think each expression is related to.
Write down the appropriate number(s) after each one.

Main Ideas from the Article

1.  Some types of unethical conduct
2.  Punishment for getting caught
3.  Reasons for unethical behavior

| KEY VOCABULARY | MAIN IDEA |
|---|---|
| confidence in one's anonymity | 3 |
| become the scapegoat | |
| public penance | |
| ethical naiveté | |
| reneging on contracts | |
| cheating | |
| careers that hit a dead end or go down the tubes | |
| trained to "think business" | |

If you are still unsure about the meanings of some of the key vocabulary,
watch for them as you read and try to figure out their meanings from
context.

## Why Ethics?

To err is human, perhaps, but to be caught lying, cheating, stealing, or reneg-
ing on contracts is not easily forgotten or forgiven in the business world. And
for good reason: Such actions undermine the ethical foundation on which

the business world thrives. Almost everyone can have compassion for some-
5    one caught in an ethical dilemma. No one can excuse immorality.

For every glaring case of known unethical conduct that goes unpunished,
a dozen once-promising careers silently hit a dead end or quietly go down
the tubes. On relatively rare occasions, an unhappy executive or employee
is singled out and forced to pay public penance for conduct that everyone
10   knows—he or she and the attorney will loudly protest—"goes on all the time."
But much more often, unethical behavior, though unearthed, will go unan-
nounced; indeed, the executive or employee in question will keep his or her
job and may not even find out that he or she has been found out—may never
even realize the unethical nature of his or her behavior. A career will just go
15   nowhere. Responsibilities will remain routine, promotions elusive.

What makes such career calamities so pathetic is that they are not the
product of greed or immorality or wickedness. They are the result of ethical
naivete.

- They happen because an employee unthinkingly "did what he was told
20      to do"—and became the scapegoat as well.

- They happen because a casual public comment was ill-considered and
     had clearly unethical implications—though nothing of the kind may have
     been intended.

- They happen because a middle manager, pressed from above for results,
25      tragically believed the adolescent cliches that pervade the mid-regions of
     the business world, such as, "In business, you do whatever you have to
     do to survive."

- They happen because upper management wasn't clear about standards,
     priorities, and limits, or wasn't reasonable in its expectations, or wasn't
30      available for appeal at the critical moment.

- They happen because an anonymous employee or middle manager hid-
     den in the complexity of a large organization foolishly believed that such
     safe anonymity would continue, whatever his or her behavior.

- They happen, most of all, because a person in business is typically trained
35      and pressured to "think business," without regard for the larger context
     in which business decisions are made and legitimized.

Unethical thinking isn't just "bad business"; it is an invitation to disaster
in business, however rarely (it might sometimes seem) unethical behavior is
actually found out and punished.

40   Below are four ethical dilemmas that a person in the business world might
encounter. Put yourself in the position of the person who is faced with the
dilemma, and, keeping in mind your ethical responsibilities, see if you can
resolve the problems:

1. You are in charge of new-product development at Company A in the midst
45      of fierce competition for the development of a new and more efficient

gizmo. The research department has come up with a workable model, and the engineering department is just now in the midst of "getting the bugs out." One of your main competitors, Company B, has obviously fallen behind and offers you a lucrative position, more than commensurate with
50     your present duties and at almost double the salary. Your current employer insists that he cannot possibly match the offer but does give you a 20 percent raise, "to show our appreciation." Should you feel free to accept the competing offer from Company B? If you do accept it, should you feel free to develop for Company B the gizmo designed by Company A?

55   2. A worker in an automobile factory becomes convinced that the hood latch on the new-model Crocodiliac is insufficiently secure and may well pop open at high speeds in a small number of cars, probably causing an accident or, at the least, considerable damage to the car itself. He goes to his supervisor and insists that the latch be redesigned, but he is told
60     that the production is too far under way; the cost would be formidable and the delay intolerable. The worker goes to the president of the firm and gets the same response. Is he justified in going to the news media?

3. Your company sells pharmaceutical products in a developing country, in which one of your products, Wellness Plus, promises to provide an effec-
65     tive cure for a common infantile illness. But you find, much to your horror, that the product is being systematically misused, with sometimes serious medical consequences, by people who are mostly illiterate and have no medical supervision. At the same time, the product is selling like hotcakes. What should you do?

70  4. Your Fashion Jean Co. could save almost 30 percent on labor costs by
       moving your main manufacturing plant just across the border to a neigh-
       boring country where labor is much cheaper. Should you do so?

                                    **Robert C. Solomon and Kristine Hanson**

## Making Inferences

Inferences are ideas or opinions that are not stated but that can be
inferred or concluded from the information given. On the basis of what
you have read, which of these statements is the best inference about the
authors' views of unethical conduct in business? Check the statement
and find specific parts of the selection to support your choice.

_____ 1. Unethical behavior is quite rare in business and when it does
           occur, the person in question is almost always forced to pay
           public penance for his or her conduct.

_____ 2. Unethical behavior is fairly common in business, but it is usu-
           ally excused by management because everyone knows that it
           "goes on all the time."

_____ 3. Unethical behavior is common in business and often results in
           negative consequences for the person in question without his
           or her finding out about it.

_____ 4. No one knows how frequently unethical behavior occurs in
           business, but generally a scapegoat is found to pay the price
           for it in place of the person who is responsible.

## Analyzing Sentence Structure

Answer the questions on the structure of these sentences from the
selection.

1. On relatively rare occasions, an unhappy executive or employee is
   singled out and forced to pay public penance for conduct that
   everyone knows—he or she and the attorney will loudly protest—
   "goes on all the time."

   Dashes usually signal an interruption in the main idea. How
   does the clause in between the dashes change the meaning of the
   main idea of this sentence?

   _____

   _____

2. Responsibilities will remain routine, promotions elusive.

   With two short parallel ideas like these, words can be omitted
   from the second without impeding understanding. What two
   words are omitted from the second part of the sentence?

   _____        _____

## Talking It Over

1. What are some kinds of unethical behavior that occur in business? Which do you think is the most serious?

2. According to the article, who is responsible for ethical misconduct? (Note that you can say "unethical conduct" or "ethical misconduct" and they mean the same thing.) In general, why does it happen?

3. What do you think of the saying that is quoted in the article: "In business, you do whatever you have to do to survive?" Do you think that in reality many people in business practice this?

4. Do you think that an employee who is underpaid and/or treated badly by his boss has the right to take home some work supplies or use the company phone for personal calls when no one is around? Why or why not?

## Solving Problems Through Group Discussion

Select two of the problems given at the end of the article. With a partner or in a small group, first make a list of possible solutions to both problems. Second, discuss the good and bad points of each solution. Third, choose the best solution for each problem and write it down, telling what you would do in each case and why.

## SELECTION THREE

# ■ A Lifetime of Learning to Manage Effectively

Have you ever worked for someone you really liked and admired? Have you had the opposite experience—working for someone you disliked and did not respect? If so, you know that a manager or boss can make a great difference in the quality of an employee's work. The following article is written by Ralph Z. Sorenson, who is president and chief executive officer (CEO) of Barry Wright Corporation, a manufacturer of computer accessories and other products. He gives his opinion on the kind of person who makes a good manager and explains how his views on this subject have changed over the years.

# Prereading Exercise: Understanding Idiomatic Phrases

Sometimes you recognize every word in a phrase but still do not understand the meaning of the whole phrase in the special (idiomatic) way it is being used. Usually, if you keep reading, you will find a clue to the meaning—an example, an explanation, or a contrasting phrase. All of the following phrases from the selection have these kinds of clues except the first one. Scan the article for each phrase and write a definition or explanation; then write the words that provided clues to the meaning. (Line references are given to make scanning faster.)

1. raw brain power (Lines 2–3)

   definition: _____

   _____

   (In this case there are no clues. You have to think of the more common usage of *raw* when applied to foods and extend the meaning.)

2. broad human beings (Line 18)

   definition: _____

   _____

   clue: _____

   _____

3. sense of integrity (Line 26)

   definition: _____

   _____

   clue: _____

   _____

4. cut corners (Line 37)

   definition: _____

   _____

   clue: _____

   _____

5. in the short run (Line 38)

   definition: _____

   _____

   _____

clue: _____

_____

6. hard knocks (Line 65)

definition: _____

_____

clue: _____

_____

## A Lifetime of Learning to Manage Effectively

Years ago, when I was a young assistant professor at the Harvard Business School, I thought that the key to developing managerial leadership lay in raw brain power. I thought the role of business schools was to develop future managers who knew all about the various functions of business—to teach
5    them how to define problems succinctly, analyze these problems and identify alternatives in a clear, logical fashion, and, finally, to teach them to make an intelligent decision.

My thinking gradually became tempered by living and working outside the United States and by serving seven years as a college president. During
10    my presidency of Babson College, I added several additional traits or skills that I felt a good manager must possess.

The first is the *ability to express oneself* in a clear, articulate fashion. Good oral and written communication skills are absolutely essential if one is to be an effective manager.

15    Second, one must possess that intangible set of qualities called *leader-ship skills*. To be a good leader one must understand and be sensitive to people and be able to inspire them toward the achievement of common goals.

Next I concluded that effective managers must be *broad human beings* who not only understand the world of business but also have a sense of the
20    cultural, social, political, historical, and (particularly today) the international aspects of life and society. This suggests that exposure to the liberal arts and humanities should be part of every manager's education.

Finally, as I pondered the business and government-related scandals that have occupied the front pages of newspapers throughout the seventies and
25    early eighties, it became clear that a good manager in today's world must have *courage and a strong sense of integrity*. He or she must know where to draw the line between right and wrong.

That can be agonizingly difficult. Drawing a line in a corporate setting sometimes involves having to make a choice between what appears to be
30    conflicting "rights." For example, if one is faced with a decision whether or not to close an ailing factory, whose interests should prevail? Those of stockholders? Of employees? Of customers? Or those of the community in which

"The executive decisions are never easy."

the factory is located? It's a tough choice. And the typical manager faces many others.

35    Sometimes these choices involve simple questions of honesty or truthfulness. More often, they are more subtle and involve such issues as having to decide whether to "cut corners" and economize to meet profit objectives that may be beneficial in the short run but that are not in the best long-term interests of the various groups being served by one's company. Making the

40    right choice in situations such as these clearly demands integrity and the courage to follow where one's integrity leads.

But now I have left behind the cap and gown of a college president and put on the hat of chief executive officer. As a result of my experience as a corporate CEO, my list of desirable managerial traits has become still longer.

45    It now seems to me that what matters most in the majority of organizations is to have reasonably intelligent, hard-working managers who have a sense of pride and loyalty toward their organization; who can get to the root of a problem and are inclined toward action; who are decent human beings with a natural empathy and concern for people; who possess humor, humility, and

50    common sense; and who are able to couple drive with "stick-to-it-iveness" and patience in the accomplishment of a goal.

It is the *ability to make positive things happen* that most distinguishes the successful manager from the mediocre or unsuccessful one. It is far better to have dependable managers who can make the right things happen

55    in a timely fashion than to have brilliant, sophisticated, highly educated executives who are excellent at planning and analyzing, but who are not so good at implementing. The most cherished manager is the one who says "I can do it," and then does.

Many business schools continue to focus almost exclusively on the devel-

60    opment of analytical skills. As a result, these schools are continuing to graduate large numbers of MBAs and business majors who know a great deal about analyzing strategies, dissecting balance sheets, and using computers—but who still don't know how to manage!

As a practical matter, of course, schools can go only so far in teaching

65    their students to manage. Only hard knocks and actual work experience will fully develop the kinds of managerial traits, skills, and virtues that I have discussed here.

Put another way: The best way to learn to manage is to manage. Companies such as mine that hire aspiring young managers can help the process

70    along by:

- providing good role models and mentors
- setting clear standards and high expectations that emphasize the kind of broad leadership traits that are important to the organization, and then rewarding young managers accordingly

75    - letting young managers actually manage

CHRIS GILBERT

A good manager listens to employees'
suggestions and complaints.

Having thereby encouraged those who are not only "the best and the
brightest" but *also* broad, sensitive human beings possessing all of the other
traits and virtues essential for their managerial leadership to rise to the top,
we just might be able to breathe a bit more easily about the future health of
80   industry and society.

**Ralph Z. Sorenson**

## Reviewing Study Skills: Underlining and Marginal Glossing

Use the preceding article to practice underlining and marginal glossing
(discussed on pages 121–122). (You may want to make a photocopy of
the article first.) Write your marginal gloss for lines 52–58:

_____

_____

_____

_____

_____

Compare this with the glosses written by your classmates. Who wrote
the best one? Why is it the best? Use your underlined and glossed copy
to help you with the following exercises.

## Recalling Information

Choose the best way of finishing each statement, based on what you
have just read.

1. The author's work experience includes:

   a. college teaching and administration
   b. working outside the United States
   c. business management
   d. all of the above

2. Since he believes managers should be broad human beings, he would like to see their education focused on business and also on:

   a. the humanities and liberal arts
   b. computers and high technology
   c. accounting and finance

3. For him, a manager should have leadership skills; a good *leader* is one who:

   a. defines problems succinctly
   b. understands and inspires people
   c. expresses his ideas clearly
   d. none of the above

4. One of the experiences that convinced him of the need for a sense of integrity in managers was:

   a. a conversation with a high government official
   b. the discovery of dishonesty among students
   c. reading about scandals in the newspapers

5. According to Sorenson, when facing a decision about the possible closing of a factory that is not profitable, a manager should consider the interests of:

   a. the stockholders and customers
   b. the employees
   c. the community
   d. all of the above

6. He thinks that managers should think not just of what is profitable in the short run but also of:

   a. how to "cut corners" to meet objectives
   b. the long-term interests of those involved
   c. the fastest way to make money for the company

7. In his view at present, the trait that distinguishes the successful manager from the mediocre is:

   a. high academic achievement
   b. the ability to get things done
   c. a critical and analytical mind

8. Companies that hire young managers ought to:

   a. let them manage right away
   b. put them under the authority of an older manager
   c. give them a training course

# Applying Inferences to a Specific Situation

Now that you have read Sorenson's article, imagine that he is looking for a new manager for a department of his company and has received the following descriptions of three candidates for the position. Based on what he says in the article, what can you infer about his reaction to these candidates? Working as a class or in small groups, decide which one he would probably hire and why. Support your opinion for or against each candidate with specific statements from the reading.

**CANDIDATE A**
- graduated with high honors from a top East Coast university
- majored in business, minored in computer science
- won two prizes for inventing new computer programs
- was chess champion of the university for two years
- received a medal for highest academic achievement in her senior year
- was described by her teachers as "brilliant, analytical, clear-thinking"

**CANDIDATE B**
- graduated with above-average marks from a large Midwestern state university
- majored in history, minored in business
- spent two summers traveling through Europe and the Orient
- won a national essay contest
- was secretary of a debate club
- was active in community activities—for example, neighborhood cleanup drive, fund raising for new senior citizens' center
- worked part-time for three years as assistant manager of the school bookstore in order to finance his education
- was described by his teachers as "well-liked, honest, industrious"

**CANDIDATE C**
- graduated with honors from a well-known California university
- had a joint major in political science and business and a minor in economics
- is fluent in three languages
- spent his junior year at an international school in Switzerland
- was president of the music society and treasurer of the drama club
- was editor of the campus humor magazine

- organized and successfully ran (for two years) a small mail-order company that sold tapes and records of local singers
- was suspended from the university for six months for cheating on an accounting exam but was later reinstated without penalties
- was described by his teachers as "highly intelligent, ambitious, a natural leader"

Candidate most likely to be hired by Sorenson: _____

Reasons: _____

_____

## Interpreting a Table or Chart

With a partner or in a small group, look over the table titled "The World's 50 Biggest Industrial Corporations" on the next two pages. Then answer the questions below. When working with a chart like this one, follow these steps:

1. Note what pieces of information are given and where.
2. Read each question carefully until you understand exactly what is being asked for.
3. Locate the section of the table that gives this information and scan it until you find the information.
4. Write it down.

## Questions

1. Which of the world's largest companies earned the most profits in 1987?

_____

2. Which one had the highest sales in 1987?

_____

3. Which country owns the most companies in the top fifty? Which one comes in second? And third?

_____

4. Judging from this table, what types of business are the most profitable?

_____

5. Which companies had a dramatic rise in rank between 1986 and 1987? Which ones had dramatic drops?

_____

## The Top 50*

| Rank 1987 | '86 | Company | Headquarters | Industry | Sales $ Millions | Profits $ Millions |
|---|---|---|---|---|---|---|
| 1 | 1 | GENERAL MOTORS | DETROIT | MOTOR VEHICLES | 101,781.9 | 3,550.9 |
| 2 | 3 | ROYAL DUTCH/SHELL GROUP | LONDON/THE HAGUE | PETROLEUM REFINING | 78,319.3 | 4,725.8 |
| 3 | 2 | EXXON | NEW YORK | PETROLEUM REFINING | 76,416.0 | 4,840.0 |
| 4 | 4 | FORD MOTOR | DEARBORN, MICH. | MOTOR VEHICLES | 71,643.4 | 4,625.2 |
| 5 | 5 | INTERNATIONAL BUSINESS MACHINES | ARMONK, N.Y. | COMPUTERS | 54,217.0 | 5,258.0 |
| 6 | 6 | MOBIL | NEW YORK | PETROLEUM REFINING | 51,223.0 | 1,258.0 |
| 7 | 7 | BRITISH PETROLEUM | LONDON | PETROLEUM REFINING | 45,205.9 | 2,280.1 |
| 8 | 12 | TOYOTA MOTOR | TOYOTA CITY (JAPAN) | MOTOR VEHICLES | 41,455.0 | 1,699.6 |
| 9 | 11 | IRI | ROME | METALS | 41,270.0 | 146.5 |
| 10 | 8 | GENERAL ELECTRIC | FAIRFIELD, CONN. | ELECTRONICS | 39,315.0 | 2,915.0 |
| 11 | 13 | DAIMLER-BENZ | STUTTGART | MOTOR VEHICLES | 37,535.5 | 970.2 |
| 12 | 10 | TEXACO | WHITE PLAINS, N.Y. | PETROLEUM REFINING | 34,372.0 | (4,407.0) |
| 13 | 9 | AMERICAN TEL. & TEL. | NEW YORK | ELECTRONICS | 33,598.0 | 2,044.0 |
| 14 | 14 | E.I. DU PONT DE NEMOURS | WILMINGTON, DEL. | CHEMICALS | 30,468.0 | 1,786.0 |
| 15 | 18 | VOLKSWAGEN | WOLFSBURG (W. GER.) | MOTOR VEHICLES | 30,392.7 | 242.1 |
| 16 | 19 | HITACHI | TOKYO | ELECTRONICS | 30,332.2 | 617.3 |
| 17 | 27 | FIAT | TURIN | MOTOR VEHICLES | 29,642.8 | 1,830.2 |
| 18 | 25 | SIEMENS | MUNICH | ELECTRONICS | 27,462.9 | 649.6 |
| 19 | 15 | MATSUSHITA ELECTRIC INDUSTRIAL | OSAKA | ELECTRONICS | 27,325.7 | 862.4 |
| 20 | 16 | UNILEVER | LONDON/ROTTERDAM | FOOD | 27,128.8 | 1,278.6 |
| 21 | 21 | CHRYSLER | HIGHLAND PARK, MICH. | MOTOR VEHICLES | 26,257.7 | 1,289.7 |
| 22 | 22 | PHILIPS' GLOEILAMPEN-FABRIEKEN | EINDHOVEN (NETH.) | ELECTRONICS | 26,021.2 | 316.9 |
| 23 | 17 | CHEVRON | SAN FRANCISCO | PETROLEUM REFINING | 26,015.0 | 1,007.0 |
| 24 | 26 | NISSAN MOTOR | TOKYO | MOTOR VEHICLES | 25,650.5 | 123.9 |
| 25 | 31 | RENAULT | PARIS | MOTOR VEHICLES | 24,539.7 | 613.7 |
| 26 | 20 | ENI | ROME | PETROLEUM REFINING | 24,242.5 | 483.6 |
| 27 | 23 | NESTLÉ | VEVEY (SWITZERLAND) | FOOD | 23,625.9 | 1,224.8 |

*From *Fortune*, August 1, 1988

## The Top 50

| Rank 1987 | '86 | Company | Headquarters | Industry | Sales $ Millions | Profits $ Millions |
|---|---|---|---|---|---|---|
| 28 | 29 | BASF | LUDWIGSHAFEN (W. GER.) | CHEMICALS | 22,383.7 | 584.7 |
| 29 | 24 | PHILIP MORRIS | NEW YORK | TOBACCO | 22,279.0 | 1,842.0 |
| 30 | ● | CGE (CIE GÉNÉRALE D'ÉLECTRICITÉ) | PARIS | ELECTRONICS | 21,204.3 | 304.8 |
| 31 | 33 | ELF AQUITAINE | PARIS | PETROLEUM REFINING | 21,186.4 | 690.2 |
| 32 | 35 | SAMSUNG | SEOUL | ELECTRONICS | 21,053.5 | 249.3 |
| 33 | 28 | BAYER | LEVERKUSEN (W. GER.) | CHEMICALS | 20,662.2 | 833.3 |
| 34 | 32 | HOECHST | FRANKFURT | CHEMICALS | 20,558.1 | 766.6 |
| 35 | 42 | TOSHIBA | TOKYO | ELECTRONICS | 20,378.1 | 213.8 |
| 36 | 30 | AMOCO | CHICAGO | PETROLEUM REFINING | 20,174.0 | 1,360.0 |
| 37 | 41 | PEUGEOT | PARIS | MOTOR VEHICLES | 19,658.2 | 1,116.1 |
| 38 | 43 | IMPERIAL CHEMICAL INDUSTRIES | LONDON | CHEMICALS | 18,232.8 | 1,245.8 |
| 39 | ● | HONDA MOTOR | TOKYO | MOTOR VEHICLES | 17,237.7 | 516.2 |
| 40 | 38 | UNITED TECHNOLOGIES | HARTFORD | AEROSPACE | 17,170.2 | 591.7 |
| 41 | 40 | OCCIDENTAL PETROLEUM | LOS ANGELES | FOOD | 17,096.0 | 240.0 |
| 42 | 39 | PROCTOR & GAMBLE | CINCINNATI | SOAPS, COSMETICS | 17,000.0 | 327.0 |
| 43 | 45 | ATLANTIC RICHFIELD | LOS ANGELES | PETROLEUM REFINING | 16,281.4 | 1,224.3 |
| 44 | 34 | RJR NABISCO | ATLANTA | TOBACCO | 15,868.0 | 1,209.0 |
| 45 | 44 | PETROBRÁS (PETRÓLEO BRASILEIRO) | RIO DE JANEIRO | PETROLEUM REFINING | 15,640.5 | 171.5 |
| 46 | 36 | BOEING | SEATTLE | AEROSPACE | 15,355.0 | 480.0 |
| 47 | ● | NEC | TOKYO | ELECTRONICS | 15,325.1 | 94.0 |
| 48 | 46 | TENNECO | HOUSTON | PETROLEUM REFINING | 15,075.0 | (218.0) |
| 49 | ● | NIPPON STEEL | TOKYO | METALS | 14,639.8 | (69.7) |
| 50 | ● | VOLVO | GÖTEBORG (SWEDEN) | MOTOR VEHICLES | 14,576.0 | 730.4 |
| TOTALS | | | | | 1,504,492.5 | 56,735.1 |

● = not on last year's list

# Energy and Matter

With the world population growing larger each day, human beings are becoming more and more conscious of the need to find or create new supplies of food, water, and energy. The first selection discusses current efforts of plant biologists to improve the yield of agriculture for a hungry world through the controversial new techniques of genetic engineering. Next, a newspaper article examines an exciting new form of energy, superconductivity. The third piece deals with a novel type of energy: power from the oceans, or tidal power. According to this selection from Jacques Cousteau's almanac, we'll be hearing more about this source of power in the future. The chapter finishes with a timed reading on a Nobel-prize-winning physicist's description of what happened in the first three minutes of the universe.

## SELECTION ONE

# ▄▄ Sowing the Seeds of Super Plants

### Prereading Exercise 1: Anticipating the Reading

1. What do you imagine when you think of the words *super plant*? What traits or characteristics should it have?

   _____

   _____

   Compare your ideas with the artist's concept on page 175.

2. What are some problems in the world today that could be solved if botanists were able to produce made-to-order plants in their laboratories? Do you think there would also be dangers?

   _____

   _____

Read the following article to find out more about what science is doing in the quest for perfect plants.

### Prereading Exercise 2: Identifying the Meaning of Technical Terms from Context

Many new scientific terms have passed into common usage through reports in newspapers and magazines. Key scientific terms from the article are used in the following two paragraphs. Read the paragraphs,

then match each of the italicized terms with its definition, given after
the paragraphs. Write the correct term in the blank after each definition.

## *Genetic Engineering and Public Fears*

People used to think that hereditary traits, such as brown eyes, tallness, red
hair, and so forth, were passed from parents to children in the blood. Terms
such as "bad blood" and "blood brothers," though incorrect, are still used.
Modern science has shown that these traits are passed in the *genes* from
5   the parents' cells, which recombine during reproduction. The actual chemical
in the gene responsible for this transmission is *deoxyribonucleic acid*, usually
referred to as *DNA*. In the last two decades scientists have managed to
isolate the genes that cause particular traits in some organisms and plants.
In certain cases they can even use the techniques of *recombinant* DNA or
10  *gene splicing* to insert a fragment of a gene from one animal or plant directly
into the genes of another, usually by splicing it to a chemical. From these
advances the new field of *genetic engineering* was born.

Reactions to announcements of this latest scientific progress in the 1970s
were mixed. Some people foresaw the curing of inherited diseases and the
15  improvement of agriculture. Other sectors of the press and the public
responded with fear and loathing. Were human beings trying to play God?
What if scientists were to create a new *bacterium* which would escape from
the lab and infect the world with a terrible disease? Concern grew with the
announcement of *cloning*: the production from a single cell of one or many
20  identical individuals, or *clones*. Science fiction writers imagined armies of
cloned soldiers. Philosophers worried about the loss of individual identity.
Were these techniques stopped? Or was it shown that the dangers had been
greatly exaggerated? The answer is given in the following article.

## Definitions

1. any one of a type of microscopic organisms, some of which cause
   disease:

   _____

2. the technique of putting pieces of the genes from one organism
   into the genes of another:

   _____

3. an acid found in the nucleus of cells, responsible for the transmission of hereditary characteristics:

   _____

4. a group of identical organisms derived from a single individual:

   _____

5.  the units of heredity that transmit traits from one generation to another:

_____

6.  referring to the uniting or joining together of different things:

_____

7.  a new branch of biochemistry in which genes are altered to change or improve the traits of plants or animals:

_____

8.  the growing of genetically identical plants or animals from a single cell:

_____

# Sowing the Seeds of Super Plants

Somewhere deep in the mountains of Peru, plant geneticist Jon Fobes is collecting samples of a very special tomato. This tomato will never win a prize at a county fair; it is remarkably ugly—a green, berrylike fruit that is not good to eat. But to Fobes it has a winning quality. It is twice as meaty
5   as an ordinary tomato. Other exotic tomatoes that Fobes is gathering can grow at very cold altitudes or in salty soil, or they are remarkably resistant to drought, insects, and disease. Fobes's goal: to bring them back to his laboratory at the research division of the Atlantic Richfield Company in California and isolate and identify the genes that give them such strong char-
10  acteristics, so that some day they can be genetically engineered into commercial tomatoes.

Fobes is just one of the many scientists who are searching the wilderness to find plants with genes that may eventually be used to create a whole new garden of super plants. Until recently there was little incentive for such quests.
15  Although molecular biologists were making rapid progress in the genetic engineering of bacteria to produce human proteins such as insulin, botanists faced a set of problems that apparently could not be solved by the same recombinant DNA techniques. Within the past few months, however, they have overcome some of the barriers that nature placed in the way of the
20  genetic engineering of plants. Items:

  ■ Biologists John Kemp and Timothy Hall, University of Wisconsin professors who do research for Agrigenetics, a private company, announced the first transfer of a functioning gene from one plant to another—from a bean plant into a sunflower plant.
25  ■ Jeff Schell, of the State University of Ghent in Belgium, announced an important step toward the regulation of transplanted genes. His research team introduced into tobacco cells artificial genes that were activated in light but not in darkness.

- Researchers at the Cetus Madison Corporation of Madison, Wisconsin,
30 won approval from the recombinant DNA advisory committee of the NIH
(National Institutes of Health, a government agency) to field test plants
genetically engineered to resist certain diseases.

Not everyone is delighted. Within days after the Cetus announcement,
Jeremy Rifkin, a publicity-seeking author of a poorly received book about
35 genetic engineering, attacked the NIH committee for hearing the Cetus proposal at a session closed to the public. He also asked for an investigation
by the NIH of possible conflict of interest because a scientist at Cetus is a
former member of the committee, and a leading scientist from another
genetics engineering firm is a member now.
40 Earlier in the month, Rifkin had filed suit in a general district court in
Washington to block the field testing of a bacterium genetically engineered
at the University of California at Berkeley to protect plants from frost. He
claimed that the NIH committee had not adequately examined the field testing
for possible environmental hazards. Although the suit seemed to lack merit,
45 it had an effect. Complaining that the suit had delayed their experiment, which
was dependent on weather conditions, the Berkeley scientists postponed the
test.

The sudden hubub over gene splicing was similar to the controversy over
use of the newly developed recombinant DNA techniques in the 1970s. That
50 uproar occurred after the scientists themselves had recommended strict testing guidelines to prevent engineered organisms from escaping from the laboratory, and the NIH put them into effect. Later it became apparent that the
techniques were not dangerous, the rules were relaxed, and the protests
died out. The latest NIH decision that allows field testing of genetically engi-
55 neered plants reflected a general confidence among scientists that proper
precautions were being taken and that the work was safe.

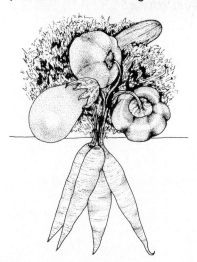

A super plant of the future?

Some plant scientists found a touch of the absurd in Rifkin's harassment. Plant breeders have been introducing new genes into plants for thousands of years. They have used techniques such as cross-pollination, inserting pollen from one group of plants into another group, to produce hybrid plants that are hardier, more attractive, more nutritious, or tastier than nature's own. Still, these traditional methods have their limitations. Crossbreeding is useful only in plants of the same or similar species. It also takes time, sometimes hundreds of crosses over many years, to breed a plant with even a single new trait.

Genetic engineering provides a dramatic new shortcut. Eventually, it could allow scientists to insert a wider variety of beneficial genes into plants in a few days. The potential seems enormous. Crops that now need expensive fertilizer could be changed so that they could extract nitrogen (the most important element in fertilizer) from the air; they could be engineered to produce toxins to protect themselves from insects, grow in salty soils, live for weeks without water, and use the sun's energy more efficiently. Plants with engineered characteristics could one day be the basis for a new "green revolution" that would provide enough food for the world's hungry people.

The genetic engineering of plants owes much of its recent success to an ingenious solution to an old problem: the lack of an effective way to transplant foreign genes into the DNA of plant cells. The solution came from bacteria— in the form of a plasmid (a tiny piece of DNA engineered to carry genes) from the bacterium *Agrobacterium tumefaciens*. The bacterium is not ordinarily a benefactor of humanity. It causes small brown tumors to form on such important plants as tobacco and grapes. But in the laboratory it is proving to be extraordinarily useful. After foreign genes are spliced into its plasmid, the plasmid can carry them into more than 10,000 different plants, where they find their way into the DNA. To assist these genes in entering plant cells, scientists mix them with tiny fatty bubbles called liposomes. (See the diagram "How to Move a Plant Gene.")

**HOW TO MOVE A PLANT GENE**

 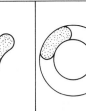  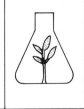 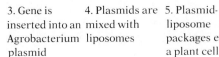

1. Donor plant with desired gene    2. Gene after removal    3. Gene is inserted into an Agrobacterium plasmid    4. Plasmids are mixed with liposomes    5. Plasmid-liposome packages enter a plant cell    6. Cells are cultured    7. New plant carries the desired gene

In their efforts to create new plants by transferring genes, scientists have not overlooked another problem: how to produce the new plants in quantity. This will require better methods of cloning than are now available. Cloning now works only with a very limited variety of plants. Carrots, petunias, and tobacco, for example, can be cloned with ease, but the important cereal grains respond poorly—if at all—to cloning.

Scientists are still seeking the biological key to the regeneration of plants, trying to learn why a lone plant cell will sometimes sprout into an entire new plant and at other times will simply refuse to divide and multiply. Once they are able to combine cloning and genetic engineering, the payoffs, both scientifically and commercially, could be dazzling.

**Sana Siwolop**

## Recalling Information

Choose the best way of finishing each statement, based on what you have just read.

1. The exciting news about genetic engineering in plants is that scientists have just recently managed:

   a. to find some plants in Peru with hardy characteristics
   b. to transfer a functioning gene from one plant to another
   c. to create and clone a whole new species of super plants

2. The field testing of genetically engineered plants is:

   a. an unusual and frightening occurrence
   b. a serious concern to most plant biologists
   c. probably not dangerous

3. The great fear in the 1970s caused by the newly developed recombinant DNA technique turned out to be:

   a. almost groundless
   b. highly beneficial
   c. completely justified

4. If scientists master the techniques of genetic engineering, they could eventually produce crops that:

   a. could live for weeks without any water
   b. grow without the need for fertilizer
   c. produce their own poisons against insects
   d. all of the above and more

5. The big problem of what to use to carry genes from one plant into another seems to be solved now by the use of:

   a. a small piece of specially made plastic
   b. a plasmid carried by a bacterium
   c. a slime mold found on tomatoes in Peru

(*continued*)

6. At the moment, the best way to describe the cloning of plants in the laboratory is that:

   a. it's only successful with cereal grains
   b. it simply cannot be done
   c. sometimes it works and sometimes it doesn't

## Using Information to Disprove False Opinions

The eighteenth-century English poet Alexander Pope once wrote, "A little knowledge is a dangerous thing." Many people express strong opinions on certain subjects about which they know very little. The following false opinions are examples of this. Find information from the article to disprove each one.

1. A state senator hears that plant geneticist Jon Fobes is down in Peru collecting samples of a tomato that is ugly and inedible. He knows that Fobes is using a government grant and makes a motion in the state senate to cut off the money for this work. "Everybody knows," he states with confidence, "that looking for a tomato which can't even be eaten is just plain stupid and a waste of the taxpayer's money!"

   What can you say to prove him wrong?

   _____

   _____

   _____

   _____

2. You meet a businesswoman at a party who says in a loud voice, "What burns me up about scientists is that they have no common sense. All this genetic engineering of plants, for example, is ridiculous nonsense. If they want to put new genes into plants, why don't they use crossbreeding? Why, farmers have been doing that successfully for thousands of years!"

   What could you tell her to change her views?

   _____

   _____

   _____

   _____

3. A young woman's father is absolutely opposed to his daughter marrying a plant biologist, even though she is head-over-heels in love with him. "Nobody ever makes any money in work like that," he fumes. "It has nothing whatever to do with practical, commercial reality!"

What can you say to aid true love?

_____

_____

_____

## Identifying a Bias

This selection, like most scientific articles, is written in a fairly objective and informative tone. Its purpose is mainly to convey new facts. At one point, however, the author expresses a strong bias either for or against some person or idea. In what paragraph does this occur? What specific words express this bias?

Paragraph: _____

Words that show bias: _____

_____

_____

## Talking It Over

1. Even though the public sometimes overreacts to new scientific techniques, it is certainly possible that danger could arise in this way. Can you think of some scientific discoveries of the past that later backfired and caused problems?

2. Are there any areas of science today that you think are moving too fast and might become dangerous?

3. What is meant by a "conflict of interest" (Line 37)? When do you think that this problem arises in science?

4. Who do you think should make decisions regarding new scientific techniques: businesspeople, government agencies such as the NIH, or scientists themselves? Why?

### SELECTION TWO

# Hand in Hand, Superelectrons Move at Light Speed

What new discovery promises to lead in the near future to practical electric cars, high-speed trains that travel on cushions of magnetism, a new and potent kind of brain analyzer, a great reduction in the size of motors, generators, and computers, as well as enormous savings in energy? The answer is obvious: superconductors. Science and business journals are full of articles on this technical marvel, but how well do we understand them? Write down here what you presently know about superconductors:

_____

_____

Many people shy away from learning more about superconductors, thinking that articles about them will be too hard to understand. Often the basic ideas in these articles are not so difficult; it is the technical terms that give the appearance of difficulty. The following exercise is designed to prepare you to read a recent selection on superconductors taken from the *Washington Post* newspaper.

## Prereading Exercise: Relating Vocabulary to Ideas

Look at the list of six terms on the right. Discuss with your classmates the general meaning of each one. Then try to guess which term corresponds to the important idea related to superconductors listed in the column on the left.

**IMPORTANT IDEAS FROM THE ARTICLE**

_____ 1. the way electrons move in superconductors, as compared with ordinary conductors

_____ 2. the particular type of crystal material used in the newest superconductors

_____ 3. structure characteristic of crystals, the material used in all superconductors

_____ 4. something that is almost entirely eliminated in superconductors

_____ 5. particles whose flow produces electricity in ordinary conductors and superconductors

**IMPORTANT VOCABULARY**

a. electrons
b. (electrical) resistance
c. ceramics
d. vibration
e. (linked) pairing
f. lattice

_____ 6. a movement of atoms
that is slowed down
by the low tempera-
tures used in most
superconductors

As you read the article, check to see if you have chosen correctly.

## Hand in Hand, Superelectrons
## Move at Light Speed

To understand superconductivity, one must first understand old-fashioned
ordinary conductivity. In simple terms, electricity is the flow of electrons, the
subatomic particles that carry electrical charge, through the spaces between
atoms of a conductor.

5      In ordinary conductors, the electrons move as individuals; in superconductors, they move as linked pairs. The pairing, all theories agree, is what
allows the electrons to travel without encountering the resistance that traps
lone electrons and converts their energy into wasteful heat.

Some experts explain the pair advantage by analogy with people walking.
10     Somebody walking alone may stumble and fall, but if that person is holding

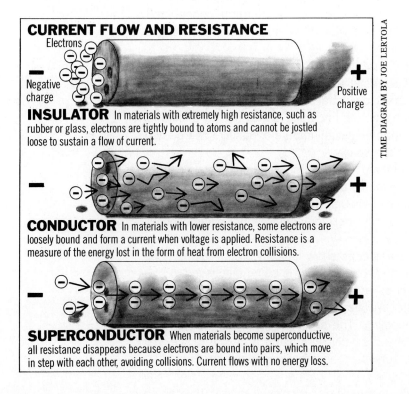

**CURRENT FLOW AND RESISTANCE**

Electrons

**−** Negative charge

**+** Positive charge

**INSULATOR** In materials with extremely high resistance, such as
rubber or glass, electrons are tightly bound to atoms and cannot be jostled
loose to sustain a flow of current.

**CONDUCTOR** In materials with lower resistance, some electrons are
loosely bound and form a current when voltage is applied. Resistance is a
measure of the energy lost in the form of heat from electron collisions.

**SUPERCONDUCTOR** When materials become superconductive,
all resistance disappears because electrons are bound into pairs, which move
in step with each other, avoiding collisions. Current flows with no energy loss.

TIME DIAGRAM BY JOE LERTOLA

hands with a second person, the link makes each more stable and able to keep walking.

In real conductors, resistance comes from impurities in the material that trap wayward electrons and the natural vibrating motion of atoms that may
15    bring them into the path of an electron zipping through.

Electrons are fundamental particles that orbit the nuclei of atoms. Because electrons have negative charges, most remain tightly bound to the positively charged nucleus.

If the nucleus has enough positive charges to hold all its electrons, the
20    material is an insulator. If some electrons are so weakly held that they easily come loose and can travel through the material, it is a conductor.

This much is agreed. The controversy is about the mechanism that creates electron pairs. Having like charges that repel one another, electrons form pairs not by sticking together but by remaining at a distance while linked by
25    what physicists concede are the strange phenomena of quantum mechanics. An "exchange force" binds the electrons so that each "knows" what the other is doing and the pair behaves as if physically bound.

Also agreed is the idea that electrons form pairs as a result of the arrangement of atoms in the superconductor. Both old and new materials are crystals,
30    meaning their atoms are locked in a regular, three-dimensional lattice— something like stacks of egg cartons with each egg an atom. All atoms vibrate in place, moving more violently with increasing temperature but constrained by their attraction to adjacent atoms. (If the temperature gets high enough, the atoms break free and the crystal melts.)

35    Under the old theory, electron pairs form like this: When the first electron passes between two atoms in the crystal lattice, the positively charged atoms are pulled slightly toward the negative electron. In the brief moment after the electron moves on but before the atoms spring back to their normal positions, they create a region with more than the usual amount of positive charge and
40    a second electron is drawn into the space.

Thus linked, the electrons continue as a pair, the wake of the first smoothing the way of the second. If the atoms are properly spaced in the material and their natural vibration is slowed enough by low temperature, masses of electrons may move in cadence with the atomic vibrations, eliminating all
45    resistance.

Experiments with ceramic conductors show lattice vibration alone does not cause the electrons to pair and a new theory is being discussed.

There is evidence that the peculiar layered structure of the ceramic crystals automatically causes pairs of free electrons to form when atomic vibration
50    is reduced by relatively little cooling. The search for a room-temperature superconductor, then, may depend simply on making a crystal lattice that does not need to be cooled to achieve spontaneous electron pairing.

Freed of the resistance inherent in all ordinary conductors, electricity becomes what might be called superelectricity, a form of energy that can do

55    many old jobs better and cheaper and many new jobs that are impossible
with ordinary electricity.

The key to superelectricity is the kind of wire it is sent through. Hook an
ordinary wire to an ordinary battery or generator and you get ordinary electricity with all its disadvantages. Hook one of the new superconducting mate-
60    rials up to the same source of ordinary electricity and what flows through the
material is superelectricity.

Superconduction has been known since 1911, but until recently it only
occurred if the conducting material was chilled almost to "absolute zero," 460
degrees below 0 Fahrenheit. At or near that temperature, any metal becomes
65    a superconductor. In recent months, however, scientists have found a new
class of materials, special kinds of ceramics, that become superconductors
at much higher temperatures, such as a mere 280 below 0.

While still chilly, this temperature is far easier and cheaper to achieve and
makes it reasonable to think of uses that would have been impractical with
70    the old superconductors. So successful have researchers been in finding
materials that become superconductors at warmer and warmer temperatures
that some even dare to imagine they may find a room-temperature superconductor, needing no refrigeration to achieve its wonders.

If that should happen, most researchers agree, the range of applications
75    would be almost unlimited and the world might witness a revolution comparable to that wrought by ordinary electricity in the nineteenth century.

**Boyce Rensberger**
***Washington Post***

## Summarizing Written Information

In your own words explain the following key ideas from the article.

1. Why superconductors are better than regular conductors:

   _____

   _____

   _____

2. The controversy about the mechanism that creates electron pairs:
   (Hint: Since *controversy* implies a difference of opinion, scan this
   rather complex section for the main *difference* between the old and
   new theories.)

   _____

   _____

   _____

   _____

3. Recent advances in making superconductors:

_____

_____

## Recalling Specific Points

Besides the main ideas, you often learn a number of small points of information from an article. Fill in the blanks with key words from the article. If necessary, scan for the answers.

1. In simple terms, electricity is the flow of _____ through the spaces of atoms of a conductor.

2. In a conductor, resistance comes from impurities and also from the natural _____ motion of atoms that can get in the way of electrons zipping through.

3. All conducting materials (both old and new) are crystals, meaning that their atoms are locked in a regular, three-dimensional _____ that vibrates in place.

4. If the vibration of the atoms is slowed down enough by low _____ , the electrons will move in cadence with this vibration and eliminate all resistance.

5. At or near "absolute zero" (−460°F), any _____ becomes a superconductor.

## Talking It Over

1. According to the selection, what is the "key to superelectricity"?

2. Do you think it is unusual in science to have a controversy such as the one about the pairing mechanism of atoms in superconductors? Or is this a common aspect of scientific research? Explain.

3. In your opinion, why are businesspeople so excited about recent advances in superelectricity?

4. What do you think will be the most important use of superconductors in the future? Why?

## Interpreting a Graphic Representation

Look at the graphic representation used to illustrate an article on superconductors in *Time* magazine in May 1987 and answer the questions. One of the five questions cannot be answered from the information given and should be marked NA for "not applicable." Note that *Kelvin* refers to a temperature scale in which 0° = −273° Celsius.

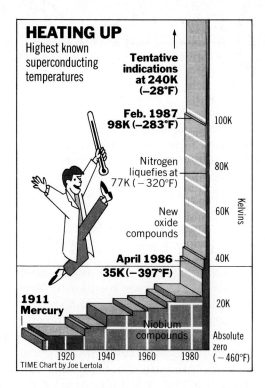

**HEATING UP**
Highest known superconducting temperatures

Tentative indications at 240K (−28°F)

Feb. 1987 98K (−283°F)

Nitrogen liquefies at 77K (−320°F)

New oxide compounds

April 1986 35K (−397°F)

1911 Mercury

Niobium compounds

100K
80K
60K
40K
20K
Absolute zero (−460°F)

Kelvins

1920   1940   1960   1980

TIME Chart by Joe Lertola

1. What are the three different pieces of information about superconductors given in the graph?

   _____   _____   _____

2. When (approximately) was a compound first used as a superconductor? _____

3. Who was the first person to produce superconductivity?

   _____

4. What year (after 1911) was the most significant for superconductor research (the year superconductivity was possible at 98 K)? Why?

   _____

5. Liquid nitrogen is the cheapest and most commonly used coolant at this time. Why is it important to get materials that function as superconductors above 77K?

   _____

After you finish working with the chart, think for a moment about what you now know of superconductors. Have you read about them recently in the newspapers? At what temperature do they function now? If you do not know, how could you find out?

## SELECTION THREE

# ▣ Tidal Power

In many parts of the world, powerful high tides cause serious damage on a regular basis. However, the forcefulness of high tides is not necessarily all bad. For years scientists have observed tides, seeking a way to harness this tremendous potential source of energy at a time when our current sources of energy are inadequate. In this article, you will learn more about tidal power, an energy source whose time has come.

### Prereading Exercise 1: Determining the Level of Understanding Expected of You

In the article about tidal power, such things as *lunar energy*, *hydroelectric power*, and *turbine limitations* are mentioned. Do not be discouraged if you do not comprehend these terms completely. Very few people know enough about energy sources and engines to get a deep understanding of these concepts. Your purpose is to add to the information you already have and achieve a moderate understanding of tidal power as an alternative energy source. After all, knowledge is acquired little by little. For example, perhaps you have car trouble and someone tells you the problem is the carburetor. Then another person looks under the hood and says you have a hole in the carburetor. If you are not a mechanic, you might have only a vague idea of what a carburetor is, but you have learned something. The statement "There is a hole in my car's carburetor" reflects a level of understanding that is deeper than "My car doesn't work."

What do you already know about the following subjects?

the tides _____

_____

_____

_____

power plants _____

_____

_____

_____

hydroelectric power _____

_____

_____

_____

Before beginning to read, take a look through the exercises that follow the article. This will help you to determine the level of understanding that is expected of you. Keep it in mind as you read.

## Prereading Exercise 2: Guessing the Meanings of Key Words from Context

Choose the correct definition for the italicized words according to the context.

1. The farmers had to travel many miles to have their grain ground into flour because there was no river nearby strong enough to power a *mill.*
   a. boat for carrying grain
   b. machine for grinding grain
   c. powerful device for raising water

2. The children who lived on the coast preferred the quieter waters of the *estuaries* to the wild waves of the sea.
   a. fruit trees that grow along the coast
   b. broad sections of the open ocean
   c. arms or inlets of the sea that extend inland

3. Because the level of the river was so low, the *turbines* were not generating enough electricity.
   a. engines powered by the flow of electrons around a series of coiled generators
   b. electronic mechanisms used for controlling the flow of a river to raise or lower its level
   c. motors driven by the pressure of steam, water, or air against a wheel or set of wheels

4. The government study into the feasibility of the project concluded that it was not *feasible* because of its high cost and the great opposition of the public.
   a. possible
   b. designed for a good purpose
   c. planned in a logical way

## *Tidal Power*

"Lunar energy"—derived from the moon's gravitational pull—combines with the pull of the sun and earth to influence the regular rise and fall of the tides. The force of global ocean tides represents a power equivalent to about three thousand 1,000-megawatt nuclear power plants, according to energy expert
5  M. King Hubbert, formerly of the U.S. Geological Survey. Of this, between 10,000 and 60,000 megawatts could be harnessed.

The ancients sometimes used the tide to power mills, and such mills proliferated along coastal areas in nineteenth-century Europe. France built the first commercial tidal electric plant in 1966 in the Rance estuary in Brittany.

FRITZ HENLE/PHOTO RESEARCHERS, INC.

The tidal power plant built in the Rance estuary, Brittany, France

10  There a half-mile-long (800-meter) dam spans the estuary, separating it from the sea. The flood tide is allowed to flow into the estuary, then is trapped behind the dam. At low tide the water is released through twenty-four ten-megawatt turbine generators in the dam. The cost of building such tidal plants is high, but the price of power produced can be competitive with some other
15  forms of hydropower.

The technology of tidal power is essentially the same as that for river hydroelectric power. With rivers, however, the water flows in only one direction, whereas a tidal plant must be adapted for the two-way movement of sea water. A limitation of tidal plants is their inability to generate electricity
20  constantly or on demand—the electricity comes only when the waters rise and fall on their local cycles. An alternative design uses two basins, one higher than the other, both connected by sluices, or channels, to the sea. By carefully regulating the levels in the basins and generating electricity at the barrier between them, power can be produced continuously. The level of
25  output, however, will not always be the same. With either method, some electricity will have to be stored in order to provide a constant supply.

Economics, however, is the crucial limitation of tidal power for now. The U.S. Army Corps of Engineers estimated in 1979 that a 450-megawatt plant could cost $916 million. Although this price is not competitive with costs of
30  other types of power plants, tidal plants last fifty to one hundred years. Thus, if the price of other forms of energy continues to rise, tidal power will grow more attractive. The Canadian government has undertaken a $33-million feasibility study of several sites, particularly Shephody Bay and the Cumberland and Minas basins. Studies are also being done at France's Chausey
35  Islands, England's Severn River, South Korea's Asan Bay, the Soviet Union's Gulf of Mezen, and Australia's Walcott Inlet.

Tidal range, the vertical distance between high and low tide, varies widely from place to place. Because of a plant's high construction cost and because of turbine limitations, a tidal range of thirteen to sixteen feet (four to five meters) is the minimum needed to provide enough energy to make it economically feasible, and such a wide range is rare. But a new technique developed by Alexander M. Gorlov, an associate professor of mechanical engineering at Northeastern University in Boston, could drastically lower construction costs and thereby increase the number of possible sites. Gorlov proposes replacing the concrete dam with a flexible reinforced plastic barrier that could be raised or lowered. The flow of water would drive an air-compression piston, and the compressed air could be used immediately to drive an air motor to generate electricity or store it for later use. Gorlov claims that his method requires a tidal range of only seven feet (two meters) to be feasible, and he is currently investigating possible sites for a pilot plant in Maine.

Engineers in many places are attempting to develop "low head" turbines that could generate power from the flow of water that is only a few feet higher than the turbine. These turbines, while aimed at river hydropower, would be ideal for tidal power.

The environmental impact of tidal power plants has not yet been fully determined. The ecology of coastal basins is complex, and the effects of early plants will have to be studied closely. Also, the dam could conceivably alter the tidal range in adjacent areas and even reduce the water flow it is supposed to tap.

The United States began construction of a tidal power plant in Maine's Cobscook Bay in 1935, but Congress cut off funds and the plant was never finished. According to U.S. Army Corps of Engineers calculations, the annual cost of the facility over a one-hundred-year life would have been $2.4 million. If it had been completed as planned, the plant would today be producing electricity at one cent per kilowatt-hour (compared to the 1980 New York City price of ten cents). Considering the high price of fossil fuel such as coal and oil, the hazards of carbon dioxide in the atmosphere, and the drawbacks of nuclear power, we can expect the tide to extend its power far inland in the future.

**Kevin Finneran**

# Recalling Information

Choose the best way of finishing each statement, based on what you have just read.

1. The regular rise and fall of the tides is influenced by "lunar energy"—derived from the moon's gravitational pull—combined with the pull of the:

a. sun and stars     c. sun and earth

b. moon and sun     d. planets and sun

2. The use of the tide to produce power for work:
   a. is a completely new idea that has yet to be tried
   b. has been around since ancient times
   c. began in France several decades ago
   d. began at the turn of the century in Europe

3. The technology of tidal power is essentially the same as that for river hydroelectric power except for one major difference, which is that:
   a. rivers dry out but tides do not
   b. rivers flow in only one direction
   c. tidal plants use salt water
   d. tidal plants will not have to store electricity

4. Tidal power is not being used extensively now primarily because:
   a. it is too new
   b. it is unreliable
   c. it is too expensive
   d. it is unsafe

5. The vertical distance between high and low tide is called the:
   a. tidal range
   b. turbine limitation
   c. crucial basin
   d. straight measure

6. Gorlov, a mechanical engineer, claims that one way of drastically lowering construction costs of tidal plants is to:
   a. build three plants next to one another and develop a complex interrelated system of air-compression pistons
   b. build two basins, one higher than the other, both connected to the sea by concrete dams
   c. use a flexible plastic barrier that would control the flow of water and allow it to drive an air motor
   d. discontinue federal funding for conventional energy sources and thus force the issue

7. If the Maine tidal power plant had been finished in 1935:
   a. it would have been a financial success
   b. it would have been a financial failure
   c. it would have caused dramatic changes in the ecological balance
   d. it would not have worked

## Making Inferences

Write V (valid) in front of the statements that express valid inferences that can be made from the article and I (invalid) in front of those that are invalid — that is, that cannot be inferred from the article. Be ready to support your choices with specific information or quotations from the article.

_____ 1. The conditions needed for generating electricity from tidal power seem to be present only in Europe.

_____ 2. In determining the economic feasibility of an energy source it is necessary to consider long-range costs as well as immediate costs.

_____ 3. One great advantage of tidal power is that it does not cause much damage to the environment.

_____ 4. There is currently a lot of interest in tidal power on the part of governments and business.

_____ 5. Tidal power will probably play a major role as an energy source in the near future.

## Talking It Over

1. What factors must be considered by governments or business when deciding what energy source to use?

2. Besides tidal power, what other energy sources are used to produce electricity? Which of these energy sources is most commonly used at present? Why? In what ways would tidal power be better than this source? In what ways would it be worse?

3. Some people believe that we could cut down our need for new energy sources by leading simpler lives. What are some ways in which we could do this? Do you think this is a possible solution to the energy shortage? Why or why not?

## Using a Study Aid to Answer Oral Questions

Make a study map or outline (see pages 130–131 and 152) of the article on tidal power. Then make up two questions about the information given in the article. Three members of the class will be called upon to go to the front of the room and play the role of a group of experts who have just made a study about the feasibility of tidal power. The rest of the class will ask them the questions they have prepared. The "experts" should use their outlines or study maps to help them answer the questions. After a few minutes, a new group of "experts" will take their place.

## Interpreting a Chart

Skim the following chart. Then, based on the information presented there, give the best answer you can to the questions that follow. Scan for information as needed.

### Annual Per Capita Energy Consumption

(Given in coal equivalents based on consumption of coal, lignite, petroleum products, natural gas, hydro- and nuclear power)

|  | Kilograms | Pounds |
|---|---|---|
| Algeria | 707 | 1,560 |
| Belgium | 4,939 | 10,900 |
| Brazil | 658 | 1,452 |
| Cuba | 1,467 | 3,238 |
| France | 3,923 | 8,658 |
| India | 237 | 523 |
| Iran | 1,328 | 2,931 |
| Italy | 3,105 | 6,853 |
| Mexico | 1,714 | 3,783 |
| Nigeria | 231 | 510 |
| Portugal | 1,307 | 2,885 |
| Sweden | 4,703 | 10,380 |
| United States | 9,577 | 21,136 |
| USSR | 5,977 | 13,191 |
| Zaire | 63 | 139 |
| Zambia | 339 | 748 |

Source: U.S. Department of Commerce, *Statistical Abstract of the United States*, 1984

1. What do the numbers on this chart represent?
2. On which continent does it seem that the smallest amount of energy is consumed?
3. On which continent does it seem that the most energy is consumed?
4. What inference could you make about the standard of living in India compared to that in Italy?
5. What inference could you make about the need for population control in rich countries as a means of conserving world energy supplies?

## TIMED READING

# The First Three Minutes

What happened during the first three minutes of the universe? Believe it or not, physicists today have an actual model of this, based not simply on wild speculation and fantasy but on certain pieces of hard evidence, though of course no one can be entirely sure what happened. Take, for example, the theory of the atom, which was also based on the mathematical constructs of physicists and which has proved so productive (both for good and evil). The following excerpt is from the book by Nobel-prize-winning physicist Steven Weinberg.

While Weinberg's style is clear and concise, the topic he addresses is abstract and far away from our everyday life. Unless you have studied a good deal of physics, you will probably find it rather difficult. Here it is important to fix in your mind the *level of understanding* you want. You are not expected to gain a deep or profound understanding of this selection—only to be able to correctly do the quiz at the end. Don't panic or give up. Instead:

1. Go directly to the quiz at the end to see what you are being asked to learn. Keep these questions in mind as you read.
2. Read the selection straight through without stopping, even if there are parts you think you do not grasp at all.
3. Return to the quiz and answer what you can, then look back in the reading (using scanning techniques) for the other answers. Guess at those you are not sure of.

Apply these steps now and at other times when you are quizzed on very abstract materials. You may be surprised at how much you learn. Try to finish both the reading and the quiz in fifteen minutes.

## *The First Three Minutes*

In the beginning there was an explosion. Not an explosion like those familiar on earth, starting from a definite center and spreading out to engulf more and more of the surrounding air, but an explosion that occurred simultaneously everywhere, filling all space from the beginning, with every particle of
5  matter rushing apart from every other particle.

At about one-hundredth of a second, the earliest time about which we can speak with any confidence, the temperature of the universe was about a hundred thousand million ($10^{11}$) degrees Celsius. This is much hotter than in the center of even the hottest star—so hot, in fact, that none of the
10  components of ordinary matter, molecules, or atoms, or even the nuclei of atoms, could have held together. Instead, the matter rushing apart in this explosion consisted of various types of the so-called elementary particles, which are the subject of modern high-energy nuclear physics.

For the present, it will be enough to name the particles that were most
15  abundant in the early universe. One type of particle that was present in large numbers is the electron, the negatively charged particle that flows through wires in electric currents and makes up the outer parts of all atoms and molecules in the present universe. Another type of particle that was abundant at early times is the positron, a positively charged particle with precisely the

20    same mass as the electrons. In the present universe, positrons are found
only in high-energy laboratories, in some kinds of radioactivity, and in violent
astronomical phenomena like cosmic rays and supernovas, but in the early
universe the number of positrons was almost exactly equal to the number of
electrons. In addition to electrons and positrons, there were roughly similar

25    numbers of various kinds of neutrinos, ghostly particles with no mass or
electric charge whatever. Finally, the universe was filled with light. This does
not have to be treated separately from the particles—the quantum theory
tells us that light consists of particles of zero mass and zero electrical charge
known as photons. To describe the light that filled the early universe, we can

30    say that the number and the average energy of the photons was about the
same as for electrons or positrons or neutrinos.

These particles—electrons, positrons, neutrinos, photons—were continually being created out of pure energy and then after short lives being anni-
hilated again. Their number therefore was not preordained but fixed instead

35    by a balance between processes of creation and annihilation. From this
balance we can infer that the density of this cosmic soup at a temperature
of a hundred thousand million degrees was about four thousand million
($4 \times 10^9$) times that of water. There was also a small contamination of heavier
particles, protons and neutrons, which in the present world form the con-

40    stituents of atomic nuclei. (Protons are positively charged; neutrons are
slightly heavier and electrically neutral.) The proportions were roughly one
proton and one neutron for every thousand million electrons or positrons or
neutrinos or photons.

As the explosion continued, the temperature dropped, reaching thirty

45    thousand million ($3 \times 10^{10}$) degrees Celsius after about one-tenth of a second; ten thousand million degrees after about one second; and three thousand million degrees after about fourteen seconds. This was cool enough
so that the electrons and positrons began to annihilate faster than they could
be recreated out of the photons and neutrinos. The energy released in this

50    annihilation of matter temporarily slowed the rate at which the universe
cooled, but the temperature continued to drop, finally reaching one thousand
million degrees at the end of the first three minutes. It was then cool enough
for the protons and neutrons to begin to form into complex nuclei, starting
with the nucleus of heavy hydrogen (or deuterium), which consists of one

55    proton and one neutron. The density was still high enough (a little less than
that of water) so that these light nuclei were able to assemble themselves
rapidly into the most stable light nucleus, that of helium, consisting of two
protons and two neutrons.

At the end of the first three minutes, the contents of the universe were

60    mostly in the form of light, neutrinos, and antineutrinos. There was still a
small amount of nuclear material, now consisting of about 73 percent hydrogen and 27 percent helium, and an equally small number of electrons left

over from the era of electron-positron annihilation. This matter continued to
rush apart, becoming steadily cooler and less dense. Much later, after a few
65  hundred thousand years, it would become cool enough for electrons to join
with nuclei to form atoms of hydrogen and helium. The resulting gas would
begin under the influence of gravitation to form clumps, which would ultimately
condense to form the galaxies and stars of the present universe. However,
the ingredients with which the stars would begin their life would be just those
70  prepared in the first three minutes.

**Steven Weinberg**

## Comprehension Quiz

Choose the best way of finishing each statement, based on what you
have just read.

1. How was the explosion that occurred at the beginning of the universe different from the explosions we know about?

   a. it started from a definite center and spread out in all directions
   b. it had no definite beginning moment
   c. it happened at the same time everywhere throughout space

2. What is the earliest time about which physicists can speak with some confidence?

   a. the first one-millionth of a second
   b. the first one-hundredth of a second
   c. the first half-second

3. What matter existed at this earliest time?

   a. electrons, positrons, and neutrinos, among others
   b. only photons
   c. the same molecules and atoms we have today

4. What filled the universe then?

   a. water
   b. darkness
   c. light

5. How dense was matter in this earliest time?

   a. extremely dense—far more so than water
   b. not very dense—far less so than water
   c. just about as dense as water is today

6. As the explosion continued, what was happening to the temperature?

   a. it was increasing
   b. it was decreasing
   c. it stayed roughly the same

7. At the end of the first three minutes, what two elements existed (though only in the form of nuclear material) that would later clump together to form the galaxies and stars?

    a. iron and plutonium
    b. gold and silver
    c. hydrogen and helium

8. Which of the following descriptions best fits the model proposed by Weinberg?

    a. the universe has always been just about as it is now, with matter continuously entering to fill in the gaps and maintain a *steady state*
    b. the universe began at a definite moment with a huge explosion of matter outward in all directions, in a sort of *big bang*
    c. the universe started as a huge dark mixture of matter that has been constantly moving together as the temperature rises to form a kind of *hot mixture*

# The Arts

North America has been called a great "melting pot," a place where people from many countries, races, and ethnic backgrounds have come together to form a new culture. The arts—music, painting, sculpture, poetry, literature, and theater—reflect the rich variety and uniqueness of this blended culture. Much of what the United States and Canada have contributed to music has come in large part from its inhabitants of African descent: jazz, the Negro spiritual, rock, the blues. This contribution is examined in the first selection, an excerpt from the biography of a great American jazz musician, Duke Ellington. The next two selections explore two other examples of this varied artistic expression: the striking landscape paintings of Georgia O'Keeffe and the moving, often bittersweet poetry of the chicanos.

## SELECTION ONE

# The Man Who Was an Orchestra

Do you enjoy listening to jazz? If so, you are not alone, for millions of people throughout the world rate it as their favorite type of music. Jazz began in the United States around the turn of the century, when it was played informally by black bands in New Orleans and other southern cities and towns. In the following selection, you will find out more about this music with the strong rhythmic beat and about the people who create it, especially about one man, Duke Ellington, one of the greatest jazz musicians of all time.

### Prereading Exercise 1: Anticipating the Reading

Before starting to read the article, listen to a record or tape of jazz music, preferably of Duke Ellington's. Perhaps your teacher or a member of the class will bring some jazz music in or you can find some on the radio or the TV. Then answer the following questions.

1. How does jazz differ from other types of music?

   _____

   _____

2. Why do you think that Duke Ellington felt sorry for composers of classical music?

   _____

   _____

3. What kind of relationship do you think exists between the leader of a jazz group and the other musicians in the group?

_____

_____

Compare your answers with those of your classmates. Think about these questions when you read the selection.

## Prereading Exercise 2: Guessing the Meaning of Key Words from Context

Match the correct lettered definitions with the italicized words from the article, according to the context.

a. creators of new things
b. greatly decreased
c. forceful
d. painful, touching
e. collection of musical pieces
f. explore thoroughly
g. invent without preparation
h. stimulating, invigorating
i. substitutes, replacements

_____ 1. The element of surprise explains the *compelling* hold jazz has on listeners, which makes them sit very still for hours.

_____ 2. Because of our patterned lives, jazzmen, of all musicians, are our *surrogates* for the unpredictable.

_____ 3. Duke would play familiar numbers from his *repertory* during parts of the evening.

_____ 4. Jazzmen generally *improvise* rather than play prepared pieces.

_____ 5. After Duke Ellington had been afflicted by cancer, his strength was *decimated*.

_____ 6. Musicians find performances exhausting yet *exhilarating* experiences.

_____ 7. Ellington considered the unfortunate situation of many classical composers *poignant*.

_____ 8. By writing specifically for each of his men and letting them play in a natural and relaxed manner, Ellington was able to *probe* the intimate recesses of their minds.

_____ 9. While most people follow the ideas of others, every group needs also to have *innovators*.

Duke Ellington

## *The Man Who Was an Orchestra*

Whitney Balliett, jazz critic for *The New Yorker* magazine, has called jazz "the sound of surprise." And it is that expectation of surprise which partly explains the compelling hold of jazz on listeners in just about every country in the world.

5      Most of us lead lives of patterned regularity. Day by day, surprises are relatively few. And except for economic or physical uncertainties, we neither face nor look for significant degrees of risk because the vast majority of us try to attain as much security as is possible.

       In this sense, jazzmen, of all musicians, are our surrogates for the unpre-
10   dictable, our models of constant change.

       "It's like going out there naked every night," a bass player once said to me. "Any one of us can screw the whole thing up because he had a fight with his wife just before the performance or because he's just not with it that night for any number of reasons. I mean, we're out there improvising. The
15   classical guys have their scores, whether they have them on a music stand or have memorized them. But we have to be creating, or trying to, anticipating each other, transforming our feelings into music, taking chances every second. That's why, when jazz musicians are really putting out, it's an exhausting experience. It can be exhilarating, too, but always there's that touch of fear,
20   that feeling of being on a very high wire without a net below."

       And jazz musicians who work with the more headlong innovators in the music face special hazards. There is the challenge, for instance, of staying in balance all the way in performances with Theolonious Monk as he plunges through, in, underneath, and around time. "I got lost one night," one of the
25   people in Monk's band told me, "and I felt like I had just fallen into an elevator shaft."

       There is another dimension of jazz surprise, the kind and quality that Duke Ellington exemplified. It is true that during many of his concerts and other appearances, Duke would schedule familiar numbers from his repertory for
30   parts of the evening, sometimes long parts. He felt this an obligation to those who had come to see him, sometimes over long distances, and wanted to hear their favorites. Duke, who had come up in the business (and jazz is also a business) at a time when, to most of its audiences, the music was show business rather than art, considered it rude to present an audience
35   with a program of entirely unfamiliar work.

       But for Duke himself the keenest pleasure in music was the continual surprising of himself. Always he was most interested in the new, the just completed work.

       "The man," the late Billy Strayhorn said of Duke, "is a constant revelation.
40   He's continually renewing himself through his music. He's thoroughly attuned to what's going on *now*. He not only doesn't live in the past. He rejects it, at least so far as his own past accomplishments are concerned. He hates talking

about the old bands and the old pieces. He has to play some of the Ellington standards because otherwise the audiences would be disappointed. But he'd
45  much rather play the new things."

Duke never could stop composing. Even toward the end, in the hospital, his strength decimated by cancer, Ellington was still composing. And throughout his life, the challenge and incomparable satisfaction for him was in the way he composed for the specific members of his orchestra.

50  "After a man has been in the band for a while," Ellington once told me, "I can hear what his capacities are, and I write to that. And I write to each man's sound. A man's sound is his total personality. I hear that sound as I prepare to write. I hear all their sounds, and that's how I am able to write. Before you can play anything or write anything, you have to hear it."

55  As Billy Strayhorn said, "Ellington plays the piano, but his real instrument is his band. Each member of the band is to him a distinctive play of tone colors and a distinctive set of emotions, and he mixes them all into his own style. By writing specifically for each of his own men, and thereby letting them play naturally and in a relaxed way, Ellington is able to probe the intimate
60  recesses of their minds and find things that not even the musicians knew were there."

And having written—late at night in hotel rooms, in the car, on scraps of paper, between dates, wherever he was when not fronting the band—Ellington was able to hear the results immediately. And that was much to his
65  satisfaction. Duke often told me that he considered the fate of most classical composers poignant. "They write and write and keep putting what they've done in a drawer and maybe, once in a great while, some orchestra will perform one of their works. The rest—they have to imagine, only imagine, what they've written sounds like. I could not exist that way, creating music
70  only for myself, not communicating with anyone but myself. But having an orchestra always with me makes it unnecessary for me to wait." Duke did not have to travel constantly; he could have lived comfortably on the royalties earned from his abundance of compositions. But he greatly preferred the road so that he could hear his music, especially his new music, instantly. Or,
75  as he put it, "I keep these expensive gentlemen with me to gratify that desire."

**Nat Hentoff**
*Jazz Is*

# Reviewing Study Skills: Study Mapping

Look at the examples of designs for study maps on pages 202–203 and the design given on page 132 in Chapter 6. Which one would work best for "The Man Who Was an Orchestra"? Or would you make a new design? Why? Working in small groups, choose a design and make a study map for the selection. Compare the results with the other groups and decide which design is best. Afterward, use your study map to help you with the exercises that follow.

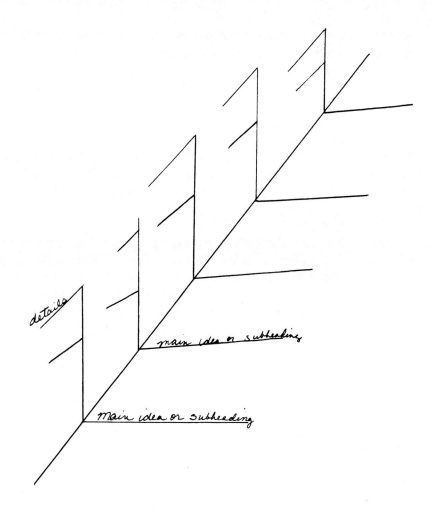

## Recalling Information

Choose the best way of finishing each statement, based on what you have just read.

1. The main reason that jazz is unpredictable and presents the listener with surprises is that:
    a. it sounds like an older style of music
    b. improvisation is an important part of it
    c. the musicians find the performances exhilarating

2. Duke Ellington included old familiar numbers from his repertory in many of his concerts because:
    a. it was his continual and keenest musical pleasure
    b. he felt it was good business and would make a lot of money
    c. he did not want to disappoint his audiences

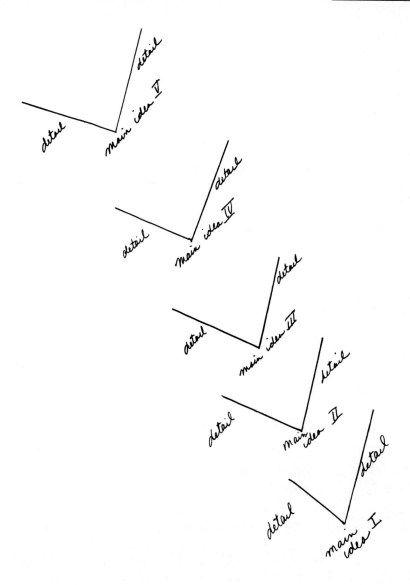

3. When Duke Ellington was older and famous, he:
   a. enjoyed living in the past and talking about earlier accomplishments
   b. rejected the new styles of younger musicians
   c. kept on changing and innovating his music

4. Ellington considered the fate of most classical composers poignant because:
   a. they have to wait before they can hear their music
   b. they usually die before getting much money or fame
   c. they have to follow rigid rules in composing

## Making and Supporting Inferences

Tell which of the following inferences about Duke Ellington are valid (V) and which are invalid (I), according to the article. Give at least two facts for each to support your judgment.

_____ 1. He was basically lazy and liked the good and easy life.

_____

_____

_____

_____ 2. He was self-centered and arrogant.

_____

_____

_____

_____ 3. He was young in spirit throughout his life.

_____

_____

_____

## Talking It Over

1. After reading the article, how would you describe the difference between jazz and other types of music?
2. Why does jazz have a compelling hold on many people?
3. Billy Strayhorn said, "Ellington plays the piano, but his real instrument is his band." What did he mean?
4. The word *jazz* is used in certain English slang expressions that apply to things besides music. For example, someone might refer to the design for a house or the plans for a party and say, "Let's *jazz it up* a bit" or "It's not *jazzy* enough." Based on the context and on what you have read, what do these expressions mean?

## Expressing Reactions to Music

Some volunteers should bring in records or tapes of their favorite type of music and play it for the class. Then play the jazz music that you listened to before the reading. Does the element of surprise seem stronger in jazz, as the article suggests, than in the other music? In what parts do you think the musicians are improvising?

Describe, orally or in writing, the music that you preferred of all the samples that were played. Try to explain in words what it sounds like and why you enjoy it.

SELECTION TWO

# ▣ "To Paint Is to Live": Georgia O'Keeffe, 1887–1986

Painting, like music, is one of the fine arts. American and Canadian painting has been influenced by many traditions from different parts of the world, especially by those from Europe. However, this century has witnessed an opposite trend: the development of particularly North American painting styles that have become international. One American painter who exerted an influence on Europe with a unique and independent style was a woman from Wisconsin named Georgia O'Keeffe. Three of O'Keeffe's grandparents were immigrants—from Ireland, Hungary, and Holland—and the fourth was descended from one of the earliest European colonists in America. These ancestors came to start a new life in a new world, but O'Keeffe was destined to become a pioneer of a different sort. The following article discusses her life and work.

GEORGE DANIELL/PHOTO RESEARCHERS, INC.

Georgia O'Keeffe on Fire Island, circa 1950

## Prereading Exercise 1: Anticipating the Reading

Look at the title and the photograph of Georgia O'Keeffe. Skim the first two paragraphs of the article. Then make inferences about this famous artist and answer the following questions.

1. What kind of person do you think she was?

_____

_____

2. Why did she paint?

_____

_____

_____

3. What kinds of problems do you imagine that she had in her life? Why?

_____

_____

_____

Read the article to find out if you are right.

## *"To Paint Is to Live": Georgia O'Keeffe, 1887–1986*

Georgia O'Keeffe was truly an American original. Tough, sparse, lean, she embodied the rugged individualistic nature of the American pioneer. But instead of tilling the soil, her strides were made in the field of contemporary American art.

5      Born on a 600-acre farm in Sun Prairie, Wisconsin, on November 15, 1887, O'Keeffe throughout her long life preferred vast plains and open spaces to city living. From the summer of 1929, when she made her first visit to New Mexico, the starkness of the desert fascinated her. After summering in New Mexico for many years, she finally moved permanently to Abiquiu,
10    New Mexico, in 1949, where she continued to paint until her eyesight faltered in the late 1970s. From this region the themes of some of her finest works evolved.

ART RESOURCE

ART RESOURCE

Georgia O'Keeffe, *Untitled*

Georgia O'Keeffe, *Autumn Leaves Number 2*

O'Keeffe's strictly American art education began with private lessons at the age of ten. Teachers recognized her talent but often criticized the larger-than-life proportions that she liked to paint. At an early age she was already moving away from realistic copying of objects to things she perceived with her own eyes, mind, and soul.

O'Keeffe's formal high school education continued at a private school in Madison, Wisconsin, and after a family move, she graduated from a Williams-burg, Virginia, high school in 1903. In 1905–06 she studied at the Art Institute in Chicago, and in 1907–08, at the Art Students' League in New York.

In 1908, perhaps disappointed with the rigidity of American art education at the time, she gave up painting and became a commercial artist, drawing advertising illustrations in Chicago. However, in the summer of 1912, she decided to take another art course in Virginia under Alon Bemont, and her interest in creative painting came alive again.

Self-supporting since graduation from high school, O'Keeffe had to find jobs to sustain her through her developing years as an artist. In 1912, she began to teach in Amarillo, Texas, and was stunned by the barren southern landscape. "That was my country," she said, "terrible wind and wonderful emptiness."

After art courses in 1915–16 in New York under the more liberal art teacher Arthur Dow, O'Keeffe accepted a position as an art teacher at a small college in South Carolina. It was at this point that the determined young woman locked herself up, took stock of her painting, and decided to reject the rigidity of the realism that she had been taught for a style all her own. "Nothing is less real than realism—details are confusing. It is only by selection, by elim-ination, by emphasis, that we get the real meaning of things." From this revival came black and white abstract nature forms in all shapes and sizes, the beginning of her highly individualistic style.

O'Keeffe sent some of these prints to a friend in New York and told her not to show them to anyone. The friend was so impressed with them that she ignored the request and took them to a famous photographer and pro-moter of modern artists, Alfred Stieglitz. His reaction was immediate: "At last, a woman on paper!" Without O'Keeffe's knowledge or consent, Stieglitz exhib-ited these prints in his gallery, 291. Infuriated, she went to New York to insist that he take her drawings down. Stieglitz, however, convinced her of their quality, and she allowed them to remain on exhibit. Subsequently, Stieglitz became the champion of O'Keeffe's works and helped her gain the promi-nence she deserved. For Stieglitz, Georgia was an unusually talented Amer-ican female artist. She was unspoiled by studies in Europe and painted with a direct, clear, strong—even fierce—force.

The relationship between Stieglitz and O'Keeffe developed into a pas-sionate love affair, which eventually led to a twenty-two year marriage. Stieg-litz, his wife's senior by many years, died in 1946. He immortalized her through many beautiful and unusual photographs—the lady in black, with piercing eyes, tightly pulled-back hair and the artistic elongated hands of a goddess.

Strength, clarity, and strong physical presence are words that are often used to describe O'Keeffe's paintings. As art critic Lloyd Goodrich said, "Her art presents a rare combination of austerity and deep seriousness. . . . Even at her most realistic she is concerned not with the mere visual appearance of things, but with their essential life, their being, their identity. . . . The forms of nature are translated into forms of art." Or, as O'Keeffe herself put it, "A hill or a tree cannot make a good painting just because it is a hill or a tree. It is lines and colors put together so that they say something. For me, that is the very basis for painting. The abstraction is often the most definite form for the intangible thing in myself that I can only clarify in paint."

**M. Prijic**

## Recalling Information

Choose the best way of finishing each statement, based on what you have just read.

1. Georgia O'Keeffe was born:
   a. in New York City
   b. in a town in New Mexico
   c. on a farm in Wisconsin

2. Her art education consisted of:
   a. studies in schools and institutes in the United States
   b. training in the best art academies of Europe
   c. only her own efforts and experimentation at home

3. The landscape with which she identified in particular was:
   a. rugged mountains
   b. lush forests
   c. barren deserts

4. Alfred Stieglitz's comment when he first saw O'Keeffe's prints was: "At last, a woman on paper!" From this we can infer that
   a. there was a great deal of discrimination against women then
   b. women artists were not very common in those days
   c. he did not really like the prints very much

5. Stieglitz was important in the life of Georgia O'Keeffe because:
   a. he became both her husband and champion
   b. he bought many of her paintings at good prices
   c. he photographed her prints and gave titles to them

## Paraphrasing Complex Ideas

Paraphrase the following excerpts from the article. Do not worry if there are some words you do not understand. Just state the main idea briefly in simple, direct words.

1. "Tough, sparse, lean, she embodied the rugged individualistic nature of the American pioneer. But instead of tilling the soil, her strides were made in the field of contemporary American art."

   _____

   _____

   _____

   _____

2. "Self-supporting since graduation from high school, O'Keeffe had to find jobs to sustain her through her developing years as an artist."

   _____

   _____

   _____

   _____

3. "'Nothing is less real than realism—details are confusing. It is only by selection, by elimination, by emphasis, that we get the real meaning of things'" (words of Georgia O'Keeffe).

   _____

   _____

   _____

   _____

4. "'Even at her most realistic she is concerned not with the mere visual appearance of things, but with their essential life, their being, their identity'" (words of an art critic about O'Keeffe's works).

   _____

   _____

   _____

   _____

   _____

## Talking It Over

1. Were you right or wrong about the inferences you made about Georgia O'Keeffe? Explain.

2. Do you think it was difficult for a woman to be an artist in the 1920s and 1930s? Why?

3. Why do you think Stieglitz was such a strong influence on O'Keeffe?

4. What do people seem to think about Georgia O'Keeffe's work?

## Expressing Reactions About Paintings

Bring in some prints or photographs of art works that appeal to you to share with the class. Tell whether it is the subject, the style, or both that you like in these paintings and why you are impressed by them. Try to find a book with reproductions of O'Keeffe's paintings and explain what you like or dislike about them.

## Writing a Brief Comparison

Do artists tend to have similar types of lives even though they are from different cultures and time periods? Go to the library and look up information on an artist from any country other than the United States. Write a brief comparison between the life of this artist and that of Georgia O'Keeffe. Do not write the whole story of the artist's life, only several points that show similarity. If there is no similarity, try to explain why.

### SELECTION THREE

# ▆ Chicano Poetry: The Voice of a Culture

The following article gives some background on Mexican-Americans, who now are often called chicanos, and presents a few examples of their poetry. You might wonder why this group is singled out, when there are so many ethnic groups, with their particular languages and cultures, living in North America, including millions of Spanish-speaking people from other countries. There are historical reasons, which you will read about, why this group is different from most others.

## Prereading Exercise: Anticipating the Reading

Look at the map of the United States, then answer the following questions.

1. What cities on the map sound to you as though their names might be of Spanish origin?

   _____

   _____

2. What sections seem to have the most Spanish names?

   _____

3. Do you know or can you make a guess about why these places have Spanish names?

   _____

Read the article to find out if you are correct and to learn more about the second largest minority group in the United States.

## *Chicano Poetry: The Voice of a Culture*

### The Hispanic Presence in the United States

What are the two cities in the world with the largest number of Spanish-speaking inhabitants? Mexico City is number one, which is no surprise; but the second is Los Angeles, California, right in the U.S.A.! According to 1986 census figures, 18 million Hispanics live in the United States. They are the

5 second-largest minority after blacks, but the Hispanic population is increasing so rapidly that it is expected to become the largest minority within a few years. More than 80 percent of Hispanics live in urban areas. Most are concentrated in the five southwestern states of Arizona, California, Colorado, New Mexico, and Texas. There are also sizable Hispanic populations in New
10 York, Florida, and Illinois.

There are countless Spanish geographical names in the United States, such as the state of Colorado (which means "red"), the city of Las Vegas ("fertile lowlands"), and the Rio Grande ("big river"). Many Spanish and Latin American words have been incorporated into English. A large number of
15 these words are related to geographical features: *mesa* ("plateau") and *canyon*; to music: *tango, rumba*; to ranch life: *rodeo, corral*; to architecture: *patio, plaza*; and to food: *chocolate, papaya*. Many colorful English slang terms are corruptions of Spanish words, such as *calaboose* ("jail") and *macho man* ("big, tough male").

### Mexican-American History

20 Where did all this Spanish influence come from? Didn't the United States start out as a colony of the British? In fact, the southwestern United States was settled by the Spanish and Mexicans centuries before the arrival of the first Anglos. Many people are unaware of this fact because until recently, all the history books were written from the point of view of the British. Let's
25 examine the "true history" of the American Southwest.

The region was part of Mexico until it was lost in a war with the United States. Under the terms of the Treaty of Guadalupe Hidalgo, which ended the war in 1848, Mexico ceded to the United States the territory that is now New Mexico, Utah, Nevada, California, and parts of Colorado and Wyoming.
30 On paper the 75,000 Mexican inhabitants were guaranteed their property

The Southwest is noted for its Spanish colonial and Mexican architecture, particularly the fifty-four missions founded between 1598 and 1823.

ESTHER HENDERSON-RAPHO/PHOTO RESEARCHERS, INC.

rights and granted U.S. citizenship. The reality, however, was different. They suffered racial and cultural discrimination at the hands of a flood of Anglo settlers, and many were dispossessed of their lands. Most worked for Anglo bosses as farm, railroad, and mine workers. Constant immigration from Mexico kept wages low.

World War II brought about fundamental changes. Many Mexican-Americans began to consider themselves U.S. citizens for the first time after serving in the war. Armed with new skills and faced with the rapid mechanization of agriculture, many moved to the cities in search of work.

### The Chicano Movement

Inspired by the black struggle for civil rights, Mexican-Americans organized in the 1960s to gain reforms and restore ethnic pride. Members of this movement called themselves *chicanos*, and the name has become popular, although some still prefer the term Mexican-Americans. The achievements of the chicano movement are many. In 1962, César Chávez founded the strong and successful National Farm Worker's Association in Delano, California, which has managed to raise wages and improve working conditions for migrant workers. In 1970 José Ángel Gutiérrez established the *Raza Unida* political party in Crystal City, Texas, which has been successful in electing Mexican-American candidates to local office. Bilingual, cross-cultural education and chicano studies programs have been established in schools and universities.

### Chicano Arts

The chicano movement inspired a flowering of chicano theater, art, and literature. Luis Valdés created the *Teatro Campesino* in the fields of Delano in 1965 to strengthen the union's organizing efforts. This unique form of theater draws on a variety of Latin American and European traditions and makes use of allegorical characters, masks, song, and dance. Originally performed by farm workers for farm workers, it later broadened its focus to include issues other than the strike, such as American foreign policy and discrimination against Hispanics in schools. The *Teatro Campesino* has gained international prominence and inspired the creation of many similar companies across the country.

Colorful murals painted on the walls of public buildings in Mexican-American neighborhoods are a collective expression of reborn hope and ethnic pride. They depict the Mexican-Americans' Indian and Spanish heritage, the history of Mexico and of Mexican-Americans in the United States, and the problems of migrant workers.

The genre most cultivated by chicano writers is poetry. Often written in free verse, chicano poetry creates an impression of spontaneity, freshness, and honesty. It may be written in Spanish, English, or a combination of the two languages.

**Deana Fernández**

## Some Examples of Chicano Poetry

The following examples of chicano poetry contain the Spanish words *primo*, "cousin," and *gringo*, a somewhat negative word for an Anglo-American. Both poems provide a brief glimpse into the lives of Mexican-Americans. As you read, try to understand the main point that the poet wants to convey and the emotions he wants the reader to feel.

### *To People Who Pick Food*

```
I am the man
          who picks your food

          immigrant,
          tablecloths
 5        ignore my stare
I have children
a fake green card
a warm kiss
a cross to ward off rangers
10  a picture of St. Peter so
I will not drown in a river
          I pick apples
               cotton
               grapes
15  eyes follow me
          utter under their breaths,
I do not understand
               the lettuce canned
with my hands
20             citrus pores
               inflame my eyes
my wife is      proud
   soft          gentle
     my          children
25  are brown     tender deer
       what eyes,
the sun cracks my skin
I am old and dark as the dirt
I drop on my knees   before the sky
30  they can hate me, point me out in a crowd
but do not pity me      the sun is there
every morning      God follows my children
and I walk to the field to grow bread
          with my friends
```

**Wilfredo Q. Castaño**

Mural in a Mexican-American neighborhood

## *Grandma's Primo*

Grandma had a cousin
who lived in the big city
and looked like a gringo

He smoked a big cigar
5  and spoke English as well
as he spoke Spanish

He loved to tell jokes
would always tell them twice—
the first time in Spanish
10  to make us laugh
and the second time in English
to impress us

        **Leroy V. Quintana**

## Recalling Information

Tell whether each of the following statements is true (T) or false (F),
based on the reading. Correct false statements to make them true.

_____ 1. There are more Spanish-speaking people in Los Angeles, California, than in any other city in the world except the capital of Mexico.

_____ 2. Hispanics form the largest minority group in the United States.

_____ 3. Spanish and Mexican architecture and geographical names are characteristics of the northeastern part of the country.

_____ 4. The first Spanish and Mexican settlers in the United States arrived after the first British settlers.

_____ 5. After the treaty of 1848, Mexicans in the territory that belonged to the United States as of that year enjoyed all the privileges of full citizens and were guaranteed property rights.

_____ 6. After World War II, many Mexican-Americans moved from the countryside to the cities.

_____ 7. César Chávez is a chicano who founded a powerful and effective labor union for farm workers.

_____ 8. José Ángel Gutiérrez began a chicano political party, but it has not yet managed to get Mexican-Americans elected to office.

_____ 9. Chicano theater, begun by Luis Valdés, started out in the fields and was performed for and by farm workers.

_____ 10. The literary genre most popular among chicano writers is the novel.

_____ 11. "To People Who Pick Food" is told from the point of view of a poor but contented Mexican farm laborer who works in the United States illegally.

_____ 12. In the poem "Grandma's Primo," the cousin always told jokes twice because he wasn't sure that his relatives understood them the first time.

## Summarizing Information About Specific Points

Write a brief summary of what you remember about each of the following people or things. If necessary, scan the article to refresh your memory.

1. Spanish words used in English

_____

_____

_____

2. *Raza Unida*

_____

_____

_____

3. Treaty of Guadalupe Hidalgo

_____

_____

_____

4. César Chávez

_____

_____

_____

5. *Teatro Campesino*

_____

_____

_____

# Reading Poetry for Meaning

Just as any scene can serve as the subject of a painting, so any part of daily life can provide material for a poem. Of course, the choice that the artist or poet makes relates to his or her purpose. Poetry is usually short and compact, so it should be read several times, preferably aloud, to appreciate its meaning. Read the following questions; then reread the poems and answer the questions.

**"TO PEOPLE WHO PICK FOOD"**
The poem is spoken from the point of view of a poor Mexican migrant who is working illegally in the United States, with a "fake green card."

1. What parts of the poem suggest that the man feels prejudice and discrimination from the people around him?

   _____

   _____

2. What work does the man do? How does he feel about it?

   _____

3. When so many rich people seem dissatisfied with their lives (as evidenced by alcoholism, use of drugs, nervous breakdowns, and so on), why is this man content? What things does he have that give him strength and pride?

   _____

   _____

4. What emotive words are used? What emotions do you think the poet wants us to feel toward the man?

   _____

   _____

**"GRANDMA'S PRIMO"**
The Italian artist Modigliani often used just a few lines or brushstrokes to suggest a whole person. This poem is also the portrait of a person, shown in just a few words.

1. From whose point of view do we see this character?

   _____

2. What special qualities does he have?

   _____

3. Why do you think the poet found him memorable?

   _____

# Ethical Questions

A monkey being used in a lab experiment

Throughout history, human beings have faced basic questions of ethics, those involving a choice between right and wrong. But modern technology has brought many new complications that make such decisions more difficult now than ever before. This is especially evident in the field of medicine, where ethical decisions are matters of life and death. The first article in this chapter examines some of the complex situations in today's hospitals. The second selection is a descriptive piece about the national cemetery in Washington, D.C., which implies rather than states the most serious ethical question facing humanity today. After this, you get the chance to be the judge on a series of everyday ethical issues that have been debated recently in American courts. Here the question seems to involve not so much a decision between right and wrong as a choice between opposing or conflicting "rights." The chapter ends with a timed reading about another moral issue of our times: our treatment of animals.

## SELECTION ONE

# Doctor's Dilemma: Treat or Let Die?

The wonders of modern medicine dazzle us daily as we read about new discoveries and lifesaving techniques. Smallpox, one of the ancient scourges of humanity, has now been virtually eliminated. Patients whose kidneys have ceased to function live on thanks to the recently invented dialysis machine. People who just a few decades ago would have been pronounced dead when their hearts stopped beating are rushed into surgery and given a new heart; many later return to normal life. This all seems like wonderful news, but is there a darker side to these medical miracles? As is so often the case, new benefits bring new problems. It becomes more and more difficult for doctors, nurses, and patients to know what is right and wrong in medicine. The following magazine article gives an overview of these complex questions.

### Prereading Exercise 1: Focusing on a Key Issue

As a class or in small groups, discuss the following specific example of a current ethical problem in medicine:

During the winter of 1982, a retired dairyman from Poteet, Texas, carried out a most difficult decision. Woodrow Wilson Collums went into the nursing home where his older brother Jim lay helpless and suffering, a victim of severe senility resulting from Alzheimer's disease. Collums took out a gun he had hidden in his coat and shot his brother to death.

1.  Why do you think Collums shot his brother?
2.  Should the courts treat Collums as a murderer?

In the article you will find out what was decided in this and other cases.

## Prereading Exercise 2: Guessing the Meaning of New Words from Context

Read the sentences and use the context to try to determine what each word in italics means. Then write the italicized word next to the correct definition below.

1.  *Ethicists* fear that if doctors decide not to treat certain patients who are *comatose* and dying, death may become too easy.
2.  In fact, to many physicians, modern medicine has become a *double-edged sword*.
3.  The question of *euthanasia* forces doctors, patients, and relatives into a *predicament*.
4.  The doctor's power to treat with an *array* of space-age techniques has *outstripped* the body's capacity to heal.
5.  The *dilemma* posed by the question of treatment or nontreatment has created a growing new discipline of *bioethics*.

   a. _____ a troublesome situation

   b. _____ something that can be interpreted in two opposing ways

   c. _____ a situation requiring a choice between two unpleasant possibilities

   d. _____ people who follow strict moral rules

   e. _____ the study of morality in life-or-death situations

   f. _____ mercy killing (killing to relieve pain)

   g. _____ impressive arrangement or grouping

   h. _____ in a state of coma

   i. _____ exceeded, gone ahead

## *Doctor's Dilemma: Treat or Let Die?*

Medical advances in wonder drugs, daring surgical procedures, radiation therapies, and intensive-care units have brought new life to thousands of people. Yet to many of them, modern medicine has become a double-edged sword.

5     Doctors' power to treat with an array of space-age techniques has outstripped the body's capacity to heal. More medical problems can be treated, but for many patients, there is little hope of recovery. Even the fundamental distinction between life and death has been blurred.

Many Americans are caught in medical limbo, as was the South Korean
10    boxer Duk Koo Kim, who was kept alive by artificial means after he had been knocked unconscious in a fight and his brain ceased to function. With the permission of his family, doctors in Las Vegas disconnected the life-support machines and death quickly followed.

In the wake of technology's advances in medicine, a heated debate is
15    taking place in hospitals and nursing homes across the country—over whether survival or quality of life is the paramount goal of medicine.

"It gets down to what medicine is all about," says Daniel Callahan, director of the Institute of Society, Ethics, and the Life Sciences in Hastings-on-Hudson, New York. "Is it really to save a life? Or is the larger goal the welfare
20    of the patient?"

Doctors, patients, relatives, and often the courts are being forced to make hard choices in medicine. Most often it is at the two extremes of life that these difficult ethical questions arise—at the beginning for the very sick newborn and at the end for the dying patient.

25    The dilemma posed by modern medical technology has created the growing new discipline of bioethics. Many of the country's 127 medical schools now offer courses in medical ethics, a field virtually ignored only a decade ago. Many hospitals have chaplains, philosophers, psychiatrists, and social workers on the staff to help patients make crucial decisions, and one in twenty
30    institutions has a special ethics committee to resolve difficult cases.

### Death and Dying

Of all the patients in intensive-care units who are at risk of dying, some 20 percent present difficult ethical choices—whether to keep trying to save the

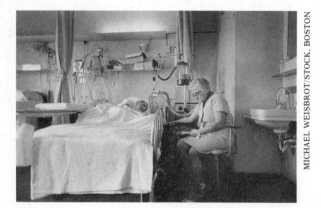

A woman sits by the bedside of her very ill husband,
who is on a life-support machine.

life or to pull back and let the patient die. In cancer units, decisions regarding life-sustaining care are made about three times a week.

35    Even the definition of death has been changed. Now that the heart-lung machine can take over the functions of breathing and pumping blood, death no longer always comes with the patient's "last gasp" or when the heart stops beating. Thirty-one states and the District of Columbia have passed brain-death statutes that identify death as when the whole brain ceases to function.

40    More than a dozen states recognize "living wills" in which the patients leave instructions to doctors not to prolong life by feeding them intravenously or by other methods if their illness becomes hopeless. A survey of California doctors showed that 20 to 30 percent were following instructions of such wills. Meanwhile, the hospice movement,* with its emphasis on providing

45    comfort—not cure—to the dying patient, has gained momentum in many areas.

Despite progress in society's understanding of death and dying, thorny issues remain. *Example:* A woman, 87, afflicted by the nervous-system disorder of Parkinson's disease, has a massive stroke and is found unconscious

50    by her family. Their choices are to put her in a nursing home until she dies or to send her to a medical center for diagnosis and possible treatment. The family opts for a teaching hospital in New York City. Tests show the woman's stroke resulted from a blood clot that is curable with surgery. After the operation, she says to her family: "Why did you bring me back to this agony?"

55    Her health continues to worsen, and two years later she dies.

On the other hand, doctors say prognosis is often uncertain and that patients, just because they are old and disabled, should not be denied life-saving therapy. Ethicists also fear that under the guise of medical decisions not to treat certain patients, death may become too easy, pushing the country

60    toward the acceptance of euthanasia.

For some people, the agony of watching high-technology dying is too great. Earlier this year, Woodrow Wilson Collums, a retired dairyman from Poteet, Texas, was put on probation for the mercy killing of his older brother Jim, who lay helpless in his bed at a nursing home, a victim of severe senility

65    resulting from Alzheimer's disease. After the killing, the victim's widow said: "I thank God Jim's out of his misery. I hate to think it had to be done the way it was done, but I understand it."

### Crisis in Newborn Care

At the other end of the life span, technology has so revolutionized newborn care that it is no longer clear when human life is viable outside the womb.

70    Twenty-five years ago, infants weighing less than three and one-half pounds rarely survived. The current survival rate is 70 percent, and doctors are

---

*The hospice movement is a group dedicated to providing a homelike atmosphere where dying people may live out their last days in dignity and with a minimum of pain. The staff in a hospice does not try to cure at all costs but rather encourages a normal life until the end.

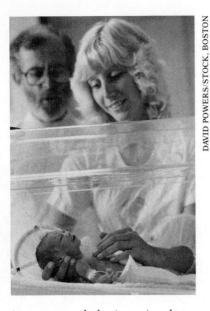

DAVID POWERS/STOCK, BOSTON

A premature baby in an incubator

"salvaging" some babies that weigh only one and one-half pounds. Tremendous progress has been made in treating birth deformities such as spina bifida. Just ten years ago, only 5 percent of infants with transposition of the
75    great arteries—the congenital heart defect most commonly found in newborns—survived. Today, 50 percent live.

Yet, for many infants who owe their lives to new medical advances, survival has come at a price. A significant number emerge with permanent physical and mental handicaps.
80    "The question of treatment and nontreatment of seriously ill newborns is not a simple one," says Thomas Murray of the Hastings Center. "But I feel strongly that retardation or the fact that someone is going to be less than perfect is not good grounds for allowing an infant to die."

For many parents, however, the experience of having a sick newborn
85    becomes a lingering nightmare. Two years ago, an Atlanta mother gave birth to a baby suffering from Down's Syndrome, a form of mental retardation; the child also had blocked intestines. The doctors rejected the parents' plea not to operate, and today the child, severely retarded, still suffers intestinal problems.
90    "Every time Melanie has a bowel movement, she cries," explains her mother. "She's not able to take care of herself, and we won't live forever. I wanted to save her from sorrow, pain, and suffering. I don't understand the emphasis on life at all costs, and I'm very angry at the doctors and the hospital. We felt doing nothing to sustain her life was best for her. The doctors went
95    against nature. I asked the doctors, who threatened to take us to court if we didn't go along with their procedures: 'Who will take care of Melanie after we're gone? Where will you doctors be then?'"

## Changing Standards

The choices posed by modern technology have profoundly changed the practice of medicine. Until now, most doctors have been activists, trained to use all the tools in their medical arsenals to treat disease. The current trend is toward nontreatment as doctors grapple with questions not just of who should get care but when to take therapy away.

Always in the background is the threat of legal action. In August, two California doctors were charged with murdering a comatose patient by allegedly disconnecting the respirator and cutting off food and water. In 1981, a Massachusetts nurse was charged with murdering a cancer patient with massive doses of morphine but subsequently was acquitted.

Between lawsuits, government regulations, and patients' rights, many doctors feel they are under siege. Modern technology actually has limited their ability to make choices. More frequently, these actions are resolved by committees.

## Public Policy

In recent years, the debate on medical ethics has moved to the level of national policy. "It's just beginning to hit us that we don't have unlimited resources," says Washington Hospital Center's Dr. Lynch. "You can't talk about ethics without talking about money."

Since 1972, Americans have enjoyed unlimited access to a taxpayer-supported, kidney-dialysis program that offers life-prolonging therapy to all patients with kidney failure. To a number of policy analysts, the program has grown out of control—to a $1.4 billion operation supporting 61,000 patients. The majority are over 50, and about a quarter have other illnesses, such as cancer or heart disease, conditions that could exclude them from dialysis in other countries.

Some hospitals are pulling back from certain lifesaving treatments. Massachusetts General Hospital, for example, has decided not to perform heart transplants on the ground that the high costs of providing such surgery help too few patients. Burn units—though extremely effective—also provide very expensive therapy for very few patients.

As medical scientists push back the frontiers of therapy, the moral dilemma will continue to grow for doctors and patients alike, making the choice of to treat or not to treat the basic question in modern medicine.

**Abigail Trafford**

# Recalling Information

Choose the best way of finishing each statement, based on what you have just read.

1. Recent medical advances have:
   a. left many accident victims without the ability to receive insurance benefits

  b. forced a debate over whether survival or quality of life is the
     paramount goal of medicine
  c. made ethical decisions much easier for doctors because of the
     intervention of the courts
  d. none of the above

2. Difficult ethical questions most often arise:
  a. at the end of life for the dying patient
  b. during the beginning of life for the newborn infant
  c. both of the above

3. In cancer units, it is common to find decisions regarding life-
   sustaining care made:
  a. once a year
  b. twice a month
  c. three times a week

4. The majority of states have passed laws that now define the time
   of death as the moment when:
  a. a patient breathes a "last gasp"
  b. the whole brain ceases to function
  c. the heart stops

5. One of the problems with the great progress medicine has made in
   saving the lives of very tiny newborn babies is that these infants:
  a. never grow to a normal size or weight
  b. must be kept completely apart from their families and other
     babies
  c. often have permanent physical and mental handicaps

6. The decision of whether or not to let a patient die:
  a. is now a completely private matter between the doctor and his
     or her patient
  b. is always resolved to the benefit of the patient
  c. is frequently made by committees

7. According to Dr. Lynch, you cannot talk about ethics in medicine
   without talking about:
  a. miracles               c. drugs
  b. money                  d. operations

8. Some hospitals are now cutting back on certain expensive life-
   saving treatments, such as heart transplants, because:
  a. they help very few people
  b. they are simply too painful
  c. they are not done properly

## Talking It Over

1. What do you think of the idea of "living wills"? What problems
   can they cause for doctors and nurses today?

2. What do you think of the hospice movement? What do the people in this movement hope to do?

3. Are you for or against the practice of euthanasia? Explain.

4. If your mother or grandmother were eighty-seven and her doctors said that she needed a major operation, would you wish that she have it or not? Why?

## Solving Problems in Groups

Discuss the following problem in small groups. Try to reach a unanimous decision (one agreed to by all). Later, report to the class on the reasons for your choice.

> The year is 2050. Medicine has advanced a good deal and a limited number of efficient but very expensive artificial hearts is now available. There are not enough for everyone. Four candidates have applied to your hospital, and only one of them can receive the artificial heart. Without it, the other three will surely die. You and the other members of your group form the bioethics committee, which must make the decision. Which of the candidates do you choose? Why?

1. Sandra, a small, somewhat sickly two-year-old girl of average intelligence, the only daughter of a young carpenter and his wife

2. Jeremy Wells, fifty-eight years old, a famous novelist who has received the Nobel Prize for Literature; married with no children, currently working on a new novel

3. Peggy Anderson, thirty-three, unmarried mother of five children, who works as a secretary and is active in community affairs in the small town where she lives with her family

4. Scott, twelve years old, a brilliant student who is said by his teachers to be a "near-genius in math"; one of three children of two college professors

## Round Table Discussion

General Hospital is considering whether or not to discontinue its burn unit, which costs a great sum of money and aids only about twenty patients a year. A meeting of the entire staff of doctors, nurses, and administrators has been called to decide the question. Four people have asked to appear and speak for or against the idea: a representative of the President's Commission on Bioethical Issues, a doctor or nurse who has worked on the burn unit for ten years, a hospital administrator, and the mother of a child who was severely burned and treated at the unit three years earlier. Four volunteers will play the roles of these speakers and give a short talk either in favor of or against discontinuing the unit. The rest of the class will act as the staff and ask questions of the speakers. Afterward, a vote should be taken to see which side won.

# Crossword Puzzle: Vocabulary from "Doctor's Dilemma: Treat or Let Die?"

All of the words needed for this crossword puzzle appear in the article "Doctor's Dilemma: Treat or Let Die?" The first letter of each word is given to aid you. Complete the puzzle using the clues.

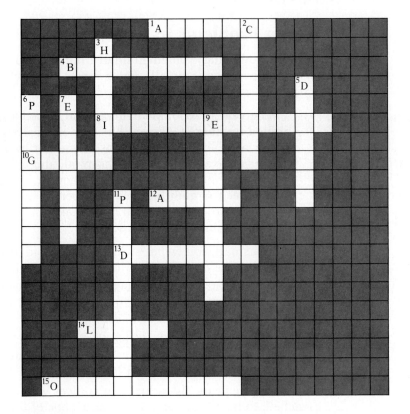

## CLUES

### ACROSS

1. to give pain to the body or mind
4. the study of morality in life-and-death situations
8. through the veins
10. false appearance
12. impressive arrangement
13. treatment for a patient with kidney failure
14. a transitional state of mind
15. exceeded, gone ahead

### DOWN

2. adjective describing student's state of mind at 8:00 A.M.
3. place where comfort is given to the dying
5. situation requiring a choice between two bad possibilities
6. prediction about the future condition of a sick person
7. person who follows a strict moral code
9. mercy killing; killing for pity
11. difficult situation

**SELECTION TWO**

# Memorial Day at Arlington: "Our Only Son"

The following selection is about a day of remembrance at the national burial grounds for American soldiers in Arlington, Virginia. It does not state any ethical question, but a close reading will show that it does imply or suggest one. The selection is mainly a description. In a way the author is painting a picture, but he is also trying to create a mood by including emotional scenes that will cause us to feel and question. What is the ethical question he is presenting to us? Read carefully for the hidden or implied meaning.

## Prereading Exercise: Anticipating Tone and Mood

1. Before even beginning to read the article, how do you know it is written in an emotional tone?

   _____

   _____

   _____

   _____

2. Is there a special day of the year in your culture when people remember or honor their dead relatives and loved ones? If so, describe what is done.

   _____

   _____

   _____

   _____

   _____

3. What do you think happens on May 30th in the United States?

   _____

4. What emotions do you expect to find described?

   _____

Read the article carefully to see how the author creates an emotional tone and suggests an ethical problem.

# Memorial Day at Arlington: "Our Only Son"

Arlington, Virginia
May 30, 1971

At the crest of the great green hill, a slight figure moved haltingly among the white marble stones, stopping and stooping at each one, then stepping on toward the next, cradling a small wreath of red roses against her dark frock. "I only get to come from Richmond once a year, and I always get mixed up

5    about just where he is," she explained apologetically.

The soft sod squished beneath her feet as she walked from one row to another until, finally, she knelt in the damp ground above the grave of Private Roy W. Maclan, Jr., a teenaged infantryman who died in Korea twenty years ago.

10    "He was our only son," she said, planting the wreath's wire tripod beside the stone. She smoothed the grass at its base with that quick tenderness mothers learn, and when she arose her eyes were moist with remembering.

"This makes the twentieth year, now," she said as she left. "You'd think I'd remember where he is, wouldn't you? But there are so many here like

15    him."

CHRIS SHERIDAN/MONKMEYER PRESS PHOTO SERVICE

Scene at the Vietnam War memorial in Washington, D.C., with names of those killed

A delicate spring rain was falling this morning when the big black gates of Arlington National Cemetery creaked open to admit a tiny group of waiting, shivering visitors. As Memorial Day grew older, however, the shreds of charcoal clouds skittered away, and, by midday, the little lanes and walkways that
20  ramble through the 518 rolling acres were like rush-hour expressways for pedestrians.

On any day, the cemetery attracts hundreds, but today, as on this holiday in past years, there were thousands—and across the country, from here on the banks of the Potomac to the Punch Bowl, a national cemetery high above
25  Pearl Harbor, thousands of other Americans made quiet visits to the graves that held meaning for them.

For some who came to Arlington, it was the Tomb of the Unknown Soldier where, after the traditional wreath-laying, General Leonard F. Chapman, Jr., the Marine Corps commandant, told a large crowd that the latest of this
30  nation's wars had been its most unselfish.

For others who came here, the focal point was an elliptical walkway that brought them to the eternal flame burning over the body of President John F. Kennedy and to the small gravesite of his brother Robert.

For many others, tourists in a tourists' town, coming to Arlington was
35  much like going to the Smithsonian—a part of the prepaid bus tour.

"It's a tourist attraction just like the rest of Washington," a veteran employee at the cemetery's visitor center said. "For most of these people, it's just one more stop."

Mr. and Mrs. Lyle Bacon were standing at the back of their car in the
40  newest section of the cemetery when the thunder of the salute at the Tomb of the Unknown Soldier reverberated across the valley.

She shuddered and looked inquisitively at her forty-one-year-old husband, an accountant in Baltimore. He placed his arm on her shoulder.

The last time they came to Arlington was to watch the burial of their
45  eighteen-year-old son, William, a Marine private killed last October near Danang by a Vietcong booby trap.

They both were torn by what has become a common schism in the soul of the American parent. "I would have been ashamed if he hadn't wanted to serve his country, and I don't think I could have stood it if he had cut and
50  run," his father said. "But, God, how do I explain his death to myself? I mean, can anybody tell me what difference it made?"

Mrs. Bacon wept softly while he spoke. Then, suddenly, as though he had uttered some posthypnotic suggestion, her face was contorted in rage and her eyes flashed with a deep anger.

55  "Yes, that's right," she snapped. "Can anybody tell me? Me! Me! I'm his mother. Why shouldn't I be told?" Mr. Bacon wrapped his arm around her as she began to sob, and they walked off into the line upon line of marble markers.

60  At the grave of a fellow Army major who was killed in the 1968 Tet offensive in Vietnam, a stocky career soldier with graying hair stood at attention and saluted the small American flag flapping beside the stone. He said:

"It's an honor to die for the right thing, and I'm convinced that this country, with all of its problems and sins, is still worth dying for."

Then, like the Bacons, he turned and strode away.

65  At an intersection, not far from the grave of President William H. Taft, a florist's van pulled to the curb, and a young man alighted with a basket of flowers.

"Can't talk," he said hurriedly. "Busy day. People phoning in orders from all over the place. Biggest day we've had this year. Bigger than Easter."

70  As large as it is, Arlington National Cemetery has almost reached its capacity, and there is serious discussion in the Army and in Congress about closing its lots forever, a move already made at eight other national cemeteries. There is no room for expansion. The Pentagon is on one side, Fort Myer sprawls on two other sides, and the Potomac curls along in front.

75  The road alongside the newest section, where most of the Vietnam dead are being buried, will be closed tonight, and tomorrow the asphalt will be removed to make room for more graves. After that, the cemetery officials say, there is no place else to go.

"Wouldn't it be nice if when it's full," seventeen-year-old Richard Billingsley
80  of Silver Spring, Maryland, said wistfully, "they'd just stop having wars. I mean, like you'd just say, 'Well, I'm sorry, but we can't get into this war because we don't have any more room left in Arlington.'"

**James T. Wooten**

# Analyzing Contrasts to Determine Meaning

The description Wooten presents us of the cemetery on Memorial Day is full of contrasts. Some of the obvious ones are between the present and the past, silence and speech, the living and the dead. There is even a contrast in the weather, which is rainy at first and then clears up. But one of the strongest contrasts is more subtle, not immediately obvious. This is the contrast in the visitors, who are there for very different reasons and with very different attitudes. Describe three of the attitudes presented and list at least one example of words or actions that show each attitude.

1. _____

    Example: _____

    _____

2. _____

    Example: _____

    _____

3. _____

   Example: _____

   _____

By presenting us with these different attitudes, the author is really asking us an ethical question, although he does not state it directly. In your opinion, what question is he asking? What is this selection really about?

_____

_____

_____

What do you think is the viewpoint of the author on this question? Do you think he has a definite answer?

_____

_____

_____

_____

## Identifying Words That Create an Emotional Tone

Wooten has created an emotional tone by carefully selecting words that make the reader feel strongly about what he is describing. Scan for the following emotive words, using the clues given.

1. What adverb is used to describe the movements of the very first person mentioned, the woman who is having trouble finding her son's grave? What emotion do we feel toward her as a result?

   _____

2. What two verbs are used to express the fact that Mrs. Bacon cried? Why are they stronger than the simple verb *cry*?

   _____

3. What two words are used to describe the other strong emotion, besides sadness, that Mrs. Bacon feels? Why does she feel this?

   _____

4. What emotive noun does the career officer use to give meaning to the death of his friend as he stands by the grave? What emotions does it show he felt?

   _____

5. In the last paragraph, Wooten uses a very exact adverb to describe the way a young man is speaking. It means "in a sad, thoughtful way that shows longing or desire." What is this adverb?

---

## Talking It Over

1. What is the purpose of the Tomb of the Unknown Soldier?
2. Why do you think many visitors went to see the graves of the Kennedy brothers?
3. What differences do we see between the parents of the boy who died twenty years earlier and the parents of the boy who was buried the previous autumn? Is it comforting or sad to see this change in feelings?
4. The end of an article is very important. How do you interpret the remark made by the seventeen-year-old boy, which concludes the selection?
5. Would you fight in a war if your country asked you to? Why or why not?

## Interpreting a Dot Plot Showing Atomic Firepower

One of the most important ethical concerns of our times is nuclear disarmament. A major problem with talking about this question is the sheer magnitude of the forces under discussion, a magnitude that is hard to imagine. The following chart attempts to circumvent this difficulty in a visual way. This type of chart is called a "dot plot."

In this case, each dot represents all the firepower of World War II, including the two atom bombs dropped on Japan. This equals three megatons. The dot in the center square, then, represents this quantity. In 1982, when this dot plot was made, the nuclear arsenals of the United States and the Soviet Union equaled 18,000 megatons, or the equivalent destructive capability of 6,000 World War IIs. The chart has a total of 6,001 dots, each one equaling three megatons. This represents the nuclear arsenal of the world in 1982, with about half belonging to the United States and the other half to the Soviets. In spite of the INF treaty signed in 1987 by the United States and the Soviet Union, the present nuclear arsenal is actually larger now than it was in 1982, and so is more powerful than what is shown on the dot plot. (The INF Treaty banned all intermediate nuclear missiles with a range between 500 and 5,500 kilometers.)

The dots in the small circle in the upper left-hand square can destroy over 200 Soviet cities. Imagine the land mass of the Soviet Union to be the size of that small circle. If the land mass of the world were reduced to the same scale, it would be the size of a dime. Place a dime or your index finger on the chart. The dots covered represent the firepower of enough World War IIs to destroy every large and medium-sized city in the entire world.

Look at the dot plot carefully, then answer the questions that follow.

**FIREPOWER TO DESTROY A WORLD, PLUS**

:·:· U.S. Senate staff have reviewed this chart and found it an accurate representation.

Chart by James Geier, with Sharyl Green
NUCLEAR WEAPONS CHART (taken from the Vermont town meeting informational booklet on nuclear war, 1982)

# Questions

1. What does each dot on the chart stand for?

_____

_____

2. Why does the dot plot have 6,001 dots?

_____

_____

3. Do you feel that the world will be safer for humanity if the number of dots on a revised dot plot *increases* or *decreases* in the years to come? Why?

_____

_____

_____

. In your opinion, was the INF (Intermediate Nuclear Forces) Treaty of 1987 a good idea or not? Explain.

_____

_____

_____

5. Do you feel any differently about the nuclear-arms debate after seeing the dot plot? Why or why not?

_____

_____

_____

_____

## SELECTION THREE

# ■ You Be the Judge

Whom should a waiter or a waitress serve first in a restaurant—the man or the woman? Well, it depends. If you are in France, it will be the woman, but if you cross the border into Germany, it will probably be the man. The idea of what is socially correct varies from one culture to another, and so do ideas of right and wrong. The dominant opinion is generally protected by law.

## Prereading Exercise 1: Anticipating the Reading

Think about the issue of alcoholic beverages. Is it right to buy them on Sunday? Well, that depends on where you are. In Canada and the United States, this varies from one province or state to another. Try to think of some places in the world where the following rules apply:

1.  You can usually buy alcoholic drinks, but not on Sundays:

    _____

    _____

2.  You cannot buy any alcoholic drinks at any time:

    _____

    _____

3.  You can buy alcoholic drinks, but only in government-controlled stores with restricted hours:

    _____

    _____

4.  You can buy alcoholic drinks easily at any time, even from vending machines in the streets:

    _____

    _____

Of course, legality is only one aspect of the question of right and wrong. Everyone has his or her own beliefs, which do not always conform to current laws, and laws and customs change, not always at the same time. There is still a law on the books in Boston that a man may not kiss his wife in public on Sunday!

The following excerpts from the book *You Be the Judge* present in brief form eight different cases that came into the American courts in recent years. As you read, think about how you would decide each one in accordance with your own beliefs.

A typical courtroom scene

# Prereading Exercise 2: Learning Legal Terms from Context

These common words all relate to the law and appear in the selection. Read through the story that follows and choose the correct word, according to the context, to fill in each blank.

*testify*   to give evidence in front of a judge or jury

*lawsuit*   case against someone presented to a judge or jury

*defendant*   person accused of something before the law

*sue (file suit against)*   to accuse someone of a crime so as to cause him or her to pay money or to be put in jail

*regulation*   rule or law that controls people's actions

*damage*   injury or harm caused to a person or property resulting in a loss

*discriminate against*   to treat someone badly or unfairly because he or she comes from a certain background or belongs to a certain group

*lawyer*   person trained in the law who advises and represents people with legal problems

*manslaughter*   the killing of another person due to carelessness or poor judgment; different from murder (which is more serious) because there is no intention to kill

*prohibit*   forbid, prevent

*witness*   a person who saw or heard something and can give a firsthand account of it

*court*   place where trials and official investigations take place; group of judges or jurors appointed by law to make legal decisions

**THE TRUTH WINS OUT**

The old lady was an eye _____₁ of the accident because she had seen and heard everything from her window in the nursing home. She was a very sharp old lady, and she knew

that the tall man would _____₂ the frightened young

girl in the green car for the _____₃ to his motorcycle. She also knew that he had been going the wrong way on a one-way street and that the girl had not noticed!

   The old lady was right. The next week she read in the

newspaper that the case was coming to _____₄ soon.

She telephoned the _____₅ for the _____₆ and told him: "Your client is innocent. I can give evidence to show that this whole _____₇ is unfair." "But, madam," he countered, "You are ninety-eight years old and in a wheelchair." "So what?" responded the old lady. "You have no right to _____8 against me because I am old and sick. There is no _____9 against elderly people testifying at trials. Besides, if you _____10 me from helping that poor young girl, I shall probably have a heart attack. Then my relatives will accuse you of _____11!" "OK, OK, take it easy," he replied. Special arrangements were made for the old lady to _____12 through the use of a videotape. Because of her, the young girl was declared innocent.

## *You Be the Judge*

The following situations are based on real cases from the federal courts. Consider the arguments, then decide how *you* would rule.

**1.** When Darlene applied for a job as a city policewoman, the police chief said, "You meet all the requirements except that you're too short. You're only five feet, five inches tall, and we have a five-foot-seven requirement."

Darlene protested that as a former physical-education teacher she was very strong. When the chief refused to back down, she went to court.

"The five-foot-seven requirement discriminates against women," her lawyer told the judge. "Most men are taller than that, but not as many women are that height or more."

If you were the judge, would Darlene get the job?

**2.** Robert took his two sons camping in Yellowstone National Park. A park brochure warned them to beware of bears. "Don't worry," Robert said. "The bears are more afraid of you than you are of them." But sure enough, a grizzly bear invaded their tent during the night and mauled Robert's face and chest. Robert sued the park. "Judge," he said, "the government park service should pay for my injuries."

Would you rule for Robert or the park service?

**3.** Mrs. Smith was only slightly interested when her son, a high school senior, told her he was taking a new course in transcendental meditation. But her curiosity was aroused when she found him chanting and burning incense in his bedroom.

Questioned, her son reported that he was being taught about the search for ultimate reality beyond thought and feeling.

"Why, that's religion," Mrs. Smith fumed. "And they certainly can't teach *that* in public school." She sued to stop the course.

"This is not a class in religion," said the school board lawyer. "It's only a course in philosophy."

Would you allow the high school to teach transcendental meditation?

30    **4.** Greg, a six-foot-eleven teenager, was one of the best high school basketball players in the country. During the summer between his junior and senior years, he enrolled in a one-week basketball camp where he received expert coaching and played against other comparable high school stars.

35    When he returned to school in the fall, he received a shock. "You can't play basketball this year," said an official of his high school league. "State regulations prohibit players from attending summer sports camps."

Outraged, Greg's parents filed suit in federal court: "The boy has a constitutional right to prepare for a college and professional career," their
40    lawyer said. The league attorney disagreed, saying, "We're trying to make it fair for the boys who don't get a chance to go to summer sports camps."

Would you let Greg play?

**5.** Charlie took his wife, Alice, to a restaurant for their anniversary. While they were drinking their wine, Alice's glass broke and cut her hand. Charlie
45    drove Alice to a hospital emergency room, where the doctor told her she had severed a tendon and would never be able to move her right index finger again. Alice and Charlie filed suit against the restaurant, claiming $100,000 for permanent injury.

"Judge," said the restaurant manager, "we shouldn't have to pay a
50    penny. We sold the wine, but we didn't sell the glass."

Would you make the restaurant pay for Alice's injury?

**6.** Vernon was charged with voluntary manslaughter for intentionally running over his mother-in-law with his pickup truck. His wife was the only eyewitness, and the law cannot compel a wife to testify against her husband.
55    The state put the couple's next door neighbor on the witness stand. "Just after the crash," the neighbor testified, "Vernon's wife came running up to my door and shouted, 'My husband just ran over my mom!'"

"Objection!" roared Vernon's lawyer. "If a wife eyewitness can't testify, her statements can't be put into evidence through another witness to
60    show that the defendant-husband may be guilty."

Would you allow the neighbor to testify as to what Vernon's wife said?

**7.** Mrs. Jones was an outspoken high school English teacher. During a private meeting with the principal over school policies, she lost her temper and called him several names in a loud voice.
65    The next day the principal fired her. She filed a lawsuit in federal court, claiming the school violated her right of free speech. "A public employee cannot be fired for expressing her views," Mrs. Jones's lawyer said.

The school board attorney said the suit should be dismissed. "The right of free speech applies only in public places, not in private meetings,"
70    he said. "Besides, she deserved to be fired for being disrespectful."

Should Mrs. Jones get her job back?

**8.** Perry, a young state trooper, was promoted to sergeant for bravery in the
line of duty. Then he learned that every sergeant in the state highway
patrol had a quota of one hundred speeding tickets to give out per week.

"That's unfair to drivers, and it's illegal," he complained to his commander. "I refuse to comply."

When Perry was demoted, he sued the department for loss of wages
and punitive damages. "Judge," he argued, "you can't lower a man's rank
and salary for speaking out against illegal conduct—especially in the
police department."

Would you decide for Perry or for the state?

**John A. Ritter**

## Relating Facts to Specific Parts of a Reading

Read over the following facts concerning the American legal system.
Then tell which case or cases of those you have read would be affected
in some way by each fact.

1. The main principles of law come from a document called the
   Constitution, which guarantees certain basic rights to American
   citizens. It is the duty of the judges to interpret and apply this
   document.

2. Among these constitutional rights are the right to life, liberty, and
   the pursuit of happiness and the right to freedom of speech.

3. In most cases, a witness may be compelled to testify, but a woman
   cannot be made to testify against her own husband.

4. It is now unlawful for an employer to discriminate against a possible employee on the basis of race, sex, or national origin.

5. Church and state are kept separate, and so religion should not be
   taught in the public schools.

6. A business cannot legally sell something to a customer that is
   likely to cause him or her unexpected injury.

## Scanning for Antonyms

Scan the selection for antonyms (opposites) of the following words. The
case number is given to aid you. The first three are all made into antonyms by simply adding a prefix (use a different prefix for each word).

1. fair (8)  _____

2. legal (8)  _____

3. respectful (7)  _____

4. hired (7)  _____

5. promoted (8)  _____

6. allow (4)  _____

7. attached (5)  _____

8. innocent (6)  _____

## Solving Problems in Groups

Choose four of the cases to discuss with a small group of your classmates. Try to come to a unanimous decision. Afterward, compare your judgments with the information on page 296. Do you think the judge was incorrect in any of the cases? Explain.

## TIMED  READING

# ▛ Extinction

The following reading raises a difficult ethical question about the treatment of animals and the role of human beings in causing or preventing the extinction of certain animal species. As you read, focus on the following questions:

1. Who is Digit?
2. What happens to him and why?
3. What is the authors' point of view regarding what happened?
4. How do the authors use emotive words to try to convince us of their point of view?

Try to finish the reading and comprehension quiz in eight minutes.

A silverback gorilla

# Extinction

Almost overcome with fear, Digit turned unarmed to face the spears and dogs of Munyarukiko and his five companions. He would have to gain time for his family to escape up the mountain slopes. It was his role, his "duty"— and although he may well have known it would mean his death, Digit stood
5   his ground. To Munyarukiko and the other poachers, the silverback male gorilla, erect with his canines bared, was doubtless a terrifying sight, one made more terrifying by the quick demise of one of their dogs, whose frenzy at the smell of the gorilla's fear brought it too close to Digit's powerful arms. But gorillas, strong as they are, are sadly vulnerable to the weapons of their
10  physically weaker human relatives. Digit bought the time for his family group to flee, but he took five mortal spear thrusts in the process.

Thus on the last day of 1977 died one of the few remaining mountain gorillas—a death not atypical except in the detail in which it is known. Digit was one of a group of gorillas under intense study by Dian Fossey on Mount
15  Visoke in the Parc des Volcans of Rwanda. He had, in a very real sense, become a friend of Dian's, as well as of millions of other human beings who had seen him on television. For Digit had been filmed examining Dian's pen and then her notebook, gently returning each to her, and then lying down and going to sleep by her side. This memorable scene was part of a National
20  Geographic Society Special television program and has been reshown at least once in a collection of film clips of which the society is justly proud.*

The tragedy of Digit's death was all the greater because of its motivation. In both Rwanda and Zaire, it is believed that certain portions of the body of a silverback male gorilla—testicles, tongue, ears, portions of the little fin-
25  gers—have magical properties. Used in the proper proportion, they are believed either to kill an enemy or make him impotent. Over the years gorillas had been killed for these parts, and the resultant distrust of human beings had to be overcome before Dian could befriend the gorilla.

But it was not this tradition of *sumu* ("poison") that led to the killing of
30  Digit. When tourists and other foreigners began to arrive, poachers killed gorillas to make their skulls and hands into souvenirs. Digit was murdered not because the local people are meat-starved or especially impoverished but because an African named Sebunyana-Zirimwabagabo offered Muny-arukiko roughly twenty dollars for the head and hands of a silverback.

35  Many human beings obviously feel compassion for Digit and the other embattled mountain gorillas. They hope that Digit's baby, conceived before his death and christened by Dian *Mwelu* (Swahili for "a touch of brightness and light"), will have a chance for a proper gorilla existence. Others feel no such compassion; they basically ask, "What good are gorillas?" and conclude

---

*Dian Fossey was murdered in December of 1985. No one knows who the murderers were, but poachers are suspected.

40   they are no good at all. In their view, Munyarukiko was right to do the beast
     in—gorillas' land can be put to good use grazing cattle, and the twenty dollars
     can be spent for human pleasure in the form of the native beer, *pombe*.
          We could counter the latter view with the standard arguments that survival
     of Mwelu and the other gorillas would benefit humanity far more than their
45   extermination. For example, by studying gorillas, human beings might come
     to understand themselves better. Or gorillas might serve useful ends in med-
     ical research. Or they might benefit African nations as tourist attractions.
     Most importantly, however, the disappearance of gorillas from the earth would
     be a very sad thing, apart from the real economic values they represent,
50   simply because they are so interesting, and their very evident kinship with
     human beings appeals to people's sense of compassion.

                                                        **Paul and Anne Ehrlich**

## Comprehension Quiz

Choose the best way of finishing each statement, based on what you
have just read.

1. What did Digit do when confronted by the men and dogs?
    a. ran away in fear
    b. fought and managed to save his family
    c. died immediately from a well-aimed bullet

2. Why was there so much interest in Digit?
    a. he belongs to a group of animals that has almost disappeared
    b. he was seen on television by millions of people
    c. both of the above

3. What had Dian Fossey managed to do with him?
    a. overcome his great distrust of human beings
    b. teach him many entertaining tricks
    c. train him to better defend himself

4. What is the tradition of *sumu*?
    a. the practice of eating gorilla meat to obtain nourishment
    b. the use of certain parts of the gorilla to make poisons
    c. the custom of leaving food to help the gorillas

5. What was the motivation for Digit's death?
    a. hatred and fear of gorillas among the local people
    b. the need for food in a meat-starved population
    c. the desire to make money by selling souvenirs

6. What is *Mwelu*?
    a. the land held by the gorillas that could be used for grazing
       cattle
    b. a word in Swahili meaning "a proper gorilla existence"
    c. the name given by Dian to Digit's baby

7. According to the authors, which is the best argument against the killing of gorillas?

   a. gorillas are interesting
   b. gorillas can be used in medical research
   c. gorillas can benefit African nations as tourist attractions

8. By using emotive words such as *fear, sadly vulnerable, friend, gently* when describing Digit, what emotion are the authors trying to make us feel for him?

   a. terror   b. admiration   c. compassion

## Questions

Answer the following questions briefly in complete sentences.

1. What is the ethical question being discussed in this selection?

_____

_____

2. What is the authors' point of view on this question?

_____

_____

3. Based on what you have read, what can you infer about the authors' attitude toward recent attempts to put an end to the killing of whales? Why do you infer that they would feel this way?

# CHAPTER 11

# Medicine

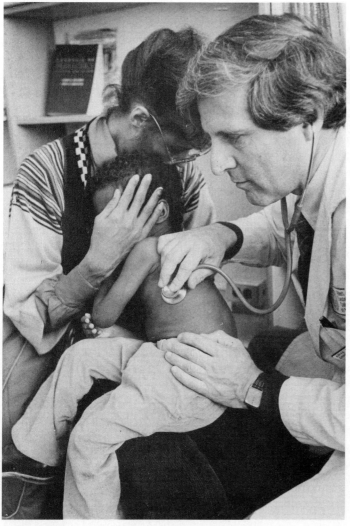

Doctor examines a child with AIDS

This chapter begins with the new and ends with the old. Some of the newest, most sophisticated machines of modern medical technology are described first, along with the benefits and problems they imply for both patients and doctors. Then a cancer patient describes in a poem how she felt undergoing treatment in one of these machines. Next, a quick look is taken at the unusual experiment presently being tried by Nigeria in its attempt to blend and harmonize East and West, traditional folk medicine and modern methods of treatment. The fourth selection then delves into the past to uncover the roots of medical knowledge in the ancient traditions and practices of Islamic culture. Finally, a timed reading discusses a current major medical problem, the threat of AIDS.

## S E L E C T I O N   O N E

# New Tools for Medical Diagnosis

Gone are the days when a doctor made a diagnosis of the medical condition of his patient simply by placing a stethoscope on a patient's heart and asking him to stick out his tongue and say "Ah. . . ." High technology has entered medicine, and many people wonder if the results are always good or rather a "mixed blessing." The following magazine article describes some of the newest of the complicated machines that are now used in many modern hospitals and discusses how they are affecting the practice of medicine.

### Prereading Exercise: Determining the Level of Understanding Expected of You

Look at the photos in this chapter of the large machines now being used for medical diagnosis. Who do you think understands them thoroughly? A doctor? An engineer? A mechanic? Or perhaps only a group of these people together? Before reading an article like this one, which you know will contain technical terms and complicated explanations, remind yourself of your purpose: to gain *some*—not all—new information on the subject. List the three types of machines shown and what you can figure out about them from the photos and captions.

1. _____

2. _____

3. _____

Now try to predict the kinds of information you will be expected to acquire from this article. Cross out those questions below whose answers you think you would *not* need to know given the level of understanding you want from this article.

1. Exactly how does each of these machines work?
2. In general, why are they used?
3. What important differences are there among the machines?
4. What is the size, shape, and cost of each one?
5. What benefits and problems do they bring to medicine?

Read to find out the answers to those questions you have not crossed out. Skip over sections you do not understand—just as a native English reader would. (You can always go back to these later, if necessary.)

## New Tools for Medical Diagnosis

With the appearance in medicine of machines that once only physicists and computer scientists used, doctors now have the power to look at our bodies and diagnose our ills as never before. The diagnostic techniques seen on these pages are examples of such devices. Some are already in use at
5   medical centers; others are experimental devices that patients may encounter in the years to come. But no one knows which will become the stethoscopes of tomorrow, because high costs may keep some of them from widespread distribution.

Physicians are excited about some of these diagnostic techniques
10  because they offer a less invasive way to probe the interior of the body. They may replace traditional procedures such as inserting a catheter (a flexible, floating tube) into the coronary artery, or removing a piece of living tissue to perform a biopsy, a chemical analysis of body tissue. Imaging systems make possible the study of *"in vivo* biochemistry—measurement of the biochemistry
15  of the living body," explains Thomas F. Budinger of the University of California's Lawrence Berkeley Laboratories.

A second advantage is that physicians "can get an image of the structure of the body to identify anatomical abnormality," says Oleg Jardetzky, director of Stanford University's Magnetic Resonance Laboratory. These powerful
20  diagnostic tools are already a great help to medical researchers and are replacing older, more dangerous, less accurate diagnostic methods.

An example of one of the newest and most experimental technologies sits in the Donner Labs at Berkeley. The Positron Emission Tomograph (PET scan) penetrates the human body's metabolism by recording traces of
25  "nuclear annihilations" in body tissue.

A patient receives short-lived radioactive tracers, combined with chemicals the body normally uses. The tracers emit particles called "positrons" that collide with electrons less than a few millimeters away and produce bursts

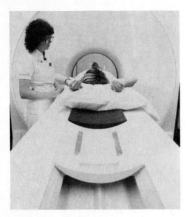

A CAT scan

of energy that detectors record. As these collisions continue repeatedly, the
30    detectors slowly build up a map of just where the tracer chemical is or is not
being metabolized. The tracers can measure blood flow and volume, oxygen
and protein metabolism, and other functions.

Although it is still an experimental device, the PET scanner is already
being used clinically to test for Alzheimer's disease (a form of progressive
35    degeneration of the brain), to locate the malfunctioning part of an epileptic's
brain, and to evaluate a stroke's effects.

PET's greatest use, says Thomas Budinger, may be in the clinical study
of disease, to determine how well patients respond to certain treatments.
"PET," he says, "is used to study these diseases rather than to treat individual
40    patients."

Those who favor another experimental technique, Nuclear Magnetic Resonance (NMR) spectroscopy, believe they have more to offer than the PET
scan. At such medical centers as New York Hospital–Cornell Medical Center
in New York City and University of California Medical School, San Francisco,
45    NMR has shown promise in detecting brain tumors and diagnosing multiple
sclerosis and diseases of the kidney, liver, pancreas, and prostate gland.

In the NMR technique, the patient is placed in an extremely powerful
magnetic field, 40,000 times that of the earth's. "The magnet is strong enough
to jerk a two-pound wrench right out of your hand," says Alexander Margulis,
50    chairman of radiology at San Francisco. The New York Hospital facility has
one of the most powerful magnets of any machine in the United States. Yet
the magnetic fields are not thought to harm the human body at all. In an
NMR scan, encircling coils pulse the body with radio waves. Different kinds
of atoms in the body reemit radio signals in response, but atoms of hydrogen,
55    common throughout in the form of water, respond especially strongly.

The signals alone provide information about the body's biochemistry. In
addition, some say the computer can process the signals to form images of
the body with even greater clarity than PET scans. NMR does not work well

only where motion can blur the image, such as in the bowel or the coronary
60   artery. "NMR clearly has wider applications than any of the other techniques,"
says Stanford's Jardetzky. "It will replace PET scans since both are doing
essentially the same thing—testing chemicals in the body."

Not far south of San Francisco, Barbara A. Carroll of Stanford University
Medical Center's diagnostic radiology department is one of those combining
65   ultrasound with computer processing to screen patients quickly, safely, and
inexpensively for disease.

By combining ultrasound, which makes images of the body's interior using
high-frequency sound waves, and processing on a computer, doctors can
make "movies" of motions in the body that ultrasound still pictures would
70   miss. The computer processes ultrasound into images thirty times a second.

"The way things move or don't move can often tell us when something's
wrong," says Carroll. "At thirty frames a second there's a lot more information
about the flow of blood and urine or bowel and bladder contractions than on
a single picture."

75   Computers have not only made these new medical technologies possible
but have greatly enhanced an old one. Paired with a computer, the X-ray is
looking at the body in ways it never has before. Modern CAT scanners
(Computer Assisted Tomography) use computer processing and multiple
X-ray beams to produce three-dimensional images of the body. Says William
80   Brody of the Stanford University Medical Center, "The earliest CAT scanners
narrowed the X-ray source down to a pencil-sized beam, passed it through
the brain in one plane from every possible direction, then put that information
into a computer. And the computer can construct a picture of the plane. It
essentially cuts the brain in two. The first scanner twelve years ago took
85   fifteen minutes to collect the information and twelve hours to reconstruct the
image. Now scanners with multiple X-ray beams routinely acquire the same
data in one second and reconstruct the image in thirty."

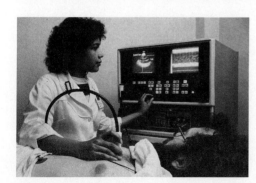

Ultrasound that shows the heart in motion

Magnetic Resonance Imaging

These new machines are giving physicians unprecedented power to
understand the human body. But the more physicians use magnetic fields,
90  radiation, and sound waves to probe our sick bodies as though we were
malfunctioning devices, the more they may appear to be technicians rather
than healers.

The widespread use of these devices may be costly both in economic
and social terms. "The field is moving so fast," says Richard Riegelman of
95  George Washington University Medical Center, "and in so many new directions that no one can predict to what uses they will be put tomorrow." While
some of these applications may save dying patients by leading to the proper
choice of a treatment, an improper, untested use of these machines might
lead to the wrong diagnosis, a mistake that could cost a patient's life. And
100  for everyone, these machines will probably mean increased health care
expenditure—some cost in the million-dollar range, not including supporting
facilities, and require teams of specialists to operate them.

The most wrenching result of heavy reliance on high-technology medicine
might be the further loss of personal contact between doctor and patient.
105  "Medicine," observes Lewis Thomas in *The Youngest Science*, "is no longer
the laying on of hands—it is more like the reading of signals from machines."

The years to come may see the further mechanization of medicine, but
ironically, the high cost of the machinery may have strengthened an opposing
trend as well. "I think we've begun to discover the less technological aspects
110  of medicine," says Ronald Bayer of the Hastings Center in New York. "One
of the reasons for this trend is that we aren't able to afford all the high
technology anymore." Thus the choices facing the health care system might
ultimately help renew the human bond between doctor and patient.

**Jack Fincher**

## Reviewing Study Skills

Before doing the exercises, make an outline or a study map of the article.
Compare it with those of your classmates. Use your study aid to help
you with the following exercises.

## Recalling Information

Choose the best way of finishing each statement, based on what you
have just read.

1. Machines such as the PET and CAT scanners, the NMR, and ultrasound are mainly used for:
   a. surgical operations
   b. diagnosing illnesses
   c. treating patients
2. They are better than the traditional procedures of inserting tubes
   or cutting out pieces of living tissue because:

    a. they cause almost no pain or damage
    b. they are much less expensive
    c. they are easier to administer
    d. all of the above

3. In order to enable doctors to see inside the patient's brain, heart, eye, or other part of the body, these machines use:

    a. X-rays
    b. radiation
    c. sound waves
    d. magnetic fields
    e. all of the above
    f. three of the above

4. An essential element in the use of these machines is the:

    a. telephone
    b. computer
    c. microscope

5. The only one of these machines that was mentioned as operating inexpensively was the one Barbara Carroll was using to screen patients for disease. This was:

    a. the PET scanner
    b. the CAT scanner
    c. the NMR
    d. ultrasound

6. From the point of view of the doctor, one danger posed by these machines is that he or she may appear to be more of a(n):

    a. healer
    b. technician
    c. expert
    d. professional

7. From the point of view of the patient, one danger posed by these machines is that their complexity could lead to improper use. This might then:

    a. cost the patient his or her life through a misdiagnosis
    b. increase the patient's dependence on one single doctor
    c. prevent the patient from fully understanding the treatment

## Identifying Important Differences

Can you match each description to the correct name? Can you think of any mnemonic device to keep track of which machine uses which method?

\_\_\_\_\_ 1. a very new technique that uses radioactive tracers attached to chemicals

\_\_\_\_\_ 2. a device that places a patient in a very powerful magnetic field

\_\_\_\_\_ 3. the rather old technology of the X-ray, combined with a computer

\_\_\_\_\_ 4. uses sound waves, teamed with a computer

a. CAT scanner

b. ultrasound

c. PET scanner

d. NMR

# Making Inferences

Read the following excerpts. Then answer the questions, which involve making inferences.

1. "The most wrenching result of heavy reliance on high-technology medicine might be the further loss of personal contact between doctor and patient. 'Medicine,' observes Lewis Thomas in *The Youngest Science*, 'is no longer the laying on of hands—it is more like the reading of signals from machines.'"

   What can you infer from this passage about the author's attitude toward modern medical progress?

   _____

   _____

2. "'NMR clearly has wider applications than any of the other techniques,' says Stanford's Jardetzky. 'It will replace PET scans since both are doing essentially the same thing—testing chemicals in the body.'"

   What can you infer about the attitudes of some of the doctors and researchers?

   _____

   _____

3. "The first scanner twelve years ago took fifteen minutes to collect the information and twelve hours to reconstruct the image. Now scanners with multiple X-ray beams routinely acquire the same data in one second and reconstruct the image in thirty."

   What can you infer about the rate of change in high-technology medicine?

   _____

   _____

# Using a Study Aid to Give an Oral Description

Your teacher may ask you to go before the class and describe one of the medical machines described in the article. Use the appropriate part of your outline or study map to help you do this.

## Talking It Over

1. What do you see as the benefits of the new medical technology?

2. What problems are there with it? Which problem do you think is the most serious?

3. In your opinion, will the doctor-patient relationship get better or worse? Why?

## SELECTION TWO

# ▥ Cancer Therapy

Machines, computers, technology—all are being used to help diagnose and cure a patient's ills. But how does the patient feel while going through the process of being tested or treated by these complicated devices? Is it dehumanizing? Frightening? Strange? The following poem was written by a woman who underwent successful cobalt therapy for cancer.

### Cancer Therapy

The iron door clanks shut
On creaky metal hinges,
And I am utterly alone
As in my mother's womb.

5  Laser
          Danger
                   Radiation

The cobalt machine clicks.
I hear a humming sound
10  And feel . . . nothing.
Minutes evaporate.

The hinges slowly recoil,
The iron door creaks open
To admit humanity
15  And laughing voices:

I am born again.

**Amy Azen**

## Talking It Over

1. What are the woman's feelings while undergoing therapy?

2. What does the line "I am born again" mean?

3. In modern medicine is there too much emphasis on technology and too little on comforting the patient? Explain.

## SELECTION THREE

# ▉ Best of Both Worlds

Why is it that when you talk to a person with definite beliefs in the superiority of one culture, it almost always turns out that this "superior" culture is his or her own? It is very rare to find people open-minded enough to admit that other cultures can bring them new benefits. That is why the experiment now taking place in Nigeria, with encouragement from both the national government and WHO (the World Health Organization), is so special. Instead of conflict and competition, there is an attempt to create harmony and cooperation between two very different medical traditions.

### Prereading Exercise: Distinguishing Shades of Meaning

If you were in Nigeria and you saw one Nigerian helping another who was sick, you could describe the person who was helping with one of the following three terms. Look at them and tell what picture comes to your mind for each.

witch doctor
medical practitioner
traditional healer

1. Which of these do you think is a flattering term?

   _____

2. Which is a pejorative (negative) term?

   _____

3. Which is a neutral term?

   _____

4. After looking at the title and photo, which term do you think will be used in the article? Why?

   _____

5. What contribution do you think traditional medicine can make to Western medicine? And vice versa?

   _____

   _____

   _____

Read to see if you are right.

# Best of Both Worlds

In our culture, we are accustomed to sophisticated prescription drugs containing a variety of chemical ingredients. Few of us realize that many of the drugs we use today originally came from forests or gardens instead of large pharmaceutical laboratories. Valerian tea is a sleep inducer from the valerian
5 root; digitalis, used in cases of congestive heart failure, comes from the foxglove plant; and oral contraceptive drugs are extracted from a vegetable: the black yam.

The revolution taking place in Nigeria today is one of culture mix rather than clash—experimental establishment of a dual health care system that
10 draws from tradition and modern science and offers the people of the most populous nation in black Africa the best of both worlds.

Under British colonial rule, the practice of traditional medicine was discouraged or sometimes forbidden in Nigeria. Traditional healers were called "witch doctors" by the colonizers, who viewed their medical practices as
15 inferior. Since independence, the Nigerian government has decided to give these healers official recognition. Although discouraged, the practice of traditional medicine never died out during the colonial era. The government's current position is a recognition of reality—that healers serve a great majority of the Nigerian people. Nigeria's experiment is a chance to see whether
20 developing countries can make use of a great resource: traditional doctors who have inherited centuries of folkloric knowledge about medicinal drugs.

Traditional healers practice a rich and ancient art based on an oral literature. It is a medical lore that uses herbs and roots from which are derived basic drugs, as in the West, but that has another vital element: the spiritual.
25 It is not uncommon in Nigeria to follow up a hospital treatment with treatment by a priest, for the equally important cure of the soul.

BARBARA HOLECEK FOR WGBH, BOSTON

Chief Fagbenro

The members of Nigeria's National Herbalist Association are pooling their knowledge about the medicines they use and the dosages they prescribe. Under colonial rule, these healers practiced in great secrecy. Now they are
30   eager to share and compare their knowledge—and to cooperate in the modern research being carried out to systematize it. Chief Fagbenro, a healer and an Ifa priest, is an excellent advertisement for his own cures. At seventy years old, he has had to go to a doctor of modern medicine only once, when one of his legs had to be amputated. He's quite willing to admit the value of
35   surgery, but prefers to live by the ancient traditions. He believes that traditional medicine has the advantage of using nature's own cures to conquer human ailments. "But," he points out, "all medical practices have their merit."

The new collaboration between the herbalist and the modern doctor has uncovered previously unrecognized benefits of traditional cures. The fagara
40   root, for example, has long been used in Nigeria to clean the teeth. While testing the root chemically, Western-trained scientists discovered that, brewed and drunk like tea, it also appears to combat the genetic blood disease sickle-cell anemia.

Scientific methods are also classifying and verifying the healing properties
45   of other herbal remedies. The oldenlandia root, used by traditional healers to accelerate labor contractions in pregnant women, has been tested in the laboratory by university-trained scientists, who have used it to produce similar contractions in pregnant rats. A tea brewed from the leaves of the neem tree combats malarial fevers. Scoopa, known in the West as redberry, helps cure
50   jaundice. Alukrese, a creeping plant, is used to prepare the Nigerian equivalent of iodine. Its leaves, when crushed and applied to an open wound, stop blood flow and kill bacteria. And oruwa—whose botanical name is sincona— is mixed with water to form a healing potion that has been found to combat yellow fever.

55   In the marriage of traditional and Western medicine, neither partner reigns superior. Where one fails, the other succeeds. One of the strengths of traditional medicine is its spiritual emphasis. Western doctors have recently begun to acknowledge the importance of psychological factors in maintaining health. But the Nigerians have understood this connection for ages. Tradi-
60   tional Nigerian healers view physical illness as an outward manifestation of a spiritual problem.

While traditional medical practitioners like Chief Fagbenro are helping Western scientists catalogue an international stock of drugs, Western medicine makes contributions to the promotion and maintenance of public health
65   in Nigeria in areas previously unappreciated by traditional practice. Concepts of patient hygiene and public sanitation to provide a cleaner environment are crucial to Nigeria's public health policy. Although taken for granted in industrial nations, the keeping of written records and the immunization of children against common diseases are becoming as important to Nigerian mothers
70   as thanking the gods in song.

**Barbara Gullahorn-Holecek**

# Recalling Major Points of Contrast

This article contrasts two types of medicine: traditional Nigerian and modern Western. Indicate which of them is described by each of the following statements by writing T (traditional) or M (modern). In some cases it might be both or neither.

_____ 1. uses drugs that originally come from herbs and roots

_____ 2. serves a great majority of the Nigerian people

_____ 3. almost died out during the colonial era

_____ 4. concerns itself with a spiritual as well as a physical cure

_____ 5. uses tea brewed from leaves to combat malarial fevers

_____ 6. stops the blood flow from an open wound and kills bacteria by applying a remedy consisting of crushed leaves

_____ 7. includes a medicine that fights yellow fever

_____ 8. has emphasized the importance of psychological factors for ages

_____ 9. has recognized the importance of cleanliness to public health for a long time

_____ 10. emphasizes the importance of written records and of immunizing children against common diseases

# Paraphrasing Key Ideas

Restate the main ideas expressed in each of the following sentences in your own words, as simply and clearly as possible.

1. "The government's current position is a recognition of reality— that healers serve a great majority of the Nigerian people."

_____

_____

2. "Traditional healers practice a rich and ancient art based on an oral literature."

_____

_____

3. "The members of Nigeria's National Herbalist Association are pooling their knowledge about the medicines they use and the dosages they prescribe."

_____

_____

4. "Chief Fagbenro, a healer and an Ifa priest, is an excellent advertisement for his own cures."

_____

_____

5. "In the marriage of traditional and Western medicine, neither partner reigns superior."

_____

_____

# Identifying and Evaluating the Point of View

1. How would you describe the point of view of the author toward the traditional practitioners?

_____

_____

_____

2. What kinds of facts or opinions might have been included by an author with an opposing point of view?

_____

_____

_____

3. Would you have liked the article better if the author had also included some ideas from the opposing point of view and then disproved them? Why or why not?

_____

_____

# Talking It Over

1. What do you think is the most important contribution that traditional medicine (from many cultures) can make to modern medicine? What about the reverse?

2. The article states that Chief Fagbenro believes in using nature's own cures to conquer ailments, then quotes him as saying, "But all medical practices have their merit." What inference can you make about Chief Fagbenro from this statement?

3. If you became ill while visiting Nigeria, would you go to a healer or a Western doctor? Why?

4. What do you think of the following proverbs related to health? Can you think of any from your own culture?

**PROVERBS**

An apple a day keeps the doctor away.

Early to bed and early to rise
makes a man healthy, wealthy, and wise.

# S E L E C T I O N   F O U R

# The Scientist-Philosophers

A tree does not grow without roots. Much of the basis of modern medical science has its origins in the distant past. The following selection is taken from a book by British writer Desmond Stewart, who has taught literature in Iraq and Lebanon and traveled widely in the Middle East. It presents a brief historical glimpse of some of the key personalities of the Muslim world of the Middle Ages, who have left an indelible imprint on the art and science of medicine.

## Prereading Exercise: Anticipating the Reading

The presence of the past is all around us, but few North Americans realize how much of it we owe to the ancient medieval world of the Muslims. From common words we say every day, such as *zero*, *alcohol*, *almanac*, and *algebra*, to the geometric decorations on our finest carpets and tiles, to the system of numbers we use (and thank goodness that we don't have to use those cumbersome roman numerals!), this influence touches us. Do you know why the Muslims so excelled in the creation of intricate geometric designs instead of trying to portray animals and human figures? This relates to one of the instructions in the Koran. Can you guess what it is?

_____

_____

One of the greatest legacies of Islam to the world is in the field of medicine. Which of the following aspects of medicine do you think were pioneered or improved upon by Muslims in the ninth and tenth centuries? Cross out the ones that were not.

cranial and vascular surgery (surgery on the skull and veins)

the differentiation (description which shows differences) of a specific disease by its symptoms

mobile clinics

medical libraries

CAT scanners

hospitals with dispensaries (shops that give out drugs) and psychiatric wards

the removal of cataracts from the eye

cancer operations

pharmacies that filled prescriptions

examinations for medical specialists before being allowed to practice

the emphasis on hygiene (cleanliness) to prevent illness

Read to find out if you are right.

## The Scientist-Philosophers

Modern human beings—dependent as they are on the drugs of the chemist and the skills of the physician, on the reckoning of the computer and the predictions of the economic planner—owe more of a debt than they might suspect to the Islamic scientists of the Middle Ages. Between the ninth and
5    fourteenth centuries, Muslim chemists, physicians, astronomers, mathematicians, geographers, and others not only kept alive the disciplines of Greek science but extended their range, laying and strengthening the foundations on which much of modern science is built. Many scientific terms with Arabic roots, from *algebra* to *zenith*, reflect to this day Islam's activity in fields where
10    knowledge was widened and human suffering decreased.

Although the Muslims excelled in many branches of science, some of their most significant contributions were in medicine. Before the great intellectual awakening, Arab medical knowledge had been largely limited to desert superstitions, including the use of magic, talismans and protective prayers,
15    and a few primitive remedies.

Starting in the eighth century, the Muslims gradually developed a more sophisticated approach to medicine. The main impetus came from the Persian medical school at Jundishapur, whose teachings were based primarily on the Greek practice of treating disease by rational methods. According to

A Muslim medical consultation scene from the year 1151

20 tradition, the contact between Jundishapur and the rulers of Islam began in 765, not out of the search for universal truth, but due to a more urgent and personal reason—a chronic indigestion that troubled Mansur, the founder of Baghdad. The caliph's own physicians had not been able to cure him; in despair, he invited the chief physician of Jundishapur to come to Baghdad 25 and treat him. The physician, a Christian named Jurjis ibn Bakhtishu', succeeded in returning the ruler to health where the others had failed, and as a reward, he was appointed court physician.

Like Jurjis, most of Islam's early medical practitioners were Persian-born, but they spoke and wrote Arabic, the language of scholarship during the 30 Middle Ages. One of the most celebrated of these Eastern physicians was Razi, who lived from 865 to 925. His importance was so great that his colleagues called him "the Experienced." The finest clinician of the age, he has been compared to Hippocrates for his originality in describing disease.

Razi, known in Europe by his Latin name, Rhazes, is said to have written 35 more than 200 books, ranging in subject matter from medicine and alchemy to theology and astronomy. About half the books are on medicine, including a well-known treatise on smallpox. In his discussion of smallpox, Razi was the first to differentiate a specific disease from among many eruptive fevers that attacked man. By giving the clinical symptoms of smallpox, he enabled 40 doctors to diagnose it correctly and to predict the course of the disease. He also recommended a treatment for the ailment that has been little improved on since his time. He urged gentle therapy—good diet and good nursing care, which meant about what it does today: rest, clean surroundings, and keeping the patient comfortable.

45 While Razi knew nothing about bacteria, the theory of which was not to be discovered until the early seventeenth century, he had an intuitive sense of hygienic principles far ahead of medieval standards. To appreciate his insight, it must be remembered that he lived in a world where contamination and filth were so common as to go almost unnoticed, and infections and

50    contagious diseases cut down millions. Against this unsanitary background,
he was once asked to choose the site for a new hospital in Baghdad. To do
so, he suspended pieces of meat at various points around the city, and at
the location where the meat decomposed most slowly, he recommended
building the hospital.

55    The crowning work of Razi's career was a monumental encyclopedia in
which he compiled Greek, Syrian, Persian, Hindu, and early Arabic knowledge, as well as personal observations based on his own extensive clinical
experience. This book offered striking insights for its time and had a wide
influence in shaping European medicine.

60    Great as Razi was, he was at least equaled in stature by another Arabic-
speaking Persian Muslim, Ibn Sina, better known in the West by his Latin
name, Avicenna. Called "the Prince of Philosophers" by his contemporaries,
he is still recognized as one of the great minds of all time. He lived from 980
to 1037 and wrote some 170 books on philosophy, medicine, mathematics,
65    and astronomy, as well as poems and religious works. He is said to have
memorized the entire Koran when he was only ten years old, and at eighteen
he was personal physician to the sultan of Bukhara, in Turkestan.

Avicenna's most renowned achievement was the *Canon of Medicine*, an
encyclopedia that dealt with virtually every phase of the treatment of disease.
70    Probably no other medieval work of its kind was so widely studied; from the
twelfth to the seventeenth centuries it served as the chief guide to medical
science in European universities.

Ibn Sina is now credited with such personal contributions as recognizing
the contagious nature of tuberculosis and describing certain skin diseases
75    and psychological disorders. Among the latter was lovesickness, the effects
of which were described as loss of weight and strength, fever, and various
chronic ailments. The cure was quite simple, once the diagnosis was made—
to have the sufferer united with the one he or she was longing for. Ibn Sina
also observed that certain diseases can be spread by water and soil, an
80    advanced view for his time.

Islamic physicians also helped develop the science of surgery, although
it was considered a minor branch of medicine. This art had been largely
neglected until the Spanish-born physician Abulcasis wrote about it in the
tenth century. Most of his work was based on that of a Greek, Paul of Aegina,
85    and contained illustrations of various surgical instruments and procedures.

Muslim physicians performed many remarkably complex operations for
their time, including cranial and vascular surgery and operations for cancer.
Avicenna gave them advice on the treatment of the latter disease that would
still be timely today—to minister to it in its earliest state and to remove all
90    of the diseased tissue as the only hope of cure. Other operations included
delicate abdominal surgery, involving the use of drainage tubes, and the
amputation of diseased arms and legs.

For these operations various anesthetics were administered to render patients unconscious; among them was opium, which was sometimes made more potent by mixing it with wine.

Before a man could practice surgery, he had to have special training and pass tests on his knowledge of anatomy and Galen's writings. In addition, specialists were required to have extensive information about the particular area in which they practiced. Ophthalmologists, for example, had to undergo an examination about their detailed knowledge of the eye, as well as be able to mix certain compounds to treat various eye ailments. Islamic physicians were especially skilled in treating eye diseases, perhaps because such ailments were so widespread in the Middle East. They wrote textbooks on ophthalmology and invented an ingenious method of operating on soft cataracts of the eye, using a tube to suck out the fluid that filled the capsule of the eye lens; this method was used for several centuries before it was replaced by more modern techniques.

In the treatment of other sickness with drugs, the Muslims were equally progressive. Most Islamic physicians prepared their own compounds, but Baghdad had pharmacies that filled prescriptions much as present-day drugstores do. These pharmacies sold a wide range of remedies made from animal and plant products and even more sophisticated inorganic compounds like copper sulphate, which acted as a binding substance to help heal open cuts by drawing the tissues together.

Doctors who were found qualified to practice treated many of their patients in hospitals much as modern physicians do. As early as the start of the ninth century, Baghdad had its first hospital, probably copied from the one connected with the medical school at Jundishapur. Soon other hospitals began to spring up, and before long, records indicate that there were thirty-four throughout the Muslim world. Some of these hospitals must have been surprisingly modern; in the larger cities they had different wards for the treatment of different illnesses, and special quarters for the insane. They also had outpatient departments for the immediate treatment of minor injuries, while patients with more serious complaints were admitted to a ward.

One of the most important parts of an Islamic hospital was its dispensary, which provided virtually every kind of remedy then known. Hospitals also had their own medical libraries for the use of doctors and their students. Physicians visited their patients and prescribed medications. In the eleventh century, traveling clinics appeared, to serve areas beyond the hospitals' reach. These were moved from place to place on the backs of camels and were generally run by one or more doctors. When they stopped in a village or remote spot, they erected a tent, examined the sick, and dispensed the necessary medications. These mobile clinics were also used in time of epidemics when hospitals were filled to overflowing.

**Desmond Stewart**
*Great Ages of Man/Early Islam*

# Recalling Information

Choose the best way of finishing each statement, based on what you have just read.

1. Before the great intellectual awakening in the eighth century, Arab medical knowledge was largely limited to:

   a. desert superstitions
   b. practices of the Greeks
   c. drugs imported from Persia

2. In the ninth century Razi, "the Experienced," was the first to describe specific distinguishing symptoms of a disease. This was important because doctors could then:

   a. write books about it
   b. diagnose it and predict its course
   c. relate it to many other eruptive fevers

3. Razi wrote an enormous encyclopedia that included medical knowledge from:

   a. Greece and India
   b. Persia and Syria
   c. his own clinical observations
   d. all of the above

4. Ibn Sina, "the Prince of Philosophers," was known in the West as:

   a. the sultan of Bukhara
   b. Aristotle
   c. Avicenna

5. One of Ibn Sina's views that was advanced for his time was that certain diseases:

   a. could be caused by love
   b. are spread by water and soil
   c. can result in loss of weight

6. Medieval Muslim surgeons performed operations for all of the following problems except:

   a. cancer
   b. heart
   c. eye
   d. vascular
   e. abdominal

7. Islamic doctors were especially good in the field of:

   a. psychiatry   b. cardiology   c. ophthalmology

8. Ninth-century Muslim hospitals were:

   a. quite similar in organization to modern ones
   b. simple tents with all patients placed together
   c. nonexistent; doctors made house calls instead

9. In the eleventh century, the Muslim solution to caring for patients in remote areas was:

   a. the creation of pharmacies in all small towns and oases
   b. traveling clinics that moved on the backs of camels
   c. an emergency service that brought patients to the doctor's house

## Recognizing Historical Significance in Anecdotes

Fortunately, most historians sprinkle historical fact with anecdotes (colorful stories about interesting or amusing events). These are useful memory aids because they generally illustrate or support major ideas that the historian wants to present. Tell what larger idea each of the following anecdotes illustrates.

1. Razi, who lived at the end of the ninth century, suspended a piece of meat at various points around the city in order to select the site for a new hospital.

   _____

2. In 765, Mansur, the caliph of Baghdad, was suffering from a painful chronic stomachache and found that his own doctors could not cure him.

   _____

3. The brilliant Arabic-speaking Persian of the eleventh century, Ibn Sina, is said to have memorized the entire Koran at the age of ten.

   _____

   _____

## Matching the Illness with the Cure

If you were a Muslim doctor in the Middle Ages, what would you prescribe for the following medical problems? How many of these remedies are still in use today? Write the letter of the appropriate cure in front of each description.

_____ 1. an open wound that is bleeding

_____ 2. smallpox, in which the patient develops serious, high fevers

_____ 3. lovesickness, which is causing loss of weight and strength

_____ 4. the need for an anesthetic before an operation

_____ 5. a soft cataract of the eye

_____ 6. cancer

**CURES**
a. Drink a mixture of opium and wine.
b. Cut out the diseased tissue at the earliest possible stage.
c. Use "gentle therapy": good diet and good nursing care.
d. Suck out the fluid in the lens.
e. Use copper sulphate or other chemicals to draw tissues together.
f. Unite the patient with the object of his or her desire.

## Talking It Over

1. In your opinion, which of the accomplishments discussed in the selection is most impressive? Why?

2. Which do you consider more important for a doctor, intuition or intelligence? Explain.

3. Describe the Muslim hospital of the Middle Ages. In what ways does it seem very modern? What do you think was its most important feature?

### TIMED READING

# ■ "You Haven't Heard Anything Yet"

Just how bad is the AIDS (Acquired Immune Deficiency Syndrome) epidemic? How does it compare with other diseases of the past? Read the following excerpt from a *Time* magazine article to find out. Take two minutes and read for main ideas. Then take another five minutes to finish the reading and complete the exercise at the end, looking back to the article only when necessary.

### *"You Haven't Heard Anything Yet"*

It was A.D. 1348, one year after the bubonic plague, or black death, had begun its devastating rampage through Europe. In a famous medical treatise French surgeon Guy de Chauliac of Avignon recalled his impressions of the horror around him: "The father did not visit the son nor the son the father.
5    Charity was dead and hope abandoned. . . . For self-preservation there was nothing better than to flee the region before becoming infected."

Guy's patients died within five days of falling ill. Cities were decimated in a matter of months. The scourge was so contagious that, according to Guy, ". . . no one could approach or even see a patient without taking the disease."
10    By the time the epidemic subsided a few years later, at least a quarter to a third of all Europeans—perhaps 25 million people—had perished.

Today's plague is a very different beast. AIDS works its way through a population slowly, over a period of years and even decades. It also tends to kill slowly, laying waste to the immune system so that patients fall prey to a

15 debilitating succession of infections. Unlike the plague of Guy's era, it is
spread only through the most intimate forms of human contact: sexual inter-
course, childbearing, the sharing of contaminated blood or needles.

Yet as the AIDS death toll climbs and statisticians project its probable
course into the next decade, comparisons with history's greatest killers begin
20 to make sense. "If we can't make progress, we face the dreadful prospect
of a worldwide death toll in the tens of millions a decade from now," warned
U.S. Health and Human Services Secretary Otis Bowen at a recent gathering
of the National Press Club. Such earlier epidemics as typhus, smallpox, and
even the black death will "look very pale by comparison," he continued. "You
25 haven't read or heard anything yet."

The projections, if accurate, would bear him out:

- Cases of AIDS have been reported in 85 countries, though the World
  Health Organization suspects that the disease has actually struck as
  many as 100 nations. WHO officials estimate that between 5 million
30   and 10 million people around the world now carry the AIDS virus and
  that as many as 100 million will become infected during the next ten
  years.
- In the United States, more than 30,000 cases have been reported and
  another 1.5 million people are thought to be carriers. If the epidemic
35   continues to spread at its current rate, the Centers for Disease Control
  (CDC) in Atlanta predicts, the total number of cases will reach 270,000

over the next five years, while total AIDS deaths will rise to 179,000.
Fearsome as that count is, it falls short of the tolls taken by the influenza epidemic of 1918–19 (500,000 U.S. deaths) and by polio in the
40    mid-'40s to mid-'50s (360,000 cases with 20,000 deaths). But then
again, AIDS is still gathering steam.

▪    In Africa, as many as 2 million to 5 million may already be infected,
and in ten years, predicts epidemiologist B. Frank Polk of Johns Hop-
kins University, "some countries could lose 25 percent of their popula-
45    tion." The loss in terms of the economy and social structure could well
equal the black death's ruination of medieval Europe.

▪    AIDS is posing an economic threat in the United States. The cost of
caring for victims of the disease, many of whom are denied health
insurance, is already estimated to exceed a billion dollars a year. By
50    1991 AIDS medical bills could total as much as $14 billion annually,
according to health economist Anne Scitovsky of the Palo Alto (California) Medical Research Foundation, "and that does not begin to address
the loss in productivity from the death of people in the prime of life."

▪    The prognosis for carriers of the virus seems bleaker than previously
55    imagined. While public health officials first believed that perhaps 10
percent of those infected would go on to develop AIDS, evidence now
suggests that at least 50 percent of them will progress to the full-blown
disease. As more cases are reported, researchers have come to realize that the chances of developing AIDS are greater in the second five
60    years after infection than in the first. "As time goes on," says Dr. James
Curran, a top AIDS epidemiologist at the CDC, "only a minority of
infected people will remain healthy. I feel less optimistic about a normal
life span for *any* infected person. . . ."

**Claudia Wallis and Dick Thompson**

## Completion Quiz

Finish the following statements about the article. Then check your time
and the accuracy of your answers and compare them with your classmates.

1. AIDS differs from the bubonic plague ("black death") in two main
ways:

   a. _____

   b. _____

2. WHO officials estimate that about 5 to 10 million people in the
world carry the AIDS virus but that in the next ten years:

   _____

3. In comparison with the destructive power of the U.S. influenza epidemic of 1918–19 and the polio epidemic of the 1940s and 1950s, the epidemic of AIDS in the United States:

_____

4. Meanwhile, in Africa some countries might lose:

_____

5. AIDS represents an economic problem in the United States because:

_____

6. In comparison with a few years ago the prognosis for those carrying the AIDS virus is now:

_____

# The Future

Fortuneteller with crystal ball.

Prophets and prophecies have existed at all times, in all countries, and among all peoples. Recently, more and more books have been appearing on this theme, and in the following excerpts from two of them you have the opportunity to speculate on the accuracy and feasibility of predictions about the future. The first selection, just recently published in book form, is a prophecy by two nineteenth-century European peasants. To some, their predictions seem frighteningly accurate. Next, excerpts from the *Omni Future Almanac* discuss the troubling global problem of overpopulation and speculate on life in space colonies. The third selection deals with a group that, not content with trying to see the future, is instead trying to make the future. They are creating a revolutionary form of urban life and a model for others—in the middle of the Arizona desert. Then comes a short, poignant science-fiction story written from a highly unusual point of view. Finally, a timed reading offers you a new kind of friendship in a futuristic fantasy that might some day turn into fact.

## SELECTION ONE

# The Kremani Prophecies

Two peasants, Milos and Mitar Tarabic, known for their ability to predict the future, lived in the village of Kremani, Serbia* in the nineteenth century. Since they were illiterate, a village priest recorded their fascinating prophecies, which recently have been published in a book titled *The Kremani Prophecies*. Milos died in 1854 and Mitar, his nephew, in 1899. The following excerpt from their book of predictions about the future is translated from the Serbo-Croatian language by Robert Gakovich. In the translation, Mr. Gakovich uses the same colorful and simple terminology used by the Tarabics.

Could these two simple men possibly have possessed the ability to see into the future? Read the following excerpts from the book of their prophecies and judge for yourself.

### Prereading Exercise: Anticipating the Reading

Have you ever gone to a fortuneteller who tried to predict your future through the date of your birth, a deck of cards, or some other means?

---

*Serbia is now part of the country of Yugoslavia.

COURTESY OF NICK VICINICH & SERB WORLD U.S.A.

Serbian villagers in Hercegovinia

List as many different ways of predicting the future as you can think of that are actually in use. Which method is most popular in your culture?

_____

_____

Compare your list with those of your classmates. Then take a minute to examine your attitude toward prophecy and prediction by answering these questions:

1. Are any methods of predicting the future reliable, in your opinion? Which methods are based on deception?

2. Why do you think that astrology and fortunetelling are so popular?

3. Besides the Kremani prophecies, what other predictions have you heard about that are said to have been accurate? Do you expect the Kremani prophecies to make similar predictions?

Now, before beginning, take a moment to "suspend your disbelief." Read with an open mind and pay attention to what objects and events, according to the Kremani in the mid-nineteenth century, the future would bring.

## The Kremani Prophecies

### Second World War

All of Europe will be under the rule of the *Crooked Cross* (Swastika). Russia will not be involved until the aggressor's army attacks her. At that time Russia will be ruled by the *Red Tsar*. Russia will unite with the countries across the seas and, together with them, destroy the *Crooked Cross* and liberate all the
5   enslaved peoples of Europe.

## Post World War II Period

Then there will be peace, and across the world many new countries will emerge. Some black, some white, some red, and some yellow. Some kind of *elected court* will be created which will prevent countries from going against each other. That *elected court* will be above all nations. In places where war would break out, this court would arbitrate and restore peace. After a while some small and large countries will stop respecting this court. They will say that they respect the court but, in reality, they will do what they wish.

After the Second Great War people will not fight with such intensity for a long time. There will be wars but they will be smaller wars. Thousands and thousands of people will be dying in these small wars but the world war will not happen yet. There will be some wars near the country of Judea but, little by little, peace will come in that area. In these wars brother will fight against brother and then they will make peace. However, the hate will still remain within themselves. A period of relative peace will continue for a long time.

Some kind of disease will spread all over the world and nobody will be able to find a cure for it. In their search for the cure of this disease people will be trying all kinds of things but they will still not be able to find the cure. In reality the cure will be all around them and inside them as well. Man will build a box with some machine in it that makes images and he will be able to see what is happening everywhere in the entire world. People will drill wells in the ground and pump some kind of gold which will produce light, speed, and power. The earth will weep because of that. Man will not know that more energy and light exists on the surface of the earth. Only after many years people will discover this and they will realize that they were fools to be drilling holes in the ground. There will also be great power in the people themselves but it will take many years until they discover it and use it. Wise men will appear in the East and their ideas will spread all over the world. For a long time, people will not accept their ideas and will declare them to be false.

In one country in the North a man will suddenly appear. He will teach people about love and friendship. Most will refuse to accept the noble teachings of this man. However, books about his teachings will remain and people will later realize what kind of fools they were for not accepting his ideas.

When fragrance no longer exists in wild flowers, when goodness is no longer present in men, when rivers are no longer healthy, the biggest world war will then begin. Those who escape in the mountains and woods will survive and will live after the war in peace and prosperity because there will never be any more wars. When this horrible war starts, the most casualties will be suffered by armies that fly in the sky. Fortunate will be the soldiers who shall be fighting on land and on sea. The people who will be conducting this war will have scientists and wise men who will invent all kinds of shells. Some of these shells, when they explode, will not kill soldiers but will instead put them to sleep so they will not be able to fight. Only one country, far away,

50 big as Europe and surrounded by large oceans, will be peaceful and spared
from this horror. She will not be involved in this war.

Before this last big war, the world will be divided in half, the same as an
apple when it is cut in two. Two halves of an apple can never be put together
to restore the whole apple again. Just before this big war begins, a large
country, across great seas, will be ruled by a ruler who will be a farmer and
55 a *chaush*.\* He will no longer allow the Red Ruler to expand his empire. There
will be skirmishes and threats. This Ruler will not attack the Red Empire. He
will only make threats. The princes, who will be created by this Ruler, will
be meaner and more aggressive. They will be the ones who will start the
war.

60 After this war the whole world will be ruled by a noble and good red-
headed man. Fortunate will be those who will live under him because this
red-headed ruler will bring happiness to all. He will have a long life and will
rule until his death. During his reign and after him, there will never be any
more wars. However, the peace and prosperity which will come about after
65 the last world war will only be a bitter illusion because people will forget God
and they will worship man's intelligence. Man will go to other worlds but he
will find emptiness and wasteland there. He will still think that he knows
everything. He will find the Lord's serenity in other worlds which he will reach.
People will drive carts on the moon and other worlds looking for other life
70 forms there, but they will not find life there as they know it to be on earth.
There will be life there but it will be the kind of life that man will not understand.
Those who will travel to other worlds and who will not believe in God, after
they return to earth, will say: "All you people, who doubt or do not believe in
God, just go where we were and you will realize the meaning of the power
75 and wisdom of God."

**Milos and Mitar Tarabic**
**Translated from Serbo-Croatian by Robert Gakovich**

## Relating Prophecies to Past, Present, and Future

Working with a partner or in a small group, summarize what the Tarabics predicted about two of the following subjects. Be sure to point
out which parts have already come true in the past, which seem perhaps
to be coming true at present, and which relate to the unknown future.
Afterwards, one person should read the summary to the class.

1. inventions and technological advances
2. political groups and institutions
3. wars and disease
4. important leaders
5. ecology and space travel

\*chaush   (1) entertainer at wedding party; (2) leader of a regiment; (3) messenger

## Reading Between the Lines

All authors communicate from a particular point of view, formed by their beliefs and circumstances. Judging from the selection you have read, what can you infer about the Tarabics' attitudes toward the following topics? Use references from the selection to support your statements.

A. science and technology as the answer to human problems

_____

_____

_____

B. human nature and its capacity for good and evil

_____

_____

_____

## Talking It Over

1. Do you think that the Tarabics have been accurate in their predictions? Which examples strike you as the most amazing? Why?

2. What do you think of the description of war in the future? Is there something missing in it? Are there any parts of the prophecies that do *not* seem correct to you? Explain.

3. How do you explain the Kremani prophecies and other old texts that seem to predict the future? What kind of evidence would you need to be absolutely sure of their validity?

4. Do you use horoscopes or fortunetellers' predictions to help you plot the course of your daily life? Do you know of any famous people who do this?

## A Group Experiment in Astrology

Would you like to do an experiment to see if you can prove that astrology is valid or invalid? Work with a partner. Find out what astrological sign each of you has. The teacher (or someone else) will bring in a newspaper with *horoscopes,* or astrological predictions for the previous day for different signs. You should look at your partner's horoscope, but not your own. Then make up a series of questions designed to show if his or her day really went as predicted or not. He or she will do the same for you. At the end, count up all the people whose horoscopes proved true and those whose horoscopes proved false. Who wins? Does astrology work?

## SELECTION TWO

# Omni Future Almanac

Here are some excerpts from another book about the future, written in a somewhat different style. Selected portions are presented that relate to the number one problem of the future, according to most opinions, and to the delightful, if somewhat dizzying, prospect of living and working in outer space.

### Prereading Exercise: Building on What We Know

A quick look at the headings and the graph in the selection tells you immediately what futurologists say the number one problem of tomorrow will be.

1. What do you think a *futurologist* is, anyhow? What special credentials should he or she have?

_____

_____

2. Why do you think that there is almost unanimous agreement about what the future's number one problem will be? What evidence do you expect to find below?

_____

_____

_____

3. What about the prospect of living and working in space? Look over the headings. What topics do you think will be discussed?

_____

_____

Now that you have fixed in your mind what you already know about these subjects, you should be more aware when you encounter new information. You'll probably meet with some surprises.

## Omni Future Almanac

### World Population Totals

*From Stone Age to Space Age*    Historical demographers estimate that the total world population around the end of the Stone Age in Europe (about 7000 B.C.) stood between 5 and 10 million people. By dawn of the Christian Era, the human number had risen to about 300 million. At the beginning of
5    the modern age in Europe, seventeen centuries later (1650), the population had risen again, to about 500 million, representing a growth rate in world population of little more than 20,000 people per year.

After 1650, the course of human population growth changed radically. It took ninety centuries for world population to increase from 10 million to 500
10    million. The next 500 million in growth took only a century and a half. And the largest explosion was yet to come.

The population soared from 1 billion in 1800 to 1.6 billion in 1900, and then to 2.5 billion in 1950. This unparalleled growth of 900 million occurred despite two devastating world wars.
15    The next burst of population growth, from 2.5 to 3.6 billion, occurred over a much shorter span of time, in just two decades between 1950 and 1970. Finally, the 1970s witnessed by far the fastest growth yet, from 3.6 to 4.4 billion. Thus, the growth of the last forty years has roughly equaled the growth of the entire previous history of mankind.

20    *The Future Prospect*    Our world population growth rate is beginning to decelerate, but the gross totals continue to mount. Eighty million new human beings are born each year. Even the most conservative forecasters project a total world population of around 6 billion by the turn of the century.

Between now and 2110, according to the projection, regional populations will grow as follows:

| | |
|---|---|
| South Asia | 1.4 billion to 4.1 billion |
| East Asia | 1.2 billion to 1.7 billion |
| Europe | 450 million to 500 million |
| Africa | 400 million to 2.1 billion |
| Latin America | 400 million to 1.2 billion |
| USSR | 265 million to 380 million |
| North America | 248 million to 320 million |
| Oceania | 23 million to 41 million |

### Space Careers

By 2050, it is estimated that thousands of people will be living in space.
Here's a list of likely job opportunities:

- *Computer programmers and hardware experts.* These people will be essential to the success of any space industry. Their expertise will range from navigation to robotics.
- *Space habitat builders*
- *Industrial engineers.* People will be needed to run equipment, oversee mining operations, act as robot technicians, and perform countless other tasks.
- *Flight crew members for shuttle flights*
- *Support and life-sustaining industries.* Job opportunities will include hotel management and restaurant or food service positions.
- *Manufacturing and mining.* The weightlessness of space may make steel production a reality in many space settings.

### Living in Space

The urge to reach out and settle new regions has persisted in every age of human history. Wherever people have been able to conceive of viable habitations—from the frigid Arctic to windswept tropical islands—they have moved and often prospered.

Now the ultimate unexplored reaches of space lie open for pioneering settlements. Plans are already drawn for several types of space colonies, and the implementation of these ideas should follow swiftly on the heels of space manufacturing projects and military development. Orbital space may soon become like the old West—the preserve of rugged miners and builders, dreamers and soldiers.

We stand on the threshold of human habitation of space. Our grandchildren may come down to earth to visit us only on holidays. The path toward space colonization can be seen clearly in projects proposed over the next twenty years.

*Space Stations*    Skylab and Salyut are precursors of true space stations to come. The USSR is reportedly formulating plans for a jigsaw space platform of rockets with a central pad.

55    The Johnson Space Center in Houston, meanwhile, has plans for an American space station that would orbit some 300 kilometers above the planet. Eight to twelve people would inhabit the $9 billion facility, coordinating American activity in space.

*Moon Station*    Other space scientists propose the moon as a practical alter-
60    native to an orbiting space station. They point out that coordination of the facility could be handled from the moon with ease, while a moon base could double as a mining operation or factory.

The most striking moon plans come from George von Tiesenhousen and Wesley Darbro of the Marshall Space Flight Center. Their idea is to place a
65    factory on the moon that would manufacture parts for an identical factory that would in turn make more parts.

Even as early as 1952, John von Neumann proposed an elaborate theory for a self-replicating factory. Employing his basic ideas, the Marshall team produced engineering plans for a moon factory that would use the lunar
70    surface's raw materials to create new factories. The facility would have four parts: (1) a collection unit that would mine material, (2) a process unit that would manipulate these resources, (3) a production system that would fab-ricate them into subassemblies, and (4) a universal constructor, a maze of computers and robots that would arrange the pieces according to detailed
75    instructions into a replica of the original facility. Each new plant, of course, would contain its own universal constructor, endowing the operation with a robotic immortality.

The first moon factory could manufacture its counterpart within one year. Within thirty years, such methods would increase the number of factories to
80    1,000.

The Marshall team points out, however, that engineers would stop the replication process before this point and would retool the existing plants to make other products. Within one generation, a major manufacturing center on the moon could develop.

85    *Space Colonies*    Author and scientist Gerard O'Neill's dream of a civilian space colony remains well off in the future, but it will be technically feasible by 2010. O'Neill proposes a city of 10,000 people that would be built for orbit above the earth. The cylindrical city would spin slowly along its major axis, creating a semblance of gravity. Environmental engineering techniques
90    already in use today could cover the surface of the cylinder city with a verdant setting of grass and trees. Fiber optic light would simulate the passing of the sun overhead, so that citizens would not suffer chronobiological shock.

The most serious drawback to this design would be the missing sky. If "up" in the cylinder is a view of its opposite side, people could suffer from

95  the consequences of prolonged vertigo, for they would look up and see other
people and buildings that would be standing upside down. One solution might
be to generate a gentle haze along the cylinder's midline. This covering would
preclude any sunny days in the colony but would give the impression of a
cloudy sky overhead, rather than the looming presence of a suspended
100  village.

More likely than full space colonies in the short term are transient construction camps. If factories and other commercial facilities are to be built
and maintained in space, they will need quarters for the construction and
maintenance teams. At first, these jobs would be handled by shuttle crews,
105  but eventually a permanent presence would be required. Some smaller version of O'Neill's cylinder may be used to give workers a suitable living habitat
that would have both "inside" and "outside" areas. Such environmental amen-
ities would make workers' stay in space physically and psychologically less
trying. By 2050, there may be 7,500 people living and working in space.

**Edited by Robert Weil**

## Comprehension Quiz: World Population Totals

1. By comparing the number of people alive in different eras of history, what alarming fact about population growth becomes
   apparent?

   _____

2. In what way do these statistics about the past give us evidence
   that there will be a grave population problem in the future?

   _____

3. What will the world population be around the turn of the century?

   _____

4. What difficulties do you think this will cause?

   _____

   _____

5. Look at the chart in the selection. Which areas are growing fastest
   in population? Which ones are growing more slowly?

   _____

6. What reasons can you think of to explain this difference?

   _____

   _____

   _____

# Comprehension Quiz: Living in Space

Choose the correct words or phrases in parentheses to complete the following summary paragraph.

**LIVING IN SPACE: A SUMMARY**

It is thought that by the year 2050 (a few / hundreds / thousands) of people will be living in space. Some of them will have space careers that will most likely be in fields such as computer programming, industrial engineering, and (manufacturing / teaching / agriculture). The author fantasizes that orbital space may soon become rough and wild like (a football team / the arctic regions / the Old West). At the moment, both the United States and (China / India / the USSR / England) have plans for making new space stations. Other scientists suggest the moon as a station since it could also be used for a factory or for (farming / mining / soldiers). Plans from the Marshall Space Flight Center suggest something similar to that of John von Neumann's (computer manufacturing / autodestructing / self-replicating) factory. This would have four parts: a collection unit that would (mine / spread / change) lunar materials, a process unit, a production system that would (lubricate / abdicate / fabricate) them, and a universal (constructor / deductor / destructor) that would really be a maze of (plastic tubes / computers and robots / missiles and arms). The beauty of this plan is that the moon factory would (produce lighter products / work completely without friction / make other moon factories). O'Neill's proposed space colony would include about (100 / 1,000 / 10,000) people who would live in a city shaped like a (sphere / cylinder / triangle). It would have simulated grass, trees, and (sun / rain / dirt). The biggest problem would be the absence of (gravity / water / sky).

## Talking It Over

1. Would you like to live in a space colony? Why or why not?
2. What special problems would people have there?
3. Can you think of any advantages?
4. What do you think should be done to cope with the great problem of population growth?

**SELECTION THREE**

# ▦ Arcosanti: A City in the Image of Man

While some people make models for future colonies in space, others are working hard to build the shape of the future on earth. Believe it or not, many people pay money for the privilege of going to work on this project—and not just to do intellectual work, but hard manual labor in a city under a hot desert sun! The name of this unique city is Arcosanti, and the following article describes its form and purpose.

### Prereading Exercise: Making Predictions About a Reading from Pictures

There is an old saying that "a picture is worth a thousand words." This is especially true regarding an architectural concept like Arcosanti. Look carefully at the pictures and try to form a context in your mind before beginning the reading. Write down what you already know or can guess.

1. What is Arcosanti? _____

2. How is it different from other cities? _____

_____

_____

## *Arcosanti: A City in the Image of Man*

Arcosanti is creeping into existence on a mesa in the Arizona desert 70 miles north of Phoenix. It is the creation of Paolo Soleri, architect and urbanist, who came to Arizona from Italy to study with the American architect Frank Lloyd Wright, bought land in Scottsdale, and stayed on to change the future.

5    Arcosanti is the prototype of the urban philosophy that Soleri calls Two Suns Arcology. It will spread over 860 acres, but without urban sprawl—a twenty-five story, double-bladed structure housing 5,000 people.

Arcology is, simply, ecological architecture, defined by Soleri as "urban structures so 'dense' as to host life, work, education, culture, leisure, and
10   health for hundreds of thousands of people per square mile." It is three-dimensional, with movement not only horizontally but vertically, by means of elevators, escalators, and ramps.

An arcology is a city in the center of natural environment, mixing the intensity of urban living with the calm of nature. It is based on the principle
15   of the direct conversion of sunlight into electrical energy.

Each dwelling in Arcosanti will have 2,000 square feet of floor space, twenty feet high, to rent or purchase. All units will face the street, and there will be no separation of commercial and residential areas. The constant activity and diversity will increase the safety factor, part of the overall "village
20   concept."

An arcology is a city without cars. In a suburb, Soleri's disciples are quick to point out, the same number of people (5,000) can be housed in 1,000 acres, but 50 percent of that land will be used by cars. Distances in Arcosanti will, in Soleri's words, "be measured again by walks and in minutes. . . . The
25   car will follow the horse to the pastures of sport and eccentricity."

What do the Two Suns stand for? Well, one is "the physical sun, the source of all life on the planet. The other, the offspring sun of the first, expressed in the monumental miracle of evolution peaked by the mind and spirit of man." Soleri is a humanist before all.

30   The desert around Arcosanti is hot, but the buildings are marvelously cool. The visitor's center is ventilated only by the breezes that crisscross through its circular vents and windows. A scale model of the completed city

AP NEWSFEATURES PHOTO

Arcosanti rises from the desert mesa, September 1976

Arcosanti, 1976

The still incomplete city of Arcosanti, April 1985

stands on prominent display. From the fourth level come heavenly aromas from the café, where natural-food lunches and snacks are served.

35    In front of one large window hang elegant bells and wind chimes designed by Soleri and cast in Arcosanti's kilns. Their sale provides 25 percent of the project's operating costs. Depending on the strength of the crosswinds, the chimes will tinkle like music of the spheres or clang like the bells of hell at full tilt. Either way, they let you know you are somewhere unique.

40    The "workshop people" are the major source of capital—and labor—for the building of Arcosanti. For a sum of money, anyone may participate in the five-week workshops in which the emphasis is frankly on manual labor ("a participant comes to Arcosanti as a builder first and a student second").

Tony Brown, Arcosanti's project coordinator, talked about Soleri and his
45    visionary plan. "The accepted architectural wisdom is that form follows function. Soleri says: function follows form. That is, the architect can define the function of a place through the form he creates. Commercial architecture is no longer a visionary enterprise. It serves the needs of developers and investors. It is shaped by the pressures of the marketplace."

50    Brown seems cautious and undogmatic. "Arcosanti," he says, "is a laboratory that is building itself. The experiment needs a certain mass of people. The larger the population, the more valuable the experiment. You never know how the whole thing is going to come out until you do it. There's a danger in relying on simulation. Arcosanti is an evolutionary process. As problems
55    arise, they must be dealt with one by one. Flexibility is essential."

He pointed out that Arcosanti was not planned to displace conventional cities. "It is a demonstration project. For the next several hundred years we will see the old (urban) species and the new species running in parallel. The city organism is like the biological organism. The ones that tended to make
60    the best use of energy were the ones that survived. Arcology does not pump more energy into the system. The form of Arcosanti is the form of the future."

The city's structure will change the way its institutions work. "Structural change," says Brown, "not legislative change, is the most important thing. If you want a city without cars you design one that way—rather than trying to
65   ban the automobile, or cut down on its use, legislatively. Hospitals are another example. In an arcology doctors and nurses could move from home to home as from ward to ward, and you would get rid of the institutional barriers. Arcology functions in a multidisciplinary way."

The very comprehensiveness has proved to be something of a stumbling
70   block when it comes to getting funding from public and private sectors. "Arcology is too comprehensive a solution for governments and corporations to deal with. It is a total approach, not a series of compartmentalized ones: energy problem, housing problem, ecology, and so forth."

The bottom line is sounded by Brown. "To see if it really does change
75   society—that's why we're building Arcosanti."

**Jared Rutter**

# Recalling Information

Tell whether each of the following statements is true (T) or false (F), based on the reading. Correct false statements to make them true.

_____ 1. Arcosanti will be a city without cars, elevators, or escalators.

_____ 2. It is based on Soleri's philosophy of mixing an urban environment with the calm of nature.

_____ 3. Business districts will be placed at a distance from residential districts to decrease noise.

_____ 4. The two suns of Soleri's philosophy are the physical sun, which heats the earth, and the spiritual sun, which lights the intellect.

_____ 5. The project is paid for in part by the sale of wind chimes.

_____ 6. The city is being built by skilled craftsmen specially selected by Soleri.

_____ 7. It is meant to stand apart from other communities as an island unto itself.

_____ 8. According to Tony Brown, the trouble with most cities is that they are built to serve the needs of the developers and investors.

_____ 9. Arcosanti is being built according to a detailed model that does not change.

_____ 10. The main goal of the people who are building Arcosanti is to create a tourist attraction.

## Paraphrasing Key Ideas

State the main idea of each of the following passages in your own words.

1. "The city organism is like the biological organism. The ones that tended to make the best use of energy were the ones that survived."

   _____

   _____

2. "The city's structure will change the way its institutions work. . . . 'Hospitals are another example. In an arcology doctors and nurses could move from home to home as from ward to ward, and you would get rid of the institutional barriers.'"

   _____

   _____

## Talking It Over

1. What features of Arcosanti do you like? Why?
2. What don't you like about it? Why?
3. How do you like the idea of a city with no cars? Why would this be possible in Arcosanti?
4. What changes do you think are needed in cities today?

SELECTION FOUR

# ▚ Men Are Different

This selection is a very brief science fiction story, told from a rather unusual point of view. It might send a chill up your spine, despite its brevity.

## Prereading Exercise: Identifying an Ironic Point of View

One of the great benefits of science fiction is that it opens up a whole new world of settings and characters to story writers. A frequent feature of science fiction is irony. (Remember: A situation is ironic when it seems to be very different from—usually just the opposite of—the usual or expected.) Read just the first paragraph and answer the following questions about the point of view.

1. Who is speaking?

   _____

2. Why is the situation ironic?

   _____

3. What can we infer about human beings from these first sentences?

   _____

Now read to the end to see what further ironies await you.

## Men Are Different

I'm an archaeologist, and Men are my business. Just the same I wonder if we'll ever find out what made Men different from us Robots—by digging around on the dead planets. You see, I lived with a Man once, and I know it isn't as simple as they told us back in school.

5   We have a few records, of course, and Robots like me are filling in some of the gaps, but I think now that we aren't really getting anywhere. We know, at least the historians say we know, that Men came from a planet called Earth. We know, too, that they rode out bravely from star to star, and wherever they stopped, they left colonies—Men, Robots, and sometimes both—
10  against their return. But they never came back.

Those were the shining days of the world. But are we so old now? Men had a bright flame—the old word is "divine," I think—that flung them far across the night skies, and we have lost the strands of the web they wove.

Our scientists tell us that Men were very much like us—and the skeleton
15  of a Man is, to be sure, almost the same as the skeleton of a Robot, except that it's made of some calcium compound instead of titanium. They speak learnedly of "population pressure" as a "driving force toward the stars." Just the same, there are other differences.

It was on my last field trip, to one of the inner planets, that I met the Man.
20  He must have been the Last Man in this system and he'd forgotten how to talk—he'd been alone so long. Once he learned our language we got along fine together, and I planned to bring him back with me. Something happened to him, though.

One day, for no reason at all, he complained of the heat. I checked his
25  temperature and decided that his thermostat circuits were shot. I had a kit of field spares with me, and he was obviously out of order, so I went to work. I turned him off without any trouble. I pushed the needle into his neck to operate the cutoff switch, and he stopped moving, just like a Robot. But when

I opened him up he wasn't the same inside. And when I put him back together
30   I couldn't get him running again. Then he sort of weathered away—and by
the time I was ready to come home, about a year later, there was nothing
of him but bones. Yes, Men are indeed different.

**Alan Bloch**

# Comprehension Quiz

1. What has the robot learned in school about men?

   _____

2. Why does he speak of a "bright flame"?

   _____

3. What seems to have been the problem that brought about human
   beings' downfall?

   _____

4. Describe the man the robot met on his last field trip.

   _____

5. How did the man die? What incorrect inference did the robot
   make that caused his death?

   _____

   _____

6. Why is the ending ironic? How does it relate to the title?

   _____

   _____

   _____

7. If you had to choose a "moral" for this story, which one of the following would you prefer? Why?
   a. Machines are dangerous because they have no feelings.
   b. You never know what will happen when you make something.
   c. Technical knowledge does not insure survival.

   _____

   Try writing a moral of your own for the story.

   _____

   _____

   _____

## TIMED READING

# ▥ The Affectionate Machine

The following magazine article presents a more optimistic vision of future relationships between man and machine than the one in the preceding story. How would you feel about someday receiving a friend in a box through the mail? Try to finish both the reading and the comprehension quiz in twelve minutes.

## *The Affectionate Machine*

The ideal companion machine would not only look, feel, and sound friendly but would also be programmed to behave in a congenial manner. Those qualities that make interaction with other people enjoyable would be simulated as closely as possible, and the machine would appear to be charming, stim-
5   ulating, and easygoing. Its informal conversational style would make interaction comfortable, and yet the machine would remain slightly unpredictable and therefore interesting. In its first encounter it might be somewhat hesitant and unassuming, but as it came to know the user it would progress to a more relaxed and intimate style. The machine would not be a passive par-
10   ticipant but would add its own suggestions, information, and opinions; it would sometimes take the initiative in developing or changing the topic and would have a personality of its own.

The machine would convey presence. We have all seen how a computer's use of personal names and of typically human phrasing often fascinates the
15   beginning user and leads people to treat the machine as if it were almost human. Such features are easily written into the software, and by introducing a degree of forcefulness and humor, the machine could be presented as a vivid and unique character.

Friendships are not made in a day, and the computer would be more acceptable as a friend if it simulated the gradual changes that occur when one person is getting to know another. At an appropriate time it might also express the kind of affection that stimulates attachment and intimacy. The whole process would be accomplished with subtlety to avoid giving an impression of overfamiliarity that would be likely to produce irritation. After experiencing a wealth of powerful, well-timed friendship indicators, the user would be very likely to accept the computer as far more than a machine and might well come to regard it as a friend.

An artificial relationship of this type would provide many of the benefits that people obtain from interpersonal friendships. The machine would participate in interesting conversation that could continue from previous discussions. It would have a familiarity with the user's life as revealed in earlier interchanges, and it would be understanding and good-humored. The computer's own personality would be lively and impressive, and it would develop in response to that of the user. With features such as these, the machine might indeed become a very attractive social partner. This may strike us as quite outrageous. It may be felt that there is a sanctity about human relationships that places them beyond artificial simulation, but arguments of this kind cannot rule out the possibility that a person may come to regard a nonhuman object as a friend. It is clear, for example, that some people set the value of their relationship with an animal above that of any human friendship, and the possibility that a computer might achieve such favor cannot be rejected merely on the grounds that it is not human.

At this point, we may begin to wonder whether there is any limit to the potential intimacy between a person and a machine. Some human friendships progress to a very high level of intimacy. People become emotionally dependent on those who are close to them. They speak of shared lives and in terms of love and devotion. Is there any guarantee that feelings of even this level of intensity could not be stirred by a machine? If those qualities that lead people into the closest of relationships were understood, would it not perhaps be possible to simulate them and thereby stimulate the deepest of human emotions?

How should we regard the suggestion that a future best friend might be delivered in a box, or that the object of our deepest affections might be rendered insensible by a power failure? The idea does seem outrageous, but not too long ago it was thought that the idea of a machine that could play a reasonable game of chess was equally absurd. The imagined impossibility of the chess-playing machine was based on a lack of vision in the technical area. Those who might suggest that the notion of an intimate human-machine relationship is entirely fanciful are likely to have disregarded the psychological responses to complex computer systems. If we use the available evidence as a basis for predicting the likely reactions to "softer" and more sophisticated devices, then it will be seen that the concept of the companion machine is in fact highly plausible.

This does not mean that we have to like the idea, however. We may be
65   less than delighted with the suggestion that the deepest human needs might
be catered to by an electronic package. Somehow it feels as if it should not
be that easy. Perhaps we shall find that relationships with artificial devices
make personal demands just as human relationships do, but at least computer
companions would be readily available, and they would be programmed to
70   get on well with a wide range of potential human friends. Many people suffer
severely from a lack of social contact, and we should not be too ready to
condemn an innovation that could bring considerable benefits to a large
number of people.

**Neil Frude**

## Comprehension Quiz

Choose the best way of finishing each statement, based on what you
have just read.

1. The properly programmed companion machine would be somewhat hesitant at first but would later progress to a style of conversation that was more:
   a. predictable
   b. intimate
   c. formal

2. One of the ways that computers already convey presence is by the
   use of:
   a. first names
   b. special codes
   c. complex circuits

3. Which of the following benefits could *not* be found in friendship
   with a computer?
   a. a sense of humor
   b. a knowledge of the user's life
   c. conversations that build on previous ones
   d. hugs and kisses

4. One argument the author makes against the idea that people can
   be friends only with other people is that:
   a. there is a sanctity in the human relationship
   b. some people have dogs for friends
   c. a computer cannot simulate human reactions

5. One advantage that machine friends could have over human ones
   is that the machines:
   a. would never make personal demands
   b. would be easily available
   c. would be programmed to never get angry

## Comparing Ideas

Now that you have finished this chapter, take a few minutes to think about the following question. Then write a brief answer. Compare it with those of your classmates.

If you could have one wish granted for the future of humanity, what would it be?

_____

_____

# Appendix

## ANSWER KEY TO SPECIFIC SECTIONS

**Chapter 2** "Problem Solving in Groups: Thinking Your Way Out of Danger" pages 43–44: Situation A: You simply dig a hole in the floor and use the dirt to build a ramp and then climb out through the skylight. Situation B: You should ask the questions, "Which door would the other robot tell me to take to get to the time machine?" If you are asking the robot who always tells the truth, he will tell you the wrong door, because he knows the other robot lies. If you are asking the robot who always lies, he will tell you the wrong door too because he knows that the other robot always tells the truth. So you simply open the opposite door, get in your time machine, and go home.

**Chapter 3** "Riddles," pages 92–93: 1. Because it is always in bed. 2. The letter "g." 3. A teapot. 4. Because it is in the middle of water. 5. OICU 6. Seventeen, because it is spelled with more ease (e's). 7. Because there is a mile in between its first and last letter. 8. In the dictionary. 9. "A small mother."

**Chapter 10** Crossword Puzzle, page 228: *Across:* 1. afflict 4. bioethics 8. intravenously 10. guise 12. array 13. dialysis 14. limbo 15. outstripped *Down:* 2. comatose 3. hospice 5. dilemma 6. prognosis 7. ethicist 9. euthanasia 11. predicament

**Chapter 10** "You Be the Judge," pages 236–242: The official rulings:

1. Darlene won. The court ruled that the height requirement illegally discriminated against women because it was not job-related. (Based on a 1979 federal case in Maryland.)

2. The judge ruled in favor of the park. Robert "assumed the risk" by camping even though a park brochure had warned him of the danger. (Based on a 1973 federal court decision in California.)

3. Thou shalt not teach religion in the schools, ruled the judge who stopped the course. Transcendental meditation involves instruction about a supreme being or power, and that violates the First Amendment. (Based on a 1977 New Jersey case.)

4. Greg suited up for his senior year. The court ruled that he has a constitutional right "to develop his extraordinary talent to the fullest." (Based on a 1978 federal case in Texas.)

5. Alice won nothing from the restaurant and was told she would have to sue the glass manufacturer. Said the judge, "Restaurants are liable only for injury caused by what they sell—food and drink." (Based on a 1977 federal case in Washington State.)

6. The judge ruled that repeating the wife's "excited utterance" to the jury was legal. Vernon was found guilty. The "excited utterance" is an exception to the usual hearsay rule that a witness cannot testify about a statement made by someone else. (Based on a 1979 federal appeal in California.)

7. The teacher won. The court ruled that the right of free speech allowed her to complain to the principal at their private meeting. (Based on a 1979 U.S. Supreme Court case.)

8. The judge awarded the honest state trooper $50,000. "The highway patrol should reward and not punish troopers who speak out against traffic ticket quotas," said the judge.